Midnight Musings
of a
Family Therapist

Midnight Musings
of a
Family Therapist

CARL WHITAKER, M.D.

Edited by

Margaret O. Ryan

W • W • Norton & Company • *New York* • *London*

Published simultaneously in Canada by Penguin Books Canada Ltd., 2801 John Street, Markham, Ontario L3R 1B4.

Printed in the United States of America

Library of Congress Cataloging-in-Publication Data

Whitaker, Carl A.
  Midnight musings of a family therapist.

  "A Norton professional book" — T.p. verso.
  1. Family psychotherapy. 2. Family. I. Ryan,
Margaret O. (Margaret O'Loghlin) II. Title.
RC488.5.W485 1989   616.89′156   89-8641

ISBN 0-393-70084-4

W. W. Norton & Company, Inc., 500 Fifth Avenue, New York, N.Y. 10110
W. W. Norton & Company Ltd., 37 Great Russell Street, London, WC1B 3NU

    3 4 5 6 7 8 9 0

To Muriel and our six—
Nancy, Elaine, Bruce,
Anita, Lynn, and Holly.
What a cuddle group!

Contents

Preface

It's 4 o'clock in the morning and I awake with a thought. In this unplanned moment of self-hypnosis, the dream-like, total Gestalt word-pictures of fifty years in the psychological world of people in pain come to me with unexpected clarity. I scribble them down. Later, in daylight, the ideas grow and take shape.

That's the way it happens to me. These musings have been nurtured during 40 years of learning the process of inducing change in people in pain and of teaching endless medical students, psychiatric residents, psychological fellows, and social work students. In the past ten years of retirement these midnight musings have been fun for me. I hope some will prime your pump.

This is not a how-to-do-it book; I'm not even sure it is a how-I-did-it book. Mostly it is a how-I-think-I-learned-to-do-it book. The problem is that I'm so suspicious of myself, I don't trust my own thinking. Maybe, taken together, these musings are just a fairytale of how I survived.

I wouldn't suggest that you gobble up this book all at once. Instead, treat it like a meal of hors d'oeuvres; taste, but don't eat anything that doesn't appeal to you.

I wrote this Preface at 4 o'clock in the morning on the 50th anniversary of the day I sat by my father's hospital bed and watched him draw his last breath. How does life happen to me? How can I get *more* to happen? May more and more happen to you.

Acknowledgments

Out of my experience as a family therapist comes the capacity to be the patient at the drop of a hat. It's a bilateral altered state of consciousness, the freedom to be more of myself by using the other. Muriel—with her integrity, her antennae always on the alert, her whole person resonance, and her capacity for locked-in-place intimacy—was my role model. Together we had six blockbuster kids in fifteen years. They still spice our life.

All of these essays carry echoes of Tom Malone, John Warkentin, Dick Felder, Milton Miller, David Keith and the endless series of trainees, colleagues, and families who rocked my boat or served as my cuddle group for the day, the week, or the year. They're to blame for the echoes. I'm only to blame for the words.

Margaret Ryan took a mountain of material and organized and edited it into the book you have here. She saved me from rambling on or repeating myself without distorting what I wanted to say. You are so lucky she did. Behind us both is the master ghost Susan Barrows.

I

Growing a Self and Evolving a Role — Whitaker Style

An Autobiographical Glimpse

Nineteen-thirty-six was a good year to get your M.D. The depression was about to be over, the war was about to start, and doctors were in high demand. But going through medical school in Syracuse had no more prepared me for a residency and internship in New York's Hell's Kitchen than growing up on the dairy farm in northern New York had prepared me for medical school. Looking back now, the family move from the dairy farm to the city when I was a freshman in high school seems like a very courageous act on the part of my parents. College-trained in agriculture, my father had been able to wire the farm and move from kerosene lanterns to electricity. But to move into the big city so that I could go to higher education seems, today, like a quantum leap. It may well be that my struggle for adventure comes out of my father's breaks, just as his move came out of *his* father's adventuresome leap from the sawmill at Whitaker's Falls in the middle of the Adirondacks to a big dairy farm up by the St. Lawrence. I often wonder what would have happened if we had done it the other way and I had grown up to be a dairy farmer instead of learning to be a student electrician when I was in high school, working summers and Saturdays rewiring old houses that had been lighted by gas.

All of our lives fell apart in the crash of 1932. The business had gone bankrupt and Dad moved back to the farm. I went on to medical school with no way of paying my tuition, and in the throes of six years of upper respiratory infections. Strange how these infections disappeared as soon as I graduated!

My childhood upbringing on an isolated dairy farm outside a small mill town in Raymondville, New York did not prepare me for the city. On the

3

The farm in Raymondville, New York, where I grew up.

farm there were no boys to play with but there was an endless load of work and a profoundly religious pressure from Mother, who believed that the only way you could get into heaven was to keep doing good. All in all, we had to take care of 100 cows, half a dozen horses, a dozen pigs, 100 chickens, and 50 sheep. The workday went from four o'clock in the morning until ten o'clock at night. My exposure to death and birth was continual. We took for granted the killing of chickens on Sunday morning for chicken dinner, the slaughtering of pigs for winter, and the growing of all our own food. Death was my companion throughout my childhood and the workaholic pattern was not a personality trait but a necessity of the world in which we lived. (This rather austere background served as a kind of "training in toughness" that turned out to be very valuable when I was working in that ghetto hospital in New York City.) Mother single-handedly maintained a ten-bedroom ex-mansion and Dad ran a 500-acre farm with one hired man. Everybody was up to their ears in struggle. There were fun times, but they were rare and special interludes of that world. Mother and Dad lived in separate worlds: she ran the inside of the house and he ran the outside world. Their days were so filled with responsibilities that it is easy to understand why I didn't see any fights—there wasn't any time! I didn't see much intimacy either, although Mother would occasionally tease Dad and he would blush like a twelve-year-old.

Our family control system was powerful but mostly nonverbal. Sunday was church and no play. Religious rituals were part of every meal, and there was a constant stream of people belonging to the family network. The daughter of one of my mother's high school chums lived with us for several years after her mother died. An orphan from Brooklyn came up and lived with us for summers. An asthmatic woman whom I have never identified lived with us for a year or so, for reasons I never knew. A woman from the community whose husband died of cancer came and lived with us for six months during her grieving period. It was almost as though we ran a kind of community halfway house. Now I think of it as a kind of psychotherapy; then it just seemed like the thing that was done.

Tracing My Addiction to Nonprofessional Agents of Change

Probably my first nonprofessional agent of change was the puppy I was given when I was two or three years old. It was clear that the puppy became my security blanket by helping to act as an intermediary between my mother's breast, and the person of my mother, and myself. Shortly thereafter came my little brother, followed by the high school boy next door whom I trailed on the way to school, followed by a negative transference to my gradeschool group to whom I was an outsider. These "agents" of change were swiftly succeeded by my fantasy of God as a foster parent, by my father's father who was aged but loved to teach me how to play checkers, and by my father's mother who needed me for little errands and paid me with warmth and tenderness. And, as with almost everyone, there was my negative transference to my mother and my utilization of my father as a way of breaking me out of the hypnosis that she had induced—certainly an example of a nonprofessional change move.

In a strange way the farm itself was like a therapist: it was Mother Nature's turf—always nurturing, comforting, and secure. From the farm, my transference (my emotional investment) moved to the adopted son of a neighbor, followed by a negative transference to my gym teacher who was very insulting about my physical inadequacies.

In retrospect, it seems as though the beginning of my adolescent schizophrenia was seeded during those solitary childhood days of hunting with

Here I am in the center, with my parents and siblings, Miriam and Lee, in 1923.

my dog, spear fishing by myself, dynamiting ditches on the farm, being buried in a load of hay, harrowing all day with the tractor out of sight of every human being. All of these experiences contained an isolation that prepared me to be even more isolated when we moved to the city and I went to high school. I spent those four years of high school very much in my own world. Occasionally I found a friend, but the relationship was usually fragmentary. I lived in a kind of strange, blank, catatonic-like emptiness. I remember once walking down the street from school and realizing that the boy coming toward me was in my class. I practiced a smile so that when we met I could at least smile, even though I didn't have enough courage to say hello.

When I went on to college (which was assumed, since both Mother and Dad had gone), I deliberately decided to break out of that painful isolation. This decision may well have amounted to another of those threshold experiences, such as moving to the city. As an undergraduate at Syracuse University, I picked the boy who was top man intellectually in my high school class, and the boy who was most revered socially, and deliberately forced us into a threesome—which lasted through all the three years of

At age 17.

Here I am at age 20, going hunting with brother Lee, age 17.

college before I went to medical school. It was as though I had structured a co-therapy team to break up my isolation. During both high school and college I lived at home, but the day that I entered medical school (also at Syracuse), the family moved back to the farm. I was alone and very much on my own, earning my room and board by washing dishes, with no known way of paying the tuition—and, from my nervous perspective, starting medical school with a bunch of strangers.

After Medical School: A Turning Point

In those days no clear divisions existed between what we now call *internships* and *residencies*. Following medical school, we were put into a two-year training program, which landed us in a variety of settings. One of these

A medical school anatomy class with Professor Henry Stiles. I am seated at right.

settings was particularly unsavory—the Sixth Avenue Hotel. The hotel looked like a fairly standard whorehouse with lush equipment, men in fancy suits, and women in nightclothes wandering the halls from room to room. Mary was waiting for me to examine her for a pain in her belly—she had an infectious pelvic disease. To my surprise, she greeted me with "Hello, Carl," after I had just put my hat upside down on the table so I wouldn't get fleas.

It turned out that I had seen her in the hospital six weeks before. She had come in to get treatment for acute gonorrhea, had stayed in the hospital for three days, and had asked if I would talk with her and her husband. This was a new experience for me and, looking back, it is probably the first psychiatric interview I ever did. They were concerned about their sexual relationships and I—being just a year out of medical school and about to begin my gynecology and obstetrics residency—was not mature enough or aware enough to do much except sit there open-mouthed while they talked about sex. This is all still powerful in my memory because the next morning, one headline in the paper reported that her husband had been murdered in a gang war.

As we took Mary back to the hospital and made plans with the ambulance driver to come back and pick up the madam (who was dying from cirrhosis of the liver), I had no sense that I would ever leave gynecology and obstetrics. Three hundred major operations later, and after a year of taking care of the Green Girls (teenagers who were acutely infected), I thought of myself as a good surgeon. I was ready to spend the rest of my days in a moderate-sized town, delivering babies and probably doing a lot of general practice. But I was also bedeviled by the horror involved in this particular specialty. Prior to the discovery of antibiotics, the healing of gonorrhea in the females usually required months of hospital bedrest. The Green Girls were locked in a big ward on top of this hopsital in the middle of the East River. It was my job to try to keep them from becoming overly excited and thus flaring up the infection which had gotten them arrested and imprisoned. The scheduling of operations and post-operation treatments was very much like life on the farm: hard work from early morning till late night. It was the flip side of the coin for me, a religious country boy, to end up dealing with the Broadway chorus girls who wanted to have their operations performed by our gynecology department because we used a special incision below the hairline, and thus they could go back on the stage and not be laughed at for exposing their operation scars. James Ricci, my gynecology Chief, would arrive straight from his Park Avenue hospital at seven o'clock in the morning, still in his pajamas and bathrobe. He was quite an idol. He would stay up all night writing *The Genealogy of Gynecology*, and then spend the forenoon supervising our operations. I can still remember the shock of my first day.

He said, "Get over on the other side. You're not going to hold retractors for me; you're going to do the operation."

I said, "I couldn't, I'm scared, and I don't know how."

He said, "That's all right. I'll stand on this little stool behind you and look down over your shoulder, and I'll guard every move you make." He was a great teacher who taught me much about human beings. In fact, he was probably one of my earliest psychotherapists!

Another threshold experience that occurred during my medical training had to do with a voluntary operation that went wrong. One of the 50 women we treated in the clinic three times a week had had chronic, intractable pain. Every menstrual period for five or six years had been hell. She became the haunt of the clinic. Nobody seemed able to help. The Chief finally decided that we should remove her uterus in the hopes of stopping the pain.

It was my job—a routine hysterectomy. I had never met her husband or her kids. All I had met was her body and her pain. The operation was comfortably finished in half an hour or so. The intern was sewing up the skin; the anesthesia resident routinely slipped the ether-filled bag off the machine to blow out the ether. He had filled it with oxygen to wash out the patient's lungs. Suddenly the machine exploded! Pandemonium! The patient began to bleed from the mouth, and four hours later she died. Nobody knew why, nobody understood the dynamics of the electrical spark; but the patient was dead. I've often wondered whether that tragedy was why I lost interest in the field when I finished the residency.

I then elected to spend a year in the psychiatric hospital, and I never turned back to ob/gyn.

A Psychiatric Career Begins

The days in the Syracuse psychopathic hospital—a little three-ward, 60-bed diagnostic unit with three staff members set up for the treatment of patients who could be returned to their homes—started out to be just a way of looking over the town. I was glad to run the neurosyphilis clinic. In those days, triparsimide was our only treatment, except for artificial fever box heat treatment, and the dangers of induced blindness and jaundice were ever-present. In the beginning I viewed psychiatric patients as curiosities. I often think about the alcoholic psychotic who said, "I saw this big white polar bear sitting on the bed, and I knew he wasn't real, but I had to call the nurse because he looked so real." Or the schizophrenic who insisted that "they" were shooting at him with machine guns out of the electric bulb. My mothering pattern of breaking the electric light bulb failed to prove there were no machine guns. My reality had nothing to do with his information and his experience with that machine gun.

As I learned more about psychosis and the vivid experience going on inside the person, I rapidly lost my interest in the mechanical carpenter work we called surgery. There was the patient who mumbled to himself but explained to me that voices were calling him horrible things and saying that he had had intercourse with his mother. I said, "That must be very upsetting," but he waved me off. "Oh, no, they've been doing that for years and I don't pay attention anymore." One nurse threatened to sink her foot up to her ankle into a patient's backside. The patient looked so sad and depressed that I thought she was being degrading. Two weeks later I discovered that he didn't want to leave her ward because she was the only person he loved.

These experiences stimulated my thinking about other people and, of course, parenthetically about myself. To experience a wily psychotic patient who was threatening to kill me suddenly collapse into a three-year-old child when I authoritatively stated that he was going to have to return to the ward surprised me more than it did him! Then there was the time I talked with an 85-year-old man who came in for molesting an eight-year-old girl. I colored it black like mother said, but when I met the girl she looked like a professional actress fresh out of Hollywood. It made huge gashes in my fantasy of what life and people were all about. This girl had been trained to act like a very seductive teenager, even though she was still very much a child. I was confused by the whole system. Who was doing what to whom? My farm life had not prepared me for such complexities.

Now my experiences in the Manhattan ghetto, which I had casually repressed, suddenly came alive in vivid color. This call of the wild—the agony and ecstasy of schizophrenia and of the whole psychotic world ballooning inside of me—was like a quantum leap. I became preoccupied with asking *why* psychosis had happened to these people, and immediately decided to go into child psychiatry and find out how to prevent it. As a psychiatric resident, I also began studying for a Master's degree at the University of Syracuse psychology department. Unfortunately, learning the mechanical administration of psychiatric diagnosis—the decision-making about whether a patient goes *in* or *out* of the hospital—gave me little chance to learn about crazy people. But at least I didn't get indoctrinated with a bunch of stale ideas.

My child psychiatry fellowship from the Commonwealth Foundation (financed by the Carnegie Foundation) assigned me to Louisville, Kentucky, for my psychiatric internship. During the intermediate period before it began, we moved to Canandaigua (near Rochester, New York), where a beautiful English mansion had been converted into a humanistically oriented, private psychiatric hospital. For seven months, my wife and I lived with ten patients in the open-door building; we played bridge with them, and we ate all our meals with them! Simultaneously, I was encountering a whole new kind of gentle humanism in the beautiful Finger Lakes region. The care and personal touch of the old asylum were pervasive. The elderly couple who ran it were warm and affectionate. One patient, a manic psychotic who had been in charge of research for a nearby chemical plant until he had gone crazy because they gave him a big department to run, was a virtual encyclopedia of knowledge about any topic imaginable. The old lady who had been sitting in her blue velvet chair in the upper hallway for the past 15 years was a joy when engaged in casual chit-chat. The massively depressed man who never got out of bed and never said a word turned out to be an exciting and powerful ping-pong player. But as soon as we stopped playing ping-pong, he would go back to his bed.

Louisville and the child psychiatry world was a whole new territory and, certainly, another threshold experience. The magic of schizophrenia—that Alice-in-Wonderland quality of spending hour after hour, sometimes all night long, with a patient whose preoccupation with delusions and hallucinations made him as fascinating as yourself—was matched by the mystery world of play therapy, where I spent month after month on the floor with little children, watching them talk about their families through my toys. Their honest replay of death and birth, of jealousy and hatred and sexuality was humbling. My discovery of Melanie Klein and her theory about infant sexuality was similar in depth and intensity to my discovery of the psychotic.

Being part of the child psychiatry training group at Louisville was like being part of another new family. When Muriel and I arrived in 1940, about to have our first baby, we were introduced to Southern culture in a delightfully personal way. The endless round of parties, the discovery of bourbon-on-the-rocks, was training in how to escape from words and regress to real life. It was lucky our first baby and my child psychiatry

Muriel and I celebrate our first wedding anniversary, 1939.

Proud parents with Elaine and Nancy in Louisville, 1943.

internship arrived at the same time. That kind of "double whammy" was probably what I needed to give me the courage to be more human. Certainly, this was augmented by the opportunity of teaching medical students and discovering how fast they retreat from humanism once they get into medical school. I can still remember the vow that, God being my helper, I would never again have anything to do with medical students. Four years later, I reversed that vow and became a full-time teacher for ten years; then I swore off for another ten years, and then came back to doing the same thing all over again!

In 1940 the child psychiatry clinic taught friendly listening as the therapeutic approach of the day. Fortunately, there was also an old social worker on staff who had been analyzed by Otto Rank. My first introduction to psychotherapy was by way of this process thinking form of Otto Rank, who was the first person to recognize and emphasize the importance of the *process* of therapy itself, in addition to the investigation of traumatic content. I became more and more intrigued by the question of what brings about change.

There was an eight-year-old boy who hadn't spoken a word since he had had whooping cough at the age of two. I spent six months seeing that boy once a week while the social worker talked to his mother upstairs. He never said anything to me either, but we threw the football out in the yard, and he did seem to listen to me talk about him. I finally gave up and admitted that I couldn't help. He and mother went away disappointed. I thought about quitting the field of psychotherapy until we got a phone call three weeks later saying that the boy had started talking!

One other boy, a ten-year-old, taught me another important lesson. He came in bitter and rebellious and stood inside the door, staring into space. I said, "I'm a doctor of people's feelings, and they must think you have hurt feelings or they wouldn't have forced you to come and see me." He said nothing. Having come from the New England silent world, I was easily induced to spend the rest of the hour sitting, meditating. I told him our time was up and he left. When he came back the next time, I said hello and we sat, or he stood and I sat. This went on for ten weeks. After the second week I didn't even say hello or goodbye, I just opened the door to let him in and out.

At the end of that time period, I got a call from his school teacher asking, "Are you the man who is treating Joe Zilch?"

"Yes," I answered.

"Well," she said, "I want you to know what a remarkable improvement he's made. He doesn't burn the curtains anymore, he doesn't hit other kids, he now studies, and he doesn't stick out his tongue at me. I don't know how you did it."

I didn't tell her. It was a professional secret because I didn't know how I had done it either!

The clinic was my first experience in rethinking past experiences. I spent the second six months going over my notes from the first six months in great detail, writing notations about what I would do again, what I should have done, what I should not have done. I had begun to sense that *thinking* about psychotherapy was almost as exciting as *doing* psychotherapy. We moved from child psychiatry training into work at Ormsby Village, a nearby delinquent school. I was exposed to 25 social workers who handled their 2,600 court assigned children while referring a few to me. I was also free to see private patients. My first patient was the four-year-old daughter of a young physician in town. Not knowing anything about families at this point, I saw the little girl for an hour, saying hello to the mother at the beginning of the hour and goodbye at the end, having no contact with the father or really with the mother, and taking no initial history since that was something the social worker did as part of her intake job. Then I got a call from the father saying how much my treatment had helped, that his daughter had changed, his wife had changed, and indeed, he himself was feeling better. I assumed, of course, that I'd found the secret of psychotherapy. I've found a dozen such secrets since, and each one disappears as soon as I find it!

During those three years I worked with delinquents and taught in the medical school part-time, I began to discover *toughness*. Tenderness had always been my thing, but toughness between people was harder to come by. I had learned about toughness with animals during my childhood on the farm. Fortunately, the arrival of our second daughter gave me access to the warmth and closeness that made it easier to forgive myself when I had to be professional or/and hard-boiled in my work with teenagers.

It became clearer and clearer that medical students were divided into those who didn't know how to be tender and those who didn't know how to be tough. How difficult it was to teach either one to have access to the other! I didn't know that I was merely talking about myself for some years, but I did discover the joys of working with delinquents. That power! I always thought of them as Cadillacs with a steering gear problem. They had lots of power but little control. (By contrast, the neurotics we saw in the medical school clinic were like old Ford cars who were only hitting on two cylinders.) Looking back, I often wonder how many of those delinquents stole cars so that they could come back and tell me about it. I had never had guts enough to do it myself, and I'm sure my enthusiasm about their adventures must have tempted them to do it again—just as they probably had been doing it for Dad and his repressed delinquency before they ever got to the institution.

The War Years: Mystery and Secrecy at the Oak Ridge Plutonium Facility

Then we moved to Oak Ridge, Tennessee, in those World War II days of terror. We listened to the bombing of London over the radio each night, and wondered whether Hitler was going to destroy England and take over the United States, as he had Poland and France and Holland and Belgium. The mysterious and eerie visits to Oak Ridge before I was hired were like something out of a Hollywood movie: the airplane flight in which the windows were covered so that you couldn't see out, the drive through the night, the floodlighted gates, and armed guards were all rather scary. Everyone used thoroughly convincing statements that "No, we don't know what we are doing here, but it is very important and we must not let the information get out." I had been referred by a child psychiatrist who knew my Chief in Louisville. All I knew was that there were 75,000 people in buildings situated on several hundred acres that had eight different security systems. The secrecy level was so high that you couldn't telephone between the two major work areas without first getting permission. When I was in one building, I was not allowed to phone anyone in the other building!

Muriel and I and the kids all lived there for two years. It was a self-contained community, complete with school and hospital. When we discovered the facility was being used to produce plutonium for nuclear bombs, we were as surprised as anyone else—although we shouldn't have been. It was an interesting example in careful memory. My Chief in Oak Ridge, who had gone to Los Alamos for the "tests," came back and told me there was a big explosion in the middle of the night but he was asleep so he didn't really know what it was about! Amid the threat of Hitler's shadow, I suppose it was easy to rouse us to patriotic service—even if we had to live not knowing exactly what we were doing.

Despite the cloak-and-dagger atmosphere, morale at Oak Ridge was astronomically high. (Observing and reporting on morale was part of our job.) There was a pervasive sense of purpose, even if most of us did not know what exactly that purpose was. There was a 300-bed hospital, and we 150 staff members worked day and night. The seven of us in psychiatry saw 20 patients each in half-hour interviews, back-to-back every day—and, with our other hand, ran a ten-bed inpatient service for acute disturbance. It was under these conditions that I discovered more of my toughness. Fighting the returning war veterans with acute psychotic episodes was hectic and scary.

I also discovered more about psychopathology and psychotherapy, albeit, rather serendipitously. Henry, a manic psychotic on the ward, was my next patient. I had just finished working with a five-year-old boy, whom I was treating with play therapy using a bottle with warm milk to help him regress. The bottle was left sitting on the desk. The manic came in, took one look at the bottle, and began a regressive sucking on it. Needless to say, I had another baby bottle with warm milk ready for him the next day. In twelve days of this intense bottle feeding experience, he completely emerged from his manic episode and, again, I thought I had discovered the secret of psychotherapy! As a matter of fact, for the next three or four years I bottle fed almost every patient I saw – man, woman, child, neurotic, psychotic, psychopathic or alcoholic – with a high degree of usefulness, if not success. It was only some time later that it dawned on me that it wasn't the patient who required the technique but the therapist. I was learning to mother, and once that awareness and skill were developed, I didn't need to use the technique.

Mating, Professionally Speaking

It was at Oak Ridge where I first discovered that, as well as needing a mate for my personal life, I also needed a partner for my professional life. Raising patients, like raising children, is horribly distorted if it is a one-parent project. John Warkentin* helped, but he wasn't always where I expected him to be. I can still recall vividly the day I was having my first interview with a South Pacific veteran. Suddenly, I became absolutely terrified that he was going to physically kill me right there and then. I excused myself, went to John's office, interrupted him and his patient, and dragged him back to my office while telling him of my fear. He took one look at the patient and said, "You know, I don't blame you. There have been times when I wanted to kill Carl myself." Then he walked out!

It is hard for me to believe even now how tremendously helpful John's behavior was for me, in the peculiar kind of paradoxical way that therapists understand so much better nowadays. It led me to structure therapy sessions so that we worked with patients together and at least could discuss the psychotherapy from the vantage point of a shared experience. It was only later that I discovered the other assets of co-therapy, which are probably even more important: assets such as the freedom to back away and look at what is happening, and the freedom to plunge in and not be afraid of what is happening – to you *and* the patient. A third asset that went unrecognized was that co-therapy also served as a secret system for learning how to talk

---

*Oak Ridge was on a "high priority" status, and we could recruit anyone we wanted from the Armed Forces. Warkentin was doing psychiatric work in an army hospital in Florida when he was selected to join our staff.

about emotional experiences, since you could objectify a subjective experience shared with someone else.

In the same sense that I enlisted two peers in college to try to be my co-therapists, I had now found a peer professionally. Dr. Warkentin and I became deeply personal in our give-and-take about patient treatment. It was as if having children (i.e., patients) together gave us a kind of professional marriage.

The Oak Ridge experience was a unique kind of growth experience for us as a family. Muriel and I were adults for the first time with two children, with no parental authority over us, and we were living in a world of mysterious surroundings comprised of tapped telephones, seven guard forces, CIA, FBI, Secret Service, local guards, police, and probably several we didn't even know about.

The psychological and emotional atmosphere of the facility was in itself something to which we had to adjust.

After the war ended, the big question for us as a family became, "Where do we go now?" Life had to be reorganized. This was when I made my first real break with a peer. Leaving Louisville was like saying goodbye to my fourth set of parents. Breaking with the Chief at Oak Ridge, who wanted to go to Minneapolis and set up a private, seven-person clinic, was quite a different kind of decision. For me, it involved developing another fragment of my own toughness to tell him that I wasn't willing to be related to him hierarchically. I would have been glad to go to Minneapolis as co-director of his clinic, even though he was 50 and I was 33, but I wasn't willing to go as only a member of his staff. So we broke, and I grieved, and then went alone (with my family) to Atlanta.

The Move to Atlanta: *Doing Therapy with Medical Students*

Once in Atlanta, I was hired by the dean of the medical school at Emory University (who was a humanistically oriented internist) to be on staff the first year and then take over the chairmanship of the psychiatry department the following year. I was hired primarily because I was young, available, and showed them a movie of the bottle feeding technique described earlier. Then, before I arrived to assume my position, the dean who had hired me left, another dean arrived, and I was rehired! Although the new dean was a very "soft," inadequate administrator, I still insisted on my massive demands: I would not teach in a medical school unless I could give every medical student two years of group therapy. Then, the second year, the same student group would be required to treat a patient in the hour before their regular group therapy but with another instructor supervising. The dean was desperate—most of the psychiatrists were overseas—so I was hired, and for ten years I got away with the policy of mandating therapy for medical students.

Actually, the school was very generous. It had never before included the field of psychiatry, so to move from two hour-long lectures every year to a situation in which *each* medical student received *400* hours of psychiatric experience was something that required adjustment! But, overall, the staff members accepted the change at face value.

The medical school had a religious affiliation and was financed by Coca-Cola on a deficit financing base. The older faculty members were very generous and warm about this "new kid on the block." The only problem was that they didn't have any money. So I went to the Rockefeller Foundation to get part of my own salary. Riding on my naive omnipotence and my previously discovered toughness, I ran head on into Alan Gregg, Medical Director of the Rockefeller Foundation. Meeting Gregg was one of those great experiences in which you find yourself in the presence of somebody who has truly found himself. We were closely related for many years and, although I only saw him on occasion, our friendship was a kind of psychotherapy of great personal significance to me. It was as though the power of the man increased your own power, like playing tennis with a professional tends to make you improve your own game.

Other men with presence followed. Lawrence Kubie, the highly respected psychoanalyst from New York, came to visit and said, "If I had a son going to medical school, I'd want him to come and be in your program." There was Dave Rioch, another respected psychoanalyst, who helped me with my decision to *not begin* psychoanalytic training and whom I especially remember for his statement, "Maturity is the capacity to be immature." There are people along the way who, when you encounter them, push you to be unified by the very fact of their own integration. This was true also of the Chairman of the Department of Medicine at Emory University, Paul Beeson, who was aloof but also a powerful, solid human being. His support of my early administrative struggles—trying to be clinician and, at the same time, play the politics of a medical school—was a sobering experience.

Unfortunately, these struggles failed to develop my toughness. In fact, I began to rebel *against* toughness and I became entangled in the typical "mother" problem. I worked to satisfy and excite the medical students rather than to belong to the faculty. This triangular conflict between the medical students and the other department chairmen was augmented by my not knowing or not being willing to play the adult-to-adult administrative role required of being chairman. Instead, I slipped into being a kind of ombudsman for the medical students: We were in collusion against the rest of the medical school faculty, as the psychotherapist tends to be in collusion against mothers. Making matters worse, there was a conflicted triangular relationship going on between the medical school (which was private), the city hospital, and Coca-Cola. Even my delusions of grandeur couldn't get me out of that corner.

Furthermore, the humanism that it required to be an effective clinician and work with schizophrenics, to work with couples, to work with cotherapists, and to teach people how to do psychotherapy, was antithetical to the kind of attitude required to handle administrative problems. I was really a clinician who was trying to be an administrator but not succeeding. I often recall how quaint it was that in this, my administrative childhood, I hired three different secretaries, all of whom turned out to be schizophrenic! The struggle with the city hospital and its master administrator—who was not going to assume any responsibility for psychiatric patients, since they were "state hospital patients"—still haunts me. The adroit way in which he helped me blueprint seven different plans for a psychiatric ward, none of which was ever built, ended in my discovery of how impotent I really was. This realization helped me develop enough toughness to get out of the medical school instead of staying on as an academic lame duck.

In those early days we continued to make clinical discoveries. For example, we discovered that the baby bottle was a valuable way to induce regression in the service of growth, but *fighting* was equally valuable. Just as the baby bottles spread from one to another within our staff group of seven, so the fighting spread so that we were apt to be involved physically with almost every patient, in one way or another. The intimacy of physical contact—of slapping games, of body wrestling, and of arm wrestling—became a means through which we continued to discover our own toughness.

Concurrent with these developments, Tom Malone* and I were in-

---

*I had first become aware of Tom Malone's work as head of undergraduate psychology at Duke University while I was at Oak Ridge, and enlisted him at Emory as soon as I was able to offer him a position and free tuition while he went to four years of medical school while a full-time faculty member.

volved in creating a secondary program of investigating the process of psychotherapy. We spent three half-days a week at a blackboard talking about psychotherapy and developing an outline. This routine continued for a couple of years until we had accrued a massive outline, and then we dictated *The Roots of Psychotherapy* (1953, Blakiston) between teaching hours. This process of give-and-take directed toward a cognitive understanding of the process of psychotherapy constituted the establishment of my third intimate peer relationship. The pinochle group in high school and the threesome in college were each a kind of therapeutic group. The peer relationships with my wife, then with Dr. Warkentin, and now with Dr. Malone were uniquely different; yet each involved a freedom to approach and withdraw, a quality of separation and togetherness. My respect and even veneration for Dr. Malone's intellectual grasp of psychoanalysis and psychological theory were paired with his respect for my intuitive understanding, and this, for me, was quite a remarkable event. It stood in rather dramatic contrast to my inherent sense of being a country bumpkin. It was as though I was learning how to think with Dr. Malone, just as I was practicing how to fight with Dr. Warkentin (in a way that also included a kind of discipline and control that was his expertise).

Just as the hospital politics and the administrative destruction of our psychotherapy there taught me something about toughness, being consultant to the Georgia Department of Mental Health, where I was expected to do something about the mental health of four-and-a-half million citizens, taught me something about impotence. My dream of bringing together the department heads in the state bureaucracy to work out mutually satisfying plans for coordinating services (so that trainees in psychotherapy could be matched to patient needs in the prisons and state hospitals) was so casually exploded by the old sophisticated administrators that I learned a whole new respect for the power of the system.

Psychiatric educators from around the country began to visit our teaching program and superimpose their theoretical structure on our teaching method. The educators quickly concluded that, if the method did not fit their theoretical model, it obviously was not working. The facts that students were *getting* psychotherapy, and that students were creatively *doing* psychotherapy, all seemed incidental to these theoreticians. It was a bitter pill for me.

Our department's hiring of Dick Felder, the chief medical resident in Grady Hospital, was a fortuitous break. He had become a psychotherapist without going through the rigors of learning psychodynamics or theoretical intrapsychic pathology. He had simply learned how to help people. Without knowing about defenses and psychic mechanisms, he developed his own frame of thinking about psychological problems. It was an extrapolation from his knowledge of the body and its physiological organization. He saw all psychopathology as an effort to heal. It was as though he would not admit that the body could be doing something bad to itself, and concomitantly, he could not admit that the mind was doing something bad to itself. Schizophrenia was an effort on the part of the child to heal the family. This reversal of the algebraic sign on emotional distress from negative to positive provided a massive input to my thinking. I became more and more preoccupied with the conviction that our professional understanding was being distorted to see everything through black glasses, just like the culture did when it put "bad" people in mental hospitals. Dr. Felder was the person who first introduced me to a gradually increasing conviction that the objective of psychotherapy is to *humanize* pathology.

Being the Patient: Symptoms Galore

Meanwhile, back at the ranch: I first went for psychotherapy during my child psychiatry days, and that brief experience was the beginning of my discovery that there was more to me than was visible. Subsequently, at Oak Ridge, I decided to be a patient to a co-therapy team. I went for a year, interrupted for a year or two, went back for another year, and so on, for the next six or eight years.

By 1946, we had three daughters and a son. The problem of trying to be an administrator and a clinician had exteriorized a great deal of my immaturity. When the stress in the hospital and medical school got high, I began to precipitate psychosomatic attacks in myself, complete with cold sweats, chills, vomiting, diarrhea, and a half-day in bed. Cuddling with my wife resolved this response, but I went back into psychotherapy to help develop competence in preventing it. (Living with our own children also convinced Muriel and me that the only "unconditional positive regard" in this world is from little children.) These psychosomatic attacks lasted for four or five years.

Then I began to have more access to my somatic symptoms in relationship to patients. These ran the gamut from intestinal spasms, hunger, full bladder, sneezing, the hair on the back of my neck standing up, tingling on one side of my body or one arm or one leg, restless walking around the office, boredom and, of course, the utterly embarrassing experience of dozing off to sleep in the middle of a session. In my early days I assumed that this was due to boredom and withdrawal on my part and I judged it to be a social misbehavior. As time went along and I survived some of my guilt and embarrassment, however, I came to a new, more positive understanding. When I went to sleep, I often dreamed about what was happening in the session. The relevance of these dreams to the ongoing therapeutic struggle made it increasingly clear that this falling asleep was a way of going

Muriel and I in Atlanta, 1948, with the first five Whitaker children. In front: Bruce and Anita; in back: Nancy, Lynn, and Elaine.

inside myself and connecting with my introjection of the patient and finding a way of communicating this to the patient. Such a communication was usually more powerful than my left-brain intellectual concepts.

For example, Bill and Mary had a daughter who was a freshman in medical school, and whom they referred for psychiatric help because she insisted on working in the black clinic that summer. The daughter revealed that father and she were linked up very tightly, while mother was the household maid. Mother was then referred to me for psychotherapy, and I tried to indoctrinate her with some of the women's liberation virus. Since this was 1953, the virus was still quite weak and didn't take. In my anxiety and concern and frustration, I went to sleep and dreamed there was a large banquet table, twelve-foot long and four-foot wide, with a huge silver tureen in the middle. Mama was sitting on this side with a large soup ladle, daughter and husband were sitting on the other side with soup bowls, and mother was dishing out soup. However, her right arm was strapped with adhesive taped from midway on the forearm to midway up the upper arm. So there was no way she could get any soup into her bowl. I woke, told her that dream, and for the first time made quite a massive assault on her male chauvinist life style.

Meanwhile, still more symptoms popped into my life: headaches, double vision, and a very stiff neck. The double vision was intriguing, since it would take place when I was preoccupied with a patient's anxiety symptoms and our relationship. In between my symptoms, I was gaining a great new freedom to be tender and maternal as well as angry and demanding. More and more I became convinced that the *relationship* was what caused change in patients rather than any insights or any unconditional positive regard. I developed a capacity not only to accept transference but, as Ronny Laing suggests, to act out the projection. If the patient looked at me and saw mother qualities, I used my intuition to carry out the role and augment this transference; then, I would violate it as it violated my own personal life space. *I tried to join the patient in her intrapsychic family, and then individuate from her into being the person I was.*

Meanwhile, I was in and out of co-therapy—alone, with my wife, with one of our kids, alone again—in a series of efforts to find more of myself. I guess I'll never finish that job.

Shifting to the Larger System

Simultaneous with my struggles to find more of myself was the struggle to move from individual psychotherapy to a larger system. At Emory we became increasingly involved with the process of using two therapists and paralleling the concept of two parents raising children. This method convinced us that the first patient-therapist contact inevitably took on the mother-child model, whereas the second therapist took on the stepfather or father role and thus was more interested in reality and more apt to set up an I-thou relationship instead of the primal, maternal "we." We began to treat more than the one, intrapsychic labyrinth.

One of my colleagues figured out why I gave up doing individual therapy. He said I was bored with individuals, and he was right! Individual therapy was often routine and unchallenging. The couple-to-couple relationship, by contrast, allowed for much more interaction, much more life, and much more fun! We soon became aware that the therapist's enjoyment of therapy was as constructive as his insightful, technical competence. It is as though the fun that the parents have becomes the nourishment from which the children grow.

One other factor that lured us from the individual context to a larger system was a series of failures in the intensive co-therapy treatment of seriously ill schizophrenics. We began treatment with bottle feeding and then progressed to a kind of induced regression (infantilization) that was physically facilitated by the therapist's use of cuddling, rubbing, positive tactile stimulation, and baby talk. We would get excellent results, but many times after the patient had been pulled out of his psychosis and was well on his way to what we thought was a good maturity, the family would intercede and destroy our therapeutic efforts. This pattern led us more and more toward a decision to *begin* with the family. I regard this fighting with schizophrenics and failing as a major watershed in my development of toughness.

In 1950, coinciding with my intensive book writing effort with Tom Malone, we (myself, Malone, Warkentin, and Felder) instigated a series of ten conferences on the psychotherapy of schizophrenia. Our "Atlanta group" was joined by the "Philadelphia group," who included psychiatrists Ed Taylor, John Rosen, and Mike Hayward. Every six months we would set up a four-day weekend, and the seven of us would work for those four days with a particular schizophrenic patient. Later in the series, we began to work with families as well as with the schizophrenic individual. The struggle for concurrence among us, the struggle for new ideas, the sharing of the exquisite joy and profound pain and suffering involved in trying to treat schizophrenia brought us close, as individuals and as a group. We stayed up many nights attempting to find our way into the unconscious perceptions we assumed were there in the schizophrenic's mind, but which were not available on a deliberate, conscious level.

Having made some therapeutic gains, we decided to include Gregory Bateson and Don Jackson in our tenth conference, with the intent of formally conceptualizing our results for publication. Don was a "brain" who sparked a lot of new thinking and Greg was an elder statesman anthropologist—a sage who smelled of people. During our intense meetings, we struggled over a definition of schizophrenia and finally decided that we could not define it. We also decided not to include a section on techniques. It was clear to us that the reason people work with schizophrenics is because they want to find their own psychotic inner-person—now referred to as the right brain part of us—the nonanalytic, total gestalt portion of our cortex. We also struggled over the role of the schizophrenogenic mother and the question, Can the father himself create schizophrenia? All this debate anteceded the advent of systems theory, which made it clear that it takes a family unit, and more, to originate such a holocaust.

Juggling Clinical and Administrative Careers

Teaching in a medical school and doing psychotherapy with groups of medical students who look like 20 carbon copies of yourself was a very stressful experience. Meantime, the big Atlanta hospital (Grady) and its endless patients were upgrading the pressure. In Oak Ridge, facing one patient after another, I had been personal, parental, loving or hateful—and had lucked onto bottle feedings whereby I had developed some capacity to be a feeding mother. But Grady Hospital was not satisfied with just a crazy mother. I was forced into becoming a reality-oriented, administrative, choice-making *father*.

An example of the crazy atmosphere: In the waiting room with 50 patients, I was accosted by a 40-year-old woman. She talked for five minutes in a chaotic, delusional way and then said, "What's wrong with me, doctor?"

It was impossible to sit down and talk at length, to be reasonable and educational, so I just said, "You're crazy."

She said, "Thank God! I've been to five doctors and I thought that was true, but none of them would tell me. Thank you so much. What do I do now?"

"Why don't you get a job, get yourself an income, go find a private psychiatrist, and sit down for a couple of years and work with him to learn how to live in the world that you're in." Follow-up many years later revealed that she had done exactly that!

Looking back on 1947, I am excited by the clinical experiences and depressed by the administrative castration experiences. Every four or five months we would work out a new blueprint for a psychiatric ward and then have it cancelled. It not only increased my sense of impotence but also my toughness. It led me towards the decision that being an administrator was a peculiar art and not my forte.

The "learning tree" of my life experiences also had branches in the V.A. Hospital with which the medical school was affiliated. Here I first became clear that the variable in psychotherapy is the *therapist*. The patient comes as a biological and psychological whole self, *albeit* with motives and impulses that are divergent. The therapist—whatever his interest, whatever his dedication—is the variable. He comes as a function: he is trying to be all of himself that is available, but he is also doing a *job*. He is not being a whole self, and the amount of himself that he can bring to this relationship determines the amount of power he and the therapeutic team can muster. The biological whole of the patient is striving towards unification, healing, growth. The functional effort on the part of the therapist depends on the situation, the constellation, the relationship of the therapist and the patient at this particular time and place. I don't trust it!

I had brought Dr. Warkentin from Oak Ridge to be head of the V.A. Hospital psychiatry department. Here, we both learned a lot more about toughness and impotence. The V.A. gradually closed in administratively to destroy our efforts at psychotherapy, forcing us to funnel 100 patients through the ward each month and making any psychotherapy useless. Meantime, we had discovered more about the process of psychotherapy: ten therapists could work well with one patient!

Among the learnings at the V.A. was the discovery of the usefulness of the soup bowl. Patients began demanding more and more sleeping pills, and in our parental panic, we finally decided to go all the way and do what is now called "paradoxical intention": We put amytal capsules on the ward table in soup bowls! Anyone could have a reserve supply. Many bowlfuls disappeared immediately, but within five days the drug consumption had diminished to one-third the nightly rate. Drugs had become a symbol of lovingness, and patients sensed they were cared for by the medication they could get from the nurse. Taking life in their hands put their control system into operation. (Control systems are very important in an inpatient ward.) Another example: one psychotic who masturbated almost 24 hours a day was clearly out of control. Nobody seemed to know what to do. One day the chief nurse walked in on her daily rounds and said, "If you don't stop that, I'm not going to come back and visit you anymore." He stopped immediately, as though he had needed some authoritative decision by this, his good mother.

The Agony and Ecstasy of Treating Schizophrenics

During those ten years at Emory, Malone and I were also deeply involved in the effort to treat individual schizophrenics by the use of co-therapy. At times, the mother of the patient was treated simultaneously by Dr. Warkentin, but essentially we were trying to find some method to resolve the horror of the psychotic process by the very power of our own two-person interventions. For a while, we used something like a halfway house setting with recovered schizophrenics. This approach was similar in its caretaking aspect to the method developed by John Rosen. Rosen had electrified and horrified the psychiatric world by treating schizophrenics in a home setting by "direct analysis"—a verbally assaultive method of dominating. (It was supposed to have cured everyone. Then the American Psychiatric Association investigated and found it wasn't true. Rosen got into very serious trouble.) We used a similar kind of process to the one he used in that the patients were cared for in a home and seen in psychotherapy on an individual basis. We were not confrontational, however. Our approach was definitely maternal.

The hell was that often, once the patient had recovered from the psychotic component, the family would find a way of dragging him or her out of therapy and re-precipitating the psychosis, even though the family lived a thousand miles away! Treatment of a chronically delusional and grossly withdrawn schizophrenic patient requires a very painful and very primitive investment of the *self*, and having the patient (child) torn away from us was a very frightening experience. Lyman Wynne talks about the agony and ecstasy of working with these patients, and I can think of no better way of describing it.

The agony is not only in the process; it is also in the outcome, and it led inevitably to my refusal to see psychotics without the family. Gradually we developed the conviction that one could define the psychotic only in the framework of his family dynamics: Father and Mother are lightly bonded; the baby becomes bonded throughout pregnancy and Mother weakens her bond to Father as she becomes more and more involved with her intrauterine, significant other. With this loosened bond, Father attaches himself to some other focus—money, his secretary, a new car, or maybe back to his own mother. Then, when the baby is born, Mother becomes more deeply attached. Father is further encouraged to bond with somebody or something else, until the baby is about a year and half old. Then, when Mother turns back to Father, he may not be available. If he's not, she begins to develop a kind of isolation. In that isolation, given her own family of origin background, she develops a fear of being crazy, of losing control of her own inner life. The symbiosis that took place between Mother and her baby in the first year and a half is then reopened, and with it, a covert arrangement is established. The child will be the primary process "half" of their one, "whole" person, and Mother then will be the control "half"—the square, the counter-schiz, if you will. Early on, the child maintains the symbiosis by staying infantile, at least in relationship to the mother, even though he may learn how to simulate social adaptation to the outer world. With the onset of adolescence, the simulation may be broken and the child goes back to the infantile primitive psychotic patterning, still protecting Mother from her fear of the psychosis that really is a malignant isolation.

The intrusion of the psychotherapist and the development of a bilateral double-binding relationship between that psychotherapist and the patient displace the mother. Once having established this (and it cannot be done by simulation—the therapist has to *be* like the mother; he can't merely *act* like her), the therapist is then in a position to flip their dyadic roles. If he becomes the psychotic "other," then the patient must reverse roles and become the sane, square, counter-schiz. This adaptation makes it possible for the psychotic to become like the rest of us—part crazy, part sane, and gradually more of each. However, this does not handle the problem of the displaced mother. That was our defeat, and resulted in our being forced into dealing with families.

The Discovery of Families

The discovery of families became a vital branch of my learning tree. The 80-year-old mother of one of our faculty was brought in for help. Because of my own interest, I stayed with her as she gradually deteriorated into being an interpersonal and psychological vegetable. I enjoyed her as a person; as in play therapy, I found that I did not need to have logical conversation with her to enjoy her. By my example, the family members also were able to go on enjoying her without needing to have her function as an intellectual, social organism. She was just their mother. Two years later, she was still living at home. The craziness that had overlaid her arteriosclerosis of the brain had long since faded into the background, and she just ate and slept and smiled and went to the bathroom. But the family still loved her and still enjoyed being with her. They had not been terrified by her craziness; they had not turned away from her because of her failing health.

I still remember the game she and I played: we were boyfriend and girlfriend and going to Bermuda for a week alone. One day, in her childlike deterioration she said, "Young man, are you playing or are you for real?" I had to laugh and say I was playing. The next week this 80-year-old grandma brought me in her little bottle of smelling salts, which she had been keeping in her pocketbook for 40 years, saying she thought I needed it more than she did!

Private Practice:
The Atlanta Psychiatric Clinic

The move from the psychiatric department of Emory University to our establishment of the Atlanta Psychiatric Clinic was a gradual one, carried out by a joint decision. The university had grown intolerant of our all-out psychotherapy orientation, and we could not resolve the administrative differences. So the group of us—Tom Malone, John Warkentin, Ellen and Bill Kiser, Dick Felder, Rives Chalmers, and I—resigned *en masse* and set up separate offices and a private clinic. Setting up a clinic, buying a building, learning how to be businessmen in the world of psychotherapy were all new experiences. We discovered the use of the routine second interview consultation. At first, use of the second interview was merely administrative: a way to get a consultant in, to get additional data, to get a more thorough-going evaluation so that we could report back to the referring doctor and to the patient, whether individual, couple, or family. Very quickly, we found that it had other uses of great significance. It seems that the initial therapist is contaminated with all of the usual problems of being a mother: he or she is all-forgiving, all-accepting and minimal in demands.

The staff of the Atlanta Psychiatric Clinic, 1961. Front row: Herbert Stone, guest Harold Searles, Ellen Kiser, Carl Whitaker. Middle row: Rives Chalmers, John Warkentin, Thomas Malone. Back row: Thomas Leland, William Kiser, Richard Felder.

On the other hand, the consultant coming into the same situation for the second interview turns out to be very much like the father: reality-oriented, demanding, intellectual; much less tempted to accept the original complaints or the original presentation; and very much freer to think about what is being presented in a conceptual, total gestalt manner.

In practice, the degree to which this process turned out to be the case was almost ridiculous. I would conduct an initial interview with a family. The following week, I would ask whomever on the staff happened to have free time available to be consultant. That person would listen while told the story in front of the patient or patients and then would expand the history during the rest of that hour. The staff meeting between the two of us would take place with the family present, unless the situation were very serious.

The consultant formulated a diagnosis of the dynamics and a proposition for therapy. We would then move to the other therapist's office, where I would be consultant to his family. In both these situations the original therapist (the primary therapist) would serve mostly as secretary. The ideas, insights, and conceptual organizational thinking would be done by the second person, the consultant.

We also discovered a dual contract. Having thus listened to the initial story, formulated a description, and reported our findings to the family, we considered the initial contract ended. We suggested that the family members not make another appointment until they took the time to sit down and talk to each other about what they wanted and whether they wanted anything. Then they might reestablish a contract for an ongoing program of therapy.

As our group of former teachers gradually became a professional clinic group whose objective was treating patients rather than teaching physicians, our pattern of interaction changed. We took to treating each other as students. We developed a professional supervision system of endless give-and-take, discussing what had happened to each other as individuals, as co-therapists, or to couples with whom we were working. This seven-member "cuddle group" also began to exercise more authority. Whenever a member got into an impasse, the problem would be presented to staff meeting and decisions would be made by the whole group rather than just by the therapist.

One other way of avoiding the routine of clinical treatment was to spend a half-a-day each week writing. Several of us would exchange ideas, and if something sparked more than one or two of us, we deemed it worth writing about. The person with the most excitement would begin the outline and others would fill in, expand, amplify and criticize. It was a very exciting collaborative experience in intimate communication and in the struggle to formulate for someone else what was our own secret language. This was not easy, because after 15 years of professional living together, we had a language with many revered code words, much like the language of twins.

Academic success had led us to move out of the university into developing a clinic. Interestingly enough, clinical success (and the financial success that accompanied it) tended to precipitate stress within our group. We gradually drifted into finding separate friendship networks. Individual territories were more and more defended rather than handled cooperatively. Our NATO defense system had worked well as long as we were in trouble with the medical school or the medical students or the patients. Once we had become comfortable and affluent, both psychologically and professionally, the work tensions became a process by which we were alienated. We could not decide whether to expand and build a psychiatric hospital. It felt as though we were beginning to dry up instead of continuing to grow.

The Move to Madison: Conceptualizing Family Therapy

In 1965 I was offered the opportunity to move to another university, which seemed like a happy escape. However, this was not only a process of escaping the professional dilemma; it was also the time to make a major change in our own family life style. The five older children were on the verge of leaving the nest—in fact, three of them already had—and our days of PTA were about over. The opportunity for Muriel and me to be a twosome again seemed very enticing. The decision to move to Madison and join the University of Wisconsin Medical School staff, then, was more of a family decision than a professional one. Certainly it was clear that moving to Madison meant I would move into being a full-time family therapist and do little or no individual therapy. The effort to shake up my own system by moving into another world to keep from going stale was also replicated in my wife's effort to get past the stage of being a mother. The two of us could be people with each other rather than just parents.

It was not clear until after we had left our clinic group how much we grieved over the loss of those loved ones. It was at least a year before the pain became prominent, and it was even longer before we became aware that in our separation, we had also tended to isolate ourselves, to withdraw from the community and reconstruct a kind of honeymoon relationship. We were helped in this area when one of our older daughters returned to live with us for a year while her husband was in Viet Nam. Every set of parents ought to have the opportunity to live through such a training period in how to be an adult with your adult child and avoid returning to the old parent-child games. It was scary, and then a very satisfying growth experience. I asked her toward the end of the year what had been important to her. She said, "The most important thing is that nobody ever came into my room without knocking."

Another preventive mental health break Muriel and I experienced was having a child in our later years. Our first five children had come two years apart; the sixth child came eight years later, in 1955. It was like having a new family; like having an only child and an opportunity for us to see across the head of that child into each other's eyes. With the first five children, we were so involved in our own living with each other as individuals and as parents that the dynamics and secondary cognitions of what we were doing were more fragmentary. Although many times we spent long hours struggling over our parenting of those five children, it was grossly contaminated by the ever-present experience of daily living. This lovely boon of our old age started her life with seven parents! The responsibilities were minimal in comparison with those previous years, and the opportunities for enjoying ourselves with her were much greater. The freedom to let her invade our lives allowed for a kind of give-and-take with less pain, less sense of responsibility, and more of the free-floating fun that should be available to younger parents but usually is not. We did not doubt ourselves as much, we did not make as many demands of her, and her right to be herself was not only more protected but even cultivated. She served as a model for our discovery of a new self in each of us.

Sixth baby Holly, 1955, with her proud Daddy.

The professional psychiatric scene in Madison was uniquely centered around Dr. Milton Miller, the chairman. Most of the department had been organized on a psychoanalytic model as a kind of satellite from Menninger's, where several of the staff had been trained. Dr. Miller had gradually moved from the psychoanalytic model towards an existential kind of psychotherapy and philosophy. My arrival was part of his effort to move into other territories in the field of psychiatry. My development of cotherapy started almost immediately, and I did work with couples or families with almost everybody on the staff at their requests and with much generous cooperation on their parts. However, my effort to establish a relationship with the residents and to kindle some interest on their part in family therapy was slow and ponderous. My own learnings were limited, and the Atlanta Psychiatric Clinic had left me with a kind of secret language which was not easy to translate into a common tongue. I seemed to be repeating the pattern of the simple farm boy moving to the sophisticated city. The clinic had been our private world, and this new world seemed far more complicated and imposing. I was besieged by the same kind of uncertainties, the same sense of awkwardness and the same temptation to be an isolate that had plagued me decades ago.

The effort to tease residents into daring to treat couples and families demanded a conceptual framework. Their endless questions, my natural self-doubt, and the long series of families coming through made conceptualization take place almost in spite of us. My decision to use residents as cotherapists was a deliberate one. I decided I could no longer tolerate playing games and trying to tease them into working with families, so I simply invited them to sit in with me in my private practice with families, and to follow their own ideas. This approach gradually developed into a fairly simplified system: they were free to participate or watch, but they automatically became part of it—many times to their own amazement. I remember one resident who had said little or nothing for five interviews. The sophisticated faculty family came back for the sixth interview and he wasn't present because he had been on call and up all night. The family stayed for five minutes and then said, "Well, if Bill isn't going to be here, we might just as well come back next week." Then they walked out! I was a bit surprised, but the resident who thought he was very unimportant was *really* shocked.

One of the conceptual understandings that came out of my work in Madison was a thorough conviction of the politics of family therapy. The initial phase of working with the family demands a political *coup d'etat* in which the therapist proves his power and his control of the therapeutic process, thus enabling the family to have the courage to change its living pattern. Other concepts, such as the importance of the detumescence of the scapegoat or the surfacing other scapegoats in the family, spreading the anxiety around the family, the necessity of using paradoxical intention to reverse the axis of responsibility so that the family would learn to carry the initiative for their own change—all of these understandings were picked up from the residents while they were working with families. Particularly important in this regard was Dr. Gus Napier, who is centrally interested in family therapy and is a very creative thinker in his own right. Each time I would propose ideas to him, he would expand, elaborate, and alter them and I was sure to get something extra in return.

One of the covert changes in thinking that I experienced was my increasing conviction that everybody is schizophrenic. Most of us do not have the courage to be crazy except in the middle of the night when we are sound asleep, and we try to forget it before we wake up. In my advancing years and tenured role I became more and more courageous and began using the word with greater nonchalance. The first six months to a year of using it was quite a shock, but after that it became gradually more and more accepted, at least in my own head.

I began to understand more clearly that there are different kinds of craziness. There is being *driven* crazy, which means that one's malignant isolationism is brought about by being forced out of his or her family. There is *going* crazy which, in the case of falling in love, is a delightful although very frightening experience, but which also takes place in the therapeutic setting. (It is sometimes called "transference psychosis" in much the same way as we use the term "transference neurosis.") Then there is *acting* crazy—the crazy responsiveness of the individual who has once been insane and who, when under stress, returns to that state of being even though he is not out of control in the same way. He is like the child who has just learned to walk: If he gets in a hurry, he'll get down on his hands and knees and crawl, even though it's slower.

There are other models of craziness, including the *quasi-craziness* that happens in social groups or in therapeutic interviews, and the *imitation craziness* that sometimes takes place when a therapist is trying to make it with a patient or a patient is trying to make it with the therapist. One of the characteristic models for quasi-craziness or maybe-going-crazy is the religious ceremony in which people "speak in tongues."

Behind these concepts about therapy is my increasing conviction that the most important task for the therapist is to preserve his own life space, to

In my department office at the University of Wisconsin Medical School, 1980.

preserve his own personhood, and to see his professional function as being different from that amateur enthusiasm with which he began his career. He isn't working for the love of it but because it is his job.

Reparenting Myself

In recent years I have been gradually more and more intrigued with the probably semi-facetious story about Plato being asked to summarize the Dialogues on his deathbed and his cryptic answer, "Practice dying." It seems to me like a logical kind of psychotherapy. Gradually I have picked up bits-

and-pieces of my own effort to kill off or, if you will, bury in dignity those parts of myself which lived in fantasy as high-flown dreams and painful disappointments. For example, my early dream that I could be an adminis-trator was partly killed off by my ten years as psychiatry chairman, and partly asphyxiated by my year as President of the AAP. (Francis Harper, who was the *de facto* president, would certainly understand this perspective.)

In Madison I was introduced to sailboats. Here I am on Lake Superior in 1984.

When I moved to Madison I declared myself unwilling to do administration, which was a way of saying, "I finally have killed off the fantasy that I could think administratively." As with each of these fragmentary suicides, I came out with a new freedom to devote myself more fully to being a clinician and more of a person.

My new life in Madison also introduced me to sailboats. I quickly developed a massive turn-on and began to fantasize a trans-Atlantic sailing voyage! The gradual realization that the amount of expertise required in navigation skills, time, and money, could not be suitably reconciled with my ongoing responsibilities and other satisfactions in life at first left me sad. Then, as I gradually became convinced that this death was acceptable to me, I found myself freer to enjoy sailing in our own lake with my wife. Having transcended this grief—or, if you will, the suicide of this daydream—life was more fun.

More crucially, but less easy to describe, are the repeated experiences with families here in my office or in the clinic. Families contain parents, grandparents, siblings, spouses and children. All reopen and jiggle around my perceptions, enjoyment, and re-experiencing of my own family life and the four generations of it in which I swim.

I discovered that suicide is a three-generational family plan. Since Joe's father didn't nourish him, he'll be damned if he'll nourish his son. If Mary's mother couldn't enjoy intimacy, then Mary feels she has no right to enjoy intimacy. I discovered that unconditional positive regard is only available from an infant, and then probably only for the first nine months of his or her life. Each of these discoveries elaborates a part of me. As I feel freer to drop bits and pieces of my fantasy world into the therapeutic hopper with my families in treatment, I am struggling to reparent myself, to prepare for my death by practicing dying, which in a strange paradoxical way is also practicing a fuller way of living in today's day and for today's joy.

Demythologizing Myself

Narcissism is the capacity to look at an image of yourself which you and your parents or your siblings or your peers have constructed and rupture that myth. "My mother thought I would be president. P.S.: She didn't say president of what!" For me to get past the delusion of her projection onto me is a large part of my struggle to individuate. Concurrent with this is my myth about *her*. My mother is the superwoman who could carry those great big chairs, who could make that lovely food, who could kiss my wounds and make them better. In my head she became a myth, and whenever that myth was not fulfilled or became ruptured, the things that ruptured it were blamed. The myth remained intact.

In psychotherapy the project becomes how to demythologize your mother, and how to demythologize those closest to you as a preliminary to demythologizing yourself.

In my professional world I create those settings which produce a myth about me in other persons and groups. I then suffer the isolation and the loneliness of not being a person and the fear of becoming only a myth. Part of the mystery is, who is the "they" who mythologize me? "They" are the people whom I set up to see me as mythological. The question then is not why *they* did it, because *I* created that dynamic, but how can I keep them from continuing with it? How can I be freed of my loneliness? My fear of being one-down, of being degraded, of being denied, makes me create a myth, an imaginary presence, which keeps *me* from being discovered. I enacted this myth with my parents by making myself the family hero; with my kids, I made myself the big-shot worker; less so, perhaps, with my spouse, but more so, perhaps with my public. Like all myths, the rupture is more painful to the person who believes the myth.

How can one explode a self-myth? Partly by inducing laughter at the fact of it, and partly by a massive injection of reality or a massive injection of some counter myth (like, "Isn't it wonderful that Freud wet his pants?"). One can learn to evolve a sense of the absurd, a capacity to laugh at the myth, to enjoy it for its fun rather than become a slave to it by taking it as a reality. Maybe the only sure way to explode a myth is to induce a counter-myth; or, make the two self-destructing; or, destroy the myth by saturating it with positive reinforcement—that is, by augmenting the myth until it is intolerable!

My Wife as Co-Therapist

Now that we've been married 50 years, I want to talk a little about the fact that my wife, Muriel, has been a covert consultant and supervisor to me from the beginning of our entrance into the world of psychotherapy. She has had no professional training, but has raised six children and, of course, has listened to my need for support and reassurance from the very beginning as I changed from one professional struggle to another. In that sense she has been my co-therapist all along, although we never talked in detail about cases. My psychological panic after the end of a difficult day, or as

With Muriel—nearing 50 years of marriage.

we proceeded to talk about a difficult patient, made her the support system. In addition, and much more important, is the fact that, for me, work is a function and a role so that my investment in my day's activities (family therapy, supervision of residents, teaching medical students) was less important than the power of her care, concern, and questioning. While the function of husband and wife moved us closer and closer to becoming peers, the undercurrent of her being my mother and my being her little boy gave greater power to her participation. Furthermore, we were two parents, and the endless give-and-take of parenthood with the one, two, three, four, five and then six children produced a kind of super-functioning that made my professional workday less critical.

My training over these many years has made me better and better in the role of psychotherapist, what I now describe most accurately as a foster parent. Muriel's job was less a role; it was a profound investment and an expression of her personhood. That is, her interaction carried a great deal more weight for her than did my professional function in the office with patients. As the empty nest phenomenon began in 1955 when our first child went off to college, I began to invite her to be co-therapist when I treated a professional therapist and spouse dealing with their marital struggles. It seemed unfair for two therapists to be paired with one therapist's spouse. It should come as no surprise that her personhood, her spontaneity, and her lack of professional distance made her very powerful and, to my surprise, much more relevant many, many times than I was. At first there was a sense of strain between us that soon became a gain in the fact of our we-ness serving as the therapist. In essence, the patients now had a set of foster parents rather than two individuals who were making believe they were a team, and/or one therapist who was making believe he could switch roles from being the nurturant parent to being the executive parent, which is not easy and frequently a total failure.

Over these last 20 years, Muriel and I have done more and more co-therapy as a team. Our own coupling becomes a metaphor for their coupling, and their coupling and marital struggles, of course, mirror those of our own marriage.

The husband-wife team adds an administrative clarity by virtue of its we-ness. For example, it becomes clear to the patient (family) that all administrative decisions (i.e., calls to report anxiety or change the schedule) must be shared with the co-therapist. This not only supplies a kind of strength but prevents the development of the usual abnormal expectations of mother love from every therapist. In addition, the marital co-therapy team adds another dimension of honesty. There is less reliance on objectivity and more necessary openness between the therapy couple. That warmth, whether it is loving, cooperative warmth or the warmth of anger or disagreement between the couple, carries over to the couple or family. To say it more openly, *love is in the air*.

Another characteristic of the marital co-therapy team is that it symbolically recapitulates the actual child-raising experiences that the patient-couple themselves went through as children. And, finally, it is important to recognize that this opportunity of working with a couple or a family in a husband-wife therapeutic team reopens learnings about the empty nest syndrome and provides ever-new experiences in saying good-bye, with all the empty-nest overtones of death, desertion, graduation, and running away from home.

Unknown—Except to the Body

Having recently come back from my open heart surgery, I have been very preoccupied with what the body knows that the mind hides. This preoccupation becomes part of a long-time curiosity I have had about dreams: Where do they come from? Why do they arrive? The body knows the total process, and we must be clear that the body is not just a new term for the unconscious. The body knows the trauma of birth. It records in muscles, in body form, and in body physiology the episodes of life—most of which are forgotten, some of which are never known.

The body also remembers the psychological death of general anesthesia. When anesthesia produces a kind of suicide or murder, and the operating table becomes only a body experience, the whole process of living is massively altered. My four-hour death during open heart surgery gave me a new sense of what a massive gap is involved. My heart didn't beat for over two hours and my lungs were collapsed like two deflated bags; yet I knew nothing about either condition in my brain. *I* only hear about it, but my *body* knows. It was there. It participated.

As my mind was slowly reincarnated, I became more and more aware of my panic as darkness set in each day, lest that Mack truck would run over me again. I began to resent the imminent return to my ecosystem and felt an increased dissociation from the culture bind of living. After those seven days that followed a six-hour paranoid delusion pattern, I came home and had three days of euphoria—first, a psychological euphoria at being reincarnated; then, a physical euphoria, as though the body had just discovered it was still alive. This was followed by 24 hours of creative, manicky-like flight of ideas, a sense of gradual ecstasy about living, and some new awareness of the slavery that living could become or, in some sense, had been. Unique for me was the realization, in a totally new way, of how much I come first. My lifetime ambivalence seemed less enslaving. I had some sense that my belief system—that part of me which is all but immovable—might be varied, even though I hadn't yet discovered how. I had some hint of where spryness comes from, of how stress operates and expands and explodes, and wondered, "Then what?" I had a new sense of time, a sense of wholeness in myself, and a new kind of opaque look at my suicidal impulses—as though the four-hour death of my mind had given my body a new access to its decision to live or die.

As the weeks have passed, I have begun to get some sense of my body and mind beginning to team again. For several weeks, it was as though my body was so dominant that my mind really wasn't operating, as though my body was somehow retaliating against the psychological death and the dissociation from the knowingness and psychological responsiveness to life. In the subsequent weeks, my body has been more and more willing to share bits of its knowledge with the psychological self. I even have felt some hint of the accumulated psychological fury of my body and its sense of retaliation for being victimized.

Old Age Is a Wonderful Time!

Someone said that youth is such a wonderful time, it is a shame to waste it on the young. I'd like to add to that my own recent discovery that old age is such a wonderful time, it is a shame you have to wait so long for it! The last five years of my teaching career (which had to end when I was 70 because of the university retirement system) and the subsequent five years of my retirement have been uniquely more exciting, more creative, and more enjoyable years than all the previous 40!

It is interesting to speculate about what accounts for the improvement. One factor is the freedom from various kinds of fear: fear of malpractice suits, fear of public disapproval, fear of professional inadequacy, and panic in general. The security of old age can be found in the attitude of really not giving a damn. Other people have a right to their opinions, but I don't see much danger of those opinions making my life either very painful or very different. I am satisfied with my life and can sit back and enjoy its process.

The process of these last ten years—five years of teaching and five years of retirement—has been quite unique. Now there is time to have new conceptual breakthroughs. These breakthroughs often begin with a single word in the middle of the night in a wakened moment, and then take sometimes several months to move to the stage of a beginning conceptual outline, and then more months before the outline becomes so clear that I get up and write it down at four in the morning. The evolution from that point to the freedom to dictate it is a very slow process—as though the experience of putting understandings together in a Gestalt is sitting there in one side of my brain, waiting for a chance to get out. Surprisingly, once this conceptual frame, this essay, this outline, of an evolving understanding of my way of operating and my way of viewing families is written up or dictated (or even put in outline form), it seems almost impossible to add anything to it, as though it has some kind of sacred quality for me that prevents my editing it or adding to it or modifying it.

Retirement itself left a good bit of panic that nothing would be asked of me, and I would be left in a rocking chair waiting for death to come up and clap its hands behind me—the sound of two hands clapping. To my surprise the requests for workshops, which had previously provided only a secondary income and a secondary teaching experience, increased. Then, there were two new mysteries. Why would people invite me back for a second time, since I said the same things? And why would I still be interested in doing the same thing over and over: interviewing a live family, formulating a pseudo-family from the audience, talking about the process of psychotherapy, talking about the question of what made a therapist mature rather than die on the vine, and so on?

Again at four in the morning in my peculiar epistemological pattern, it dawned on me that the reason I was invited back was that watching my craziness in the workshop gave other people the freedom to be more spontaneous, to be more intuitive, to be crazy in their own ways.

The answer to the second question of why it was all still so alive for me was slower in coming, but the breakthrough was very clear. It dawned on me that *I had become the patient to the audience*. I had somehow developed so much trust in people that when I was in front of a group who had paid money to hear my ideas about family therapy, I was able to expose not only my professional understandings but more and more of my personal self, more and more of my creativity, my free associative stories, case fragments, and other bits of my inner self. This makes it more possible for workshop participants to dare to face more of their culture-bound understandings, which they tend to hide or forget or only see through a glass darkly.

Finally, it has become clearer and clearer to me that the stage fright and the pre-workshop anxiety are still very much alive and are very important in producing creative breakthroughs into new ways of thinking, new ways of saying the same things, and even new perceptions of key concepts.

Youth is a nightmare of doubt; middle age is a sweaty, rock-breaking marathon; and old age is the graceful enjoyment of a well-choreographed dance (perhaps a little stiff in the joints, but the timing and the finesse are automatic, not studied). Old age is indeed a joy. Old age knows more than it can say, and best of all, has little need to say it! More and more, life is for *living*. My wife and I know each other. Life with her is like the joy of walking around inside the house with all the lights out: Every step is filled with the welcome security of belonging. Those six who were our children

The six Whitaker children, all grown-up and married: Nancy, Elaine, Bruce, Anita, Lynn, and Holly.

are our deepest friends, the eleven grandchildren, a flower garden to walk in and sniff the fragrance.

As I watch talented and dedicated young therapists try to find the next rung on the ladder, I often wonder how can they prevent burnout. One asked me sadly, "What can I do? I'm already burned out." How did I avoid burnout? Was it the luck of switching from an ob-gyn residency to psychiatry on an uncritiqued impulse? Was it the luck of a full year of play therapy, and three more years of psychotherapy with delinquents? Was it the chance of teaching psychiatry to medical students before I knew anything about psychiatry? Was it never being exposed to hard psychiatry? Everybody who should have been teaching in 1941 was overseas. If you don't go to the AA meetings, you can't be an alcoholic—you're just an ordinary drunk. The next ironic twist flipped us to Oak Ridge. That secret city, where we were told to save the world, was an adrenalin high—burnout was unthinkable.

The next twist of life's screw left us originating a four-year crash training program in the psychotherapy of medical students. I was too inexperienced to know that all medical students shouldn't be forced to take two years of group therapy. The dean was too new to know that they should have been forced to learn the facts of psychodynamics, not the humanism of a good listener. It worked for ten years before "they" (who is *they?*) realized that psychotherapy was not a science. They had my head! It was a bloody scene, but a profound learning experience. Is defeat the only good teacher?

Co-therapy for individual schizophrenics was successful — until they went back to the original family. That defeat was more than a pound of flesh, but fueled the next twist of my life, the move into family therapy. Will that be the final touch that produces a burnout? I defy it, not in this life!

My Delusion System:
The "Whitaker Manifesto"

I have become convinced that my orientation, which has emerged out of many years of treating schizophrenics, has evolved a peculiar definition of health. I have become convinced that the socially adapted citizen — the culturally adjusted individual — is essentially duplicitous. He lives the socially dishonest game, making believe that his vision of the world and the vision of the world held by other people is identical, that altruism is a valid concept, and that the people who practice dishonest politics are really unusual. My conviction is that we are all as dishonest as the standard politician; we are all talking out of both sides of our mouths, making believe that we are not the center of our own worlds. We carefully conceal our personal lives and maintain an artificially constructed social facade that is essentially dishonest.

Concomitant with this viewpoint is my conviction that *psychopathology is proof of psychological health*. The individual who is distorted in his thinking is essentially carrying on an open war in himself rather than capitulating to the social slavery. His delusion system and his hallucinations are a direct result of this war with his lifetime situation — the stresses of his living and his efforts to defeat those stresses rather than become a non-person and a social robot. Schizophrenics are individuals who are pathologically determined to live up to their own world view. They have a disease of abnormal integrity, they are trained to be scapegoats; whether heroes or villains, they dedicate themselves to trying to change the world and trying to massively disturb the system that so duplicitously surrounds them.

I believe the depression we view as individual pathology is actually a response to a real perception of the pathology in others. It is an effort which is recognized as a failure to do something about the pain in the world. The manic attack is an effort to escape into things as a way of avoiding the depression. It is the essential counter-move to the delusion of altruism.

Being is Becoming

Each of us works in the framework of a set of beliefs, most of which are unstated but powerfully dominating in our lifestyle and in our relationships with other people. I should like to say something about my convictions in this territory.

First of all, nothing that is worth knowing can be taught. It has to be learned. It has to be discovered by each of us. The process of learning how you learn, of discovering your own epistemology—your method of handling discoveries, new thoughts, new ideas, new opinions—is something you must struggle for in order to evolve more and more of who you are. Tillich wrote a book entitled *Being is Becoming*. This title was a koan for me. For several years I wondered what the rest of it was, and then it dawned on me. *Doing* is to keep from *being*, meaning that if you keep busy enough, you don't have to *be* anybody. You can keep trying harder and harder to be somebody different than you are, either better, more powerful, more like somebody else, less like what you've discovered of yourself in the past.

But *being is becoming* means that you must learn to be all of what you are. This is a dangerous process, of course, because the social structure only tolerates certain versions of personhood. If you turn out to be sadistic, you need to be careful to be sadistic in the right time, in the right way, with the right people, lest you cut your own throat.

One of the reasons for psychotherapy is that by going "one-down" to a stranger, you may discover the kind of freedom that makes it possible for you to be more of yourself. A psychotherapist is one of those people you can hate without guilt. He is one of those people you can be fully yourself with and still be acceptable—or, to say it another way, he or she can probably tolerate your being fully yourself for an hour or so a week. Daring to expose yourself to someone else makes it easier or more possible to expose more of yourself to yourself.

So, the first step is learn to listen for yourself. Dare to have time when nothing is happening except that you're waiting for something to happen *from inside of you*, not from outside, not from somebody else. Creativity demands isolation and time. One psychotherapist I know goes up to the top of a particular mountain and puts up a tent and stays there for a week or two weeks each year, with nothing to do except be with himself. You know about meditation, spending 20 minutes once a day, or the process of knowing that a friend is someone with whom you can be silent. *So listen for yourself.* As Freud discovered and publicized in the psychoanalytic evolution, nothing is too unimportant. All expressions of yourself are symbolic and, therefore, significant (*symbolic* meaning that they represent more than they specify). You should be aware that anything that comes out of yourself is the beginning of a conceptual exercise which, I believe, is important for its own sake. Part of that process is the recognition that there is no truth. There are only approaches to truth, so that anything that you think of or wonder about is powerfully truthful, whether it sounds good or bad or unimportant.

The Panic of Dialectic

The effort to solve living as a problem is impossible. The process of facing the dialectic life poses is endless, irresolvable, and poorly understood. My effort to describe it begins quite graphically.

Let's begin before birth. The intrauterine infant says, without using words, *I'm too big to stay here*, and is suddenly faced with the panic that *it is pushing me out*. The comfort which has become too much as the baby grows bigger and bigger is itself a stimulus for individuation, for separateness. Once the birth has taken place, the pain and trauma of that experience leave an even greater panic. The crash of cold air and the lack of oxygen are premonitions or previews of things to come. The baby is put to the breast and says, *I'm too hungry to be all alone. She's wonderful.* Then there comes the next step, *It's fun to move*, and then, *I won't let her capture me*. Next, the other half of the dialectic appears, *Oh, I didn't want her to go away for good*, and then as she returns, *It's so good to get warm, to eat, to hear the happy thump-thump that I've been listening to for nine months.*

Now the reversal, the dialectic flip again. *I want to wiggle more*, and then the return, *I want to feed, I want to be warm.* With each return to the breast, to the mother, the baby acquires a little more courage to move further. And then comes the discovery of two-ness on a different level. *Wow, she'll wiggle with me*, which is followed by even more courage to separate. *Crawling is very exciting. I'm going to get way away. I hope she doesn't drag me back. Oh well, it's fun to be back with her. I guess I'll go further, cuz I think she'll come and get me, and we'll play*. As time passes, the baby also discovers a second person to play with: *Hey, he's warm, too*.

Then comes the individuation. *I want to walk. Wow, he helped me. I can go farther from her with him, but he's not as much fun as Mommy. Somewhere along here, she didn't come and get me as soon as I cried, but he did. I'll cry for him next time and she'll be sorry. I hope she doesn't stay away or look funny. Hey, I can get warm with both of them. That's great! I'll get right in the middle. Gee, I can go and then come back and get warm again. I can even hide just like she does, and he does it, too. Are we all alike? I guess we belong. That's great, but I think I'll hide again. We do belong, but who are those others. Do we all belong? I'll hide and then come back. Maybe they'll play with me too*.

The dialectic has begun: I-ness and we-ness in flux; security and exploration, each with its joys and its panic, an irresolvable dialectic. Security alone equals slavery. Exploration alone equals danger and death. The flux is always exciting but never an answer, only a courage-inducing impetus to more of the individual's right to decide on the next move and to discover more and dare more.

An Existential Shift
to the Present

The panic of the dialectic eventually fades into the limbo of what I call "metaliving." The essential component in psychotherapy and the challenge we all struggle with endlessly is that most of us live a fragmented life: we are either preoccupied with the horrors or the glories of the past, or we are preoccupied with the horrors and the glories of the future. We don't *live*; we just use our left brains to endlessly *think about* living. This kind of metaliving is just like metacommunication—the disease that plagues all psychotherapists. We spend our lives dealing in a framework in which we talk about talking and many times never say anything. And if we're not very careful, that process (or non-process) contaminates the rest of our living and the rest of our talking. Medical students who are learning psychotherapy commonly complain, "The problem with this racket is that whenever I go on a date, I end up being a psychotherapist instead of a boyfriend and I don't know how I get there!"

What is even worse is that we do it with each other. If I can't be your therapist, I flip the other side of the coin and become your patient; I either say I want to talk about what's wrong with you, or I turn it around and say, "Why don't you tell me what's wrong with me." There is that old joke about the two psychiatrists who meet on the street and one of them says, "You're fine, how am I?"

We contaminate our world. We not only have the disease ourselves, but we're *carriers*. We contaminate our patients and that's bad by itself. Worse, almost all marriages in America now are bilateral pseudotherapy projects. She's just the girl for him as soon as he gets her over her compulsiveness, and he's just the man for her as soon as she gets him over his alcoholism. Then they spend the first five years of their marriage (it used to be ten years) trying to be better psychotherapists and better patients until it becomes a therapeutic impasse, and then they ask for help. So when you see a couple, it's really not psychotherapy, it's supervision. They're trying to learn to be better psychotherapists, or better patients, or both!

I deduce, therefore, that the essential objective of all psychotherapy is to get rid of the past, good and bad, and the future, good and bad, and to just *be*. That means developing your personhood or your capacity to live, your capacity to be all of who you are, whenever and wherever you are. It is generally a process by which the individual reorganizes his total lifestyle by virtue of a massive emotional experience. It may have close resemblance to what Franz Alexander called "the corrective emotional experience," or it may have similarities to the old religious term "conversion." Either way, it is a specific entity, and a very exciting one when it takes place.

Every once in a while I get patients who have "it" happen to them. The language change is dramatic: They talk in the present. One of my patients, the mother of two anorexic daughters and the wife of a systems analyst husband said to me recently, "I called my daughter to talk about the appointment today, and then I called you and you were upset about it, so I called her back knowing that if it was to be different, she would be there and if it wasn't to be different, she wouldn't be at her apartment." For her, this statement reflected a kind of strange arrival of the present tense world to her living process. It was alright with her whichever way the world turned. She would be accepting of it, even ahead of time. The thing that was strange was not that she did it but that it was such a surprise. There was no aura—no warning. The present isn't something that we ever seem to "live" in.

The existential shift may happen in the recovery of a chronic alcoholic who suddenly makes a declaration of change in his orientation that is not just one more good resolution but a massive reorganization of his own living style and experiencing of life rather than just his behavior. However, there also can be unexpected repercussions. In one couple I was seeing many years ago, the wife, who had been a chronic alcoholic for 10 or 15 years, made this sudden shift. It was so conspicuous to me and to her husband that the next weekend, without his realizing what had happened, he went on a four-day drinking binge—the first time he had ever been drunk in their 10 years of marriage. It was as though the role switch in the family was so specific that he had to take up her pattern within the matter of one week, much to his horror and her amusement. Fortunately, he did not continue this pattern.

A similar existential shift took place in a sociopathic female, age 32, married for eight years, who had slept with her previous therapist and struggled to *not* get into couples therapy. Once in couples therapy, she retreated into a kind of catatonic-like withdrawal for a matter of many months, seething with rage at her husband's dependent confessions to the therapy team. Finally, after six or eight months, she said to me, "Why don't you talk to me?" I responded out of deep honesty, "I don't trust you"—at which point she threw a cup of coffee at me, hitting me in the face! In my rage, I then backed her into the corner and verbally laced her until she was quite terrified, probably the first time she'd been emotionally raped since she was a child. Subsequently, our relationship became a very warm one. The situation of the therapy was quite constructively altered, and the patient went on to live very creatively during at least the next two years, when follow-up was possible.

If you study the few grownup people in the world who have managed to make an existential shift to the *present*, you will find that the most dramatic aspect about them is their personhood—that is, their *presence*. Barbara Betz says, "The dynamics of psychotherapy are in the person of the psychotherapist." My way of saying it: "I've known three or four or five people in the world with whom I've had personal contact and who, I think, could say the A, B, C's and it would be a personally significant experience." One was Alan Gregg, who was medical director of the Rockefeller Foundation. One was Isaac Bashevis Singer, the Nobel Prize winning Jewish writer. One was a Welsh preacher whom I met when I was in college. I'd heard him lecture and I was impressed and went up to meet him. I went to talk about what to do with my life. We had a very quiet talk. As I got through with our time and I said good-bye, he said, "Give my regards to your father." The comment came out of nowhere—it was an eerie sort of validation of me. We had said nothing about my father, but it was like I was zonked by his peculiar kind of perception.

I had a similar experience with Gregory Bateson in 1939 when I was a psychiatric resident. I wrote to several leaders in the field asking to meet them at the annual meeting of the American Psychiatric Association. I met with Bateson at the meeting two or three years. He and I would go to the hotel bar and have a drink. I didn't have to say anything to Gregory—he was self-priming! I think I was learning from him how to focus myself, how to be all in one place, how to be all in one direction. And that is the existential shift: *How to narrow your world until you are in the present tense.*

I think the change of language that comes with this existential shift has to do with the disappearance of the conditional quality, the disappearance of the mythological "I wish it could be," "I think it should have been"—all the *shoulds, woulds, coulds, ought to's, ought not to's.* It has some of the quality of the manic patient who will name 250 things in the office. It is as if he's not *thinking*; he's just seeing and putting into words. The present-tense person is letting the unconscious stream flow, reserving only the process of crossing the corpus callosum to the verbal analytic side for communication. There is no programming in the computer to see whether it agrees with past conclusions, conceptual frameworks, parental orders, cultural demands, and so forth. It's really very exciting but like a sexual turn-on that you can respond to or not respond to, as you choose. I'm amazed that when I do hear it, others who are present may not hear it.

Being Childish:
The Antidote to Metaliving

The only thing sadder than seeing children who are abnormally old—who at the ripe age of four are talking and behaving and carrying the responsibility of adults—is to see adults who are emotionally child-like yet intellectually struggling to play the game of being adults. Watching this painful process has led me to an increasing conviction that there is a way to make life more livable. If the parents can be childish (read *child-like*) with their children, then the children can be themselves. Not only do they have the fun of being children when they *are* children, not only do they have the fun of playing with their parents who are also playing, but they discover the inside of themselves—and if the parents get courage from this, the parents also may discover the inside of themselves. The parent can play at being four years old, whether it's playing horsey or playing silly on-the-floor games; and the child can play grownup, cutting the meatloaf and serving the vegetable and the potatoes while Daddy sits over in the little boy's chair and whines about having to eat all his food. Or the parent can have the joy of whining and becoming a little child when he comes home with a stiff neck from a big day at the office and says to his four-year-old little girl, "Would you rub my neck? I feel terrible."

This role reversal is such a joy to the child; she has the fun of watching Daddy play at being a little boy, and she has the experience of playing at being a mommy. I'm not sure whether it's more helpful for her to play at being a mommy and thus getting the courage that she'll need some day to be a mommy, or whether it's more important that Daddy play at being a four-year-old when, indeed, he feels like one—since I suspect that will postpone his coronary at least five years if he really can learn how to do it.

It is even better, of course, if Mommy can join in and be the little girl while Daddy is being the little boy. The little brother and sister can be the father and mother, and the parents can be sent to bed at eight o'clock while the children stay up to watch TV. Or the parents have to go to bed in the youths' beds and the children can play at being daddy and mommy in the big bed. These role reversals probably are more important for mother and father than they are for the children, but certainly for the children they are a kind of pilot project in learning how it is to be grownup.

Secondary benefits arise from this flexibility of roles, from this right to change the family scene so that the gradual deterioration to the state of that famous American Gothic painting is interrupted. Playing has a unique role in the human living structure. It allows for relaxation of blood vessels and muscles; it allows for a relaxation of that endless power-driven *purposefulness* that is a major disease of our culture. It even allows for a gradual immunization against that other disease of our culture, the disease of metaliving and metacommunication. As I said, sometimes we sophisticates talk so much about talking that we never say anything. It is as if we were endlessly playing analytic games without knowing they are games or without ever giving the signal that this is for fun. The other person therefore thinks it's all "for real" and soon we get to the place where nobody knows the difference between imitation make-believe and real make-believe.

Furthering the development of children's rights to be themselves is probably the most important function of parenthood. There is no other relationship which we can be as honest or as close as we are to our parents. Therefore, the more emotional nakedness the child sees in his parents, the more prepared he is to face the moments and fragments of nakedness that he will see in himself and others in his adult world. The discovery that mother's temper can go completely out-of-control relieves the child of the nightmare terror that he himself will kill somebody, or that his bad thoughts about other people make him uniquely horrible. The discovery that Mother is physically afraid of Daddy and that Daddy is physically afraid of Mother makes the child's fear of those two giants just part of the human condition, not some special horror that he lies awake at night haunted by or wakes up screaming from in a nightmare.

The child who discovers maleness in his mother and femaleness in his father has made a profoundly valuable discovery about himself. The child who discovers the silly sexuality between his parents and can have fun with his sexy-like feelings about his mother or about her father, and the sexy-like feelings of the parents toward the children—that child has a whole new set of "race horses" for his future living. In fact, our taboo about incest is so primitive and sometimes so profound that the fun of being sexy in the family is oftentimes completely hidden, yet it exerts a long-term effect on the marriage of the children. *Family flirtation is one of the immunizing values that makes adult loving more human and less tinged with delinquency.*

Intimacy: The Golden Calf

Assuming that intimacy is one pull of the dialectic of togetherness and individuation—and assuming that, for most people, the need or desire or yen for intimacy is much greater than the tolerance of it—most of us are public-relations-dominated victims in the world of our private relationships. Postulating that schizophrenia is a disease of pathological integrity and pathological need for intimacy, and that hallucinations are really a way of evolving an intimacy that needs no other person, it becomes interesting to postulate how our capacity for intimacy develops.

The evolution of intimacy certainly must begin with the profound intimacy of the intrauterine and birth experiences with the mother. It is obvious that that trauma makes bonding with the mother a most profound counter-move from the paranoid panic of birth, the pain and the shock of the cold, outside world, and the profound stress of air hunger. All is countered by the fondling, the closeness, the warmth, the nonverbal but profoundly felt intimacy with the mother.

As the child grows, intimacy becomes a process of fondling the self (the fingers, the toes, the face, the whole body), and as that self-fondling becomes dominant, the desire to fondle another (hopefully the father, if not, some other person than the mother) emerges. In each case, there is the undercover paranoid panic that a break in the we-ness will result. "Mother is turning her back," "Mother is leaving the room": Each reawakens the terror of birth, the fear that mother will never come back, and that the coldness of the world will be all there is.

If the child's fondness for another person (the father, grandmother or grandfather, siblings or nurse) becomes acceptable and enjoyable, there then evolves the intimacy of perceiving the fondling that takes place between mother and father, or the fondling of the child by both parents. This is a primarily *physical* perception; as the child is developing, however, it also becomes possible for the *visual* experience of the parents' fondling to cause a satisfying stretch in the child's evolution of intimacy.

It should be clear that all intimacy is conditional; its understructure is paranoia. Even the intimacy with the self is conditional upon a clear recognition that one cannot trust oneself because the self is always tricky. The freedom to endure this paranoia as part of living develops the kind of capacity to laugh at oneself that Harold Searles says makes for the cure of schizophrenia.

It should also be stated that *all* roles—the role of intimacy as well as the role of paranoia—are a way of avoiding *beingness*. Beingness is the fact that underlies all roles, the fact that underlies all doingness, all functional operations, be they simple, complex, superficial, or profound. *Beingness* is a way of expressing the degree of integration between the left brain and the right brain, the degree of freedom to be oneself. This freedom to express oneself infers a courage and a recklessness, because there is no such thing as trust. Trust is merely a make-believe game covering the courage to take a chance on being vulnerable and suffering the consequences.

One can see or assume or suspect personhood, but it is not possible to prove its existence. It is only an obvious fact that one is more or less a whole, and that whole depends upon the situation and the individual. However, the fact of *being* does not arise or disappear or become larger or smaller in response to the contingencies of situations. Beingness is a fact, in and of itself.

Although *intimacy* is a word that is used quite frequently, it has the same vague definition as the word *love*. Actually, there are three kinds of intimacy: the *delusion of intimacy*, the *illusion of intimacy*, and the *fact of intimacy*.

The delusion of intimacy, like most psychotic states, involves a euphoric sensation of flooding whereby the beloved is seen in a highly accentuated glow. It's a kind of psychological hallucination that frequently precipitates a two-person psychosis. As in most *folie à deux*, the delusion builds slowly and fades in a fairly short time (hours, days, or weeks). As in most psychotic states, it is all but untouchable by reality or rationality, even though other aspects of living and other aspects of reality may be seen correctly. If it is bilateral, it may be augmented by the additional force of a second person, but in either case it is not available to contradiction or to intellectual, verbal, or even quite personal input.

The *illusion of intimacy* is probably best illustrated by the biblical expression of being of "one flesh." It is usually a factor in the mysterious turn-on of strange flesh, which is itself highly complicated by the process of triangulation as a way of breaking out of the dialectic of belonging and individuating. The illusion of intimacy is like most illusions: it is a misperception of the situation that is not really hallucinatory in nature but that does involve a minor kind of alteration of consciousness. It is, in fact, an excellent example of the symbolic experience. This is a kind of experience that tends to make a modification in the individual's lifestyle, and/or personhood, and/or quality of interpersonal relationships.

The *fact of intimacy* is probably best illustrated by the relationship between the mother and her intrauterine infant; yet even here, they are never complete in the intimacy (the infant is always isolated in the umbilical sac). Nonetheless, this intrauterine intimacy is most profound. The mother psychologically experiences the intrauterine other as *herself*. The baby's birth, and its profound intimacy during breastfeeding are physiological and psychological replicas of the mother's experience when she was intrauterine, being birthed, and being breastfed. In other words, the mother is reliving, physiologically and psychologically, her own origins and the profound intimacy that she shared with her mother.

The fact of intimacy is something which initially occurs between child and mother. It then becomes gradually diluted, internalized, more and more covert; it is challenged and repeated at least to some degree in the intimacy with the father, then in the intimacy with the parents as a *we*, then with the siblings, and then with less profound combinations of two or more people. The fact of intimacy becomes a lifetime motive. First, intimacy with one's self is sought, then intimacy with an identical other, and finally the search for intimacy with a heterosexual partner. This demands an increasing willingness to break through the *illusion of intimacy* and face the dialectic of we-ness and me-ness, each of which is painful in its own way. In *me-ness* is the horror of isolation (schizophrenia), and in *we-ness* is the panic of enslavement or loss of self.

The factual process of evolving intimacy necessitates the gradual decision to experience a level of whole person to whole person relating with one different other. To sacrifice one's freedom, one's initiative, one's indoctrination in a lifestyle for the strength, freedom, security and ecstasy of belonging in a much more secure way is an endless compromise.

Quantifying Intimacy

Any discussion of intimacy is hampered by the problem of degree or quantity. It is difficult to find a method of measuring intimacy. Friends say, "We are not very intimate," or "We are very close." We assume husband and wife are very intimate. The mother and child attain the greatest intimacy in *interpersonal* relationships, and an individual's greatest intrapersonal intimacy is obviously with the self.

It seems possible to talk about intimacy in terms of the framework of *temperature*. We say: "He's hot for her," "He's hot-headed," "She's cold," "He's cold." We connote that interpersonal relationships (mainly sexual and/or hostile) are describable in degrees of temperature. We see the peculiar, reversible quality of the relationship. The temperature is regulated by the couple. If one is cool, the other is hot; if something should happen to change the temperature of one, the temperature of the other will change to keep the "couple temperature" stabilized.

The relationship temperature increases during courtship and during marriage. We say that marriage becomes increasingly sexual. We might better say that marriage becomes increasingly heated, whether this heat is increasingly *sexual* in nature or increasingly *hostile* in nature. In fact, increasing temperature on the hostile side of marriage is one way to avoid increasing the temperature of the sexual relationship. If we accept this analogy of temperature, it would be easy to say that the fundamental objective of psychotherapy is to increase the temperature of the couple relationship, or to increase the individual's temperature in his relationship to himself.

The Intimacy of Isolation

In our book, *The Roots of Psychotherapy*, Malone and I suggested that isolation was one of the prime requirements for an intimate relationship between therapist and patient. The intimacy of isolation is significantly useful to the therapist in the initiation of transference and in the development of a purposeful concentration on the project of psychotherapy. A kind of uniting takes place between two people who are separated from the rest of the social structure, and who are involved in a significant joint endeavor. The significance may be great for both of them, or it may be great for one and less so for the other. This aspect of psychotherapy is basically no different from Robinson Crusoe and his man Friday, or the mythical boy and girl marooned on a desert island, or the real-life husband

and wife who are brought together powerfully by the buying of a home, their first new automobile, or the arrival of the new baby.

Earlier I described my experience with the ten-year-old boy, "Jim," who spent session after session in complete silence with me. For ten weeks, I sat while he stood, silently, meditatively, throughout the sessions. I certainly had no clue that he was being helped. Yet his teacher phoned me to praise my "remarkable" work, as evidenced by the boy's sweeping improvements.

One could make various hypotheses about the process that took place in this experience between the two of us. Certain it is that this ten-year-old's relationship with other people had contained great quantities of hostility. His anger evoked dependency in other kids (and perhaps his mother) who were frightened by this hostility; or it met with more hostility from those kids and from adults he couldn't bully. The treatment situation was new and different. A person obviously more powerful than Jim was allowing him to express his hostility, and was not hostile nor dependent nor frightened in return. The fantasies which Jim ordinarily had in relationship to other people were disrupted by the presence of one person to whom they did not apply. His philosophical resolution of life's mysteries was disrupted. The fact that he could not formulate these fantasies in words seems unimportant. His behavior changed. Period. Everybody wants to belong to the social structure.

Was Jim changed by the experience of guiltless hatred? What happened to his fantasy? I assume that this fantasy, like a nighttime dream, was altered by the mere fact that someone else was in it, and that someone else did not conform to Jim's social myth. The isolation of the office made it impossible to keep me out of his fantasy. Regression (for, indeed, such fantasy should be called *regression* as it begins and is characteristic of childhood) may be possible because all one-to-one relationships are essentially a return to the mother-child state of the first two or three years. It also could be possible that this boy's isolation from the social structure was gross, and that anyone who helped him avoid this isolation became very significant to him on an existential, adult level.

Work in the areas of co-therapy, group therapy, and family therapy may seem to contradict the importance of the isolation aspect of intimacy, but I do not think this is unanswerable. Co-therapy can and frequently has been shown to consist, not in two separate people doing therapy with a patient, but in the formation of a twosome which then becomes the therapist. The therapist is a single entity, as evidenced when the patient interchanges the names of the two therapists, assuming that their attitudes are identical, even after intimate experience with the fact that this is not true. The patient may be an individual, a couple, a family, or a group. In each case, the evidence of isolation is very frequent and very simple to confirm. One can be isolated with 30 people in a blinding snow storm, or one can feel a sense of intimacy even with the entire country (as occurred when Pearl Harbor was attacked in 1941).

Various mechanisms can be utilized to describe the phenomenon of intimacy associated with isolation. Calling it *transference* puts it into the intimate child-parent perspective, but it is just as appropriate to speak of it in reference to a *cross-identification*. The exposure of one individual to the physical, visual presence of the other automatically sets up a sense of difference; "He's taller, he's fatter, he's older, he's smarter." But it also activates in a much more powerful way the identification that "he's human like me, he's suffered, he feels badly, or he feels happy, as I do."

The Intimacy of the
Doctor-Patient Relationship

For many years the relationship of physician to patient has been one of the models of intimacy our society has respected, sanctioned, and reinforced. Since it emulates the model of the mother-child and/or father-child relationship, it has gradually become more sacred than all other models except its biological prototype. The fact that the physician-patient relationship involves the examination and care of the physical body, the concomitant physical contact, and relatively unquestioned obedience has made it even more sacred.

The mother-child relationship, as symbolized by the physician, is nurturing, caring, warm, and typically carries a quality of softness. The father-child pattern indicates protection, defense, and partnership with strength. The physician is seen as being so clearly on the side of the patient that he is the recipient of secrets which may not be questioned, even by the society as a whole (until recent years). His rules have been regarded as unchallengeable and his strength as being so far above the ordinary member of the social structure that he "can do no wrong." In many communities and in the minds of many people, the physician is still very God-like.

The physician elects to go into his profession because of his "concern for others," his desire to prevent and cure disease, and his zeal to attack those things which are destroying the human body. Confirming the intimate quality of this role is the peculiar incest-like taboo that is built into the

Hypocratic oath, "Do no harm"—as though the physician, in his peculiar intimacy with the patient, were like the parent, capable of a kind of damage not available to the ordinary person. The physician is thus accorded special rights. In some sense, his role combines that of the parents, the priest, and the teacher.

Model form: The patient says, "Nobody loves me," and the doctor answers, "I will." The patient says, "My head aches," and the doctor says, "I'll fix it" (mother will kiss it). The patient says, "All is lost except for your magic," and the doctor answers, "I have the magic." The patient says, "I'm dying," and the doctor says, "I'll save your life."

A Group Model of Intimacy

The models of group work by psychiatrists are almost as varied as the kinds of groups described by people who participate. Part of the problem in conceptualizing what goes on in a group may well have to do with a lack of clarity about the possible group models. Groups can be concerned with the *interpersonal model*, the pattern of experimenting with, learning how to, and watching the disruption of the process of being with another (or, as a variant, being with others). As the group becomes freer, and the function of the group as a therapist becomes more available, the members move gradually and with great eagerness into the process of each person being with himself. Intrapsychic intimacy is one ultimate goal, of equal weight with the interpersonal intimacy on which it is dependent. A group which spends many hours struggling with the questions of "How can a person express anger with another?" "How can a person express love with another?" evolves into the stage where each individual can use the group for the purpose of self discovery—through dreams or through psychological and psychosomatic experiences. During the hour, the group member discovers that it is feasible to be with others and simultaneously be even more with oneself. In this sense, being with another is not only a way of *filling* oneself but also a way of *expanding* oneself. Beyond the completion of one's intrapsychic intimacy is the psychological joining of one's entire self with that of a significant other.

These two states of beingness are always present in us, albeit usually in diluted form, or in badly contaminated form. In a group setting, they are grossly disrupted when the group process focuses only on *talking*. Whenever the intimacy between the group members is restricted to *doing* things, the process becomes stale. *Doing things* with each other—whether it be intellectual exercises, psychological games, or verbal ballet—sustains our roles on a fairly superficial level. The manipulation of others via the presentation of self to others can be subsumed under the general pattern of worshiping a graven image. The individual constructs an image of himself and tries to learn methods of getting others to worship it, as he himself does. After all, mother believed he could be president. (P.S. She didn't say president of what.)

That is not intimacy!

The Intimacy of Suicide as a Two-Person Event

We assume that people who are suicidal either want to be dead, wish someone would kill them, or want to kill themselves. Further presumption is that murder is murder, whether you are murdering somebody else or murdering yourself, and that many times the suicide is a reversal of murderous impulses. There is someone else you want to kill, and you kill yourself instead. I further assume that one of the characteristics of suicidal people is that they live a life full of rancor, and that the physical suicide is merely the ultimate end point for one who has been self-destructive socially, psychologically, affectively, economically. One of the other components that contributes to the suicide threat or attempt is the person's struggling emergence from hopeless despair. The individual who has descended into a massive depression and finally begins to emerge from it is then confronted by the horrible stress of having to reconstruct a life and a lifestyle. Under such pressure, he or she may decide that it would be simpler to commit suicide than to go through the tremendous reconstruction effort.

Parenthetically, the process of psychotherapy may follow much the same course. The individual descends into his intrapsychic self and struggles with his craziness, his sense of impotence and futility, his fears of his own death, and his lack of self-esteem due to the discovery of how little a person he is. Having dared this plunge, he faces the responsibility and the tremendous task of reconstructing his personhood. Instead, he decides that it isn't worth the struggle. At that point, like emerging from a depression, he has enough energy to deliberately destroy himself.

What can be done about it? Any effort to change such a massive descent requires a better understanding of systems theory. No person is a self-contained unit. *Anyone who wants him- or herself dead may have a significant other who wants him or her dead.* This wanting the person dead may be a minor affect or a covert impulse in the significant other, whether it is father, mother, sibling, or spouse. Or, it may be a fairly overt sentiment on the part of a whole group. The therapist's function is to bring the group together to determine in the presence of the patient the murderous component in the family that makes suicide possible. Having exteriorized that component, the therapist may then help this group face not only their murderous impulses, but also their feelings for the patient.

One of the ways of helping the patient cope with suicidal urges is to engage her in a future projection fantasy. What would happen if she were successful in her suicide? How long would Daddy cry? Who would come to the funeral? How long would Mother and siblings cry? Who has plans for new relationships after she is dead? Does her husband have another woman on the waiting list? What would the family do about her personal effects—would there be a big hope chest nailed shut with her name on the top? Would the family have to move out of the home because of the haunt? Would they have a fancy funeral with tons of flowers? This is a process of converting her *intra*psychic fantasy of "They'll be sorry when I'm dead and gone" into an *inter*personal fantasy, thus making it impossible for her to get wrapped up all alone in the horrible fascination of "What would it be like after I died?"

Some therapists make use of a "no-suicide" contract: "Promise me that you won't kill yourself before we meet again." This seems mechanical to me, but for some therapists it is quite beneficial. One technique that has been useful to me is to verbally attack the patient. This is a natural approach for me, and it is supported by the "punishment therapy" techniques that the American GI's devised while interned in the Japanese prison camps. Those soldiers who had a thanatotic impulse and were going to die from self-induced psychosomatic causes in a few days were deliberately beaten up by the other GI's; amazingly, they emerged from their depression and did not retreat again.

I have had several patients respond well to this kind of threat. One patient was threatening suicide in what I considered to be a very serious way: I told her if she killed herself, I would jump up and down on her grave and curse her! Later she said that this statement kept her from killing herself. Another patient who said that nobody in her family knew that she felt suicidal and that they wouldn't care anyway was told that, if she died, I would go to the funeral and tell all the family members that I thought they were responsible for her death. On the basis of that threat, she brought them in for therapy and her suicide was at least postponed.

Yet another methodology is the use of paradoxical intention: you deliberately turn over to the patient her decision about death. Many times this is a way of getting out from underneath the horror of feeling partially responsible for her life. One suicide threat was resolved by a consultant I brought in who helped my patient doubt that his homosexual partner would be upset by his threat of suicide. The patient, having been forced to question whether the murderous retaliation impulse in his suicide would be of any use, gave up the effort.

Quite frequently I have positively reinforced the suicide impulse by suggesting that if they were going to kill themselves, they might just as well get an automatic shotgun and kill some other people first. It would make their own suicide a great deal more fun if they could kill off those people they hated before finally killing themselves. "There is no sense in doing a halfway job! If you have murderous impulses, you might as well enjoy them before you destroy yourself." This augmentation of the pathology many times serves to make it impossible for patients to handle the affect load, so they move out of the whole suicide game and into a less fatal one.

Some therapists use themselves as the murder victim. They say to the patient, "If you're going to kill yourself, maybe it's because you want to kill me first." Perhaps it is also true that some patients kill themselves because the therapist cannot extricate her/himself from the relationship and also cannot tolerate being in a relationship involving that much pain. The commonsense fear that the therapist may bring about the suicidal act by suggesting something absurd is countermanded by the fact that such pathological functioning in the culture is only tolerable when there is massive support from the intrapsychic fantasy. If the therapist has needs that are quite primitive in her/himself for this kind of destructiveness, then the patient may help carry out the therapist's fantasy. However, if the therapist is personally concerned with the patient and is humanly non-murderous, then the patient will not pick up erroneous affect from the absurd offer. That is, on the overt level he hears it as a suggestion, but on the personal level it is an invasion of his fantasy life and, as such, disrupts its programmed circuit. Once the programmed circuit has been disrupted, it is not possible for the patient to continue spiraling the circuit downward in suicidal descent.

The Outer Limits
of Psychotherapy

The power of man over his own life and his own death has been proven many, many times. Each of us is free to kill himself—suddenly with a gun, or gradually via obesity, starvation, alcoholism—or, for a few people, with a somatized decision to stop living. The reality of psychosomatic death implies the possibility of many other axes (parameters) of potential for each of us in relation to our own lives and our own deaths. To some degree each of us is able to control the quality of our lives. How much control we exercise varies widely. If my mother wants me to be healthy and live forever, will that make me live 20 years longer than if, for reasons having to do with her life, she wanted me dead? We know that if she wills me to be female, it has an influence on my living style. Many of us believe it can even influence my body structure. I know one mother, who clearly hated men and her ex-husband, had a daughter with broad shoulders, narrow hips, and no breasts, while her son had broad hips, narrow shoulders, and a distinctly feminine habitus. Those of us who knew the family and the significance of her feelings about men clearly suspected that she had pressured her son to grow up feminine and her daughter to grow up with a masculine physiology.

Major life and situational experiences can dramatically change the physiology of the individual. One patient had no problem with his three-night-a-week liaison with his mistress in town for the eight years he had relations with her. Yet after his wife conveniently died of cancer and he had married the mistress, he suddenly stopped having erections. We can easily accept the somatic aspect of impotence. But is it also true that his wife died of cancer in somatic compliance with the husband's desire to marry the

68

girlfriend? Is it possible that the wife died for the hostile purpose of making her husband impotent with the other woman? Greater hate hath no woman than to die to frustrate her husband's affair!

Yes, our own physiology changes greatly in response to life stress. Can we change it by deliberate intent? There is the young bride who decides that her temper tantrums are more than her husband can stand. Does she deliberately decide to stop having her temper tantrums and start having headaches? Or is this a result of the stress in her relationship with her husband, with whom she plays the role of a victim rather than of a deliberate instigator? The young man who tries to become an Atlas by weight-lifting with barbells certainly can produce muscles. Does he thus produce better health? What about the young woman who is intensely anxious to have her children be healthy and vigorous? Does she deliberately alter her life to become healthier? Or is her improved health a by-product of her loving relationship with her husband and beyond her deliberate control?

If we can ruin our own lives as well as better them to some degree by our own intent, what is the scope of our influence over others? Certainly one of us can kill another, either by deliberate physical destruction, or by acts of bitter, malevolent hatred. Although hex deaths are not common in our civilized world (or at least not identified), *there is no question in my mind that craziness is a two-person event, and that suicide is a two-person event.* Probably all suicides necessitate the presence of one person who is willing to be dead, and another person who wants him or her dead. The *summation of their affects* then brings about the gradual or the sudden suicidal experience—whether it is the alcoholic who is dying from sclerosis because his wife can't stand living her life with the sole purpose of being his mother, or the crippled son who decides to shoot himself as a way of retaliating against his hated mother, while she wants him dead to relieve her guilt about the birth trauma that left him with a limp.

Do mothers, fathers, and siblings deliberately drive an individual crazy? Certainly, the system of the family and the culture bring it about. Certainly, some persons are more susceptible to craziness than others. Maybe all the susceptible people do not go crazy because the system doesn't demand it, or because someone else interrupts the system, thus weakening its hold. Why does a family that has the power to produce one crazy child not produce craziness in the other three? Or, in contrast, why does one family produce craziness in two children and not in the third? Is this discrepancy merely a factor of susceptibility, or does the *system* change so that it doesn't force psychosis on the equally susceptible third child? Or, is the third child merely unsusceptible?

Do some people really have the capacity to bring about deliberately destructive physiological influences on someone else? Is the hex death of primitive societies based upon the victim's belief, or is it possible that some people really carry this kind of psychological or psychophysiological power? At a conference on the treatment of schizophrenia, Jay Haley once suggested that the next conference should consider the question, "Can we produce a schizophrenic on purpose?" The next five minutes of dead silence did not produce any freedom on the part of the assembled experts to even talk about such a horrible thought. Yet, this is the kind of question we need to answer.

Where along this continuum of influence is the psychotherapist—the person who is deliberately trying to improve his power over another? Our profession has gone through a series of breakthroughs. Freud broke through the belief that neurosis was a crime, and he set the wheels in motion for learning how to help the individual grow past the neurosis. Many years later, John Rosen broke through the professional's conviction that schizophrenia was psychologically untreatable. In his own crazy way, Rosen shocked us out of our delusional dependence on social convictions and on Freud's idea that schizophrenia was untouchable by psychotherapy. How far can we go? What are the limits for psychotherapy? Would we be delusional to agree with my schizophrenic patient who said, "When you get good enough, you can cure any schizophrenic in three days"? We know that many people grow out of epilepsy and asthma; and we know about the physiological sterility that disappears as soon as the couple adopts a baby. What are *our* limits? What should we expect of ourselves and at what point should we give up trying?

Many years ago our group in Atlanta decided to hold a series of meetings for the purpose of hammering out our basic assumptions about the possibilities in psychotherapy. One of the early questions raised was, "If we were adequate, could we help the individual re-grow an amputated leg? The planaria do it; some amphibia do it; why can't we?" We do know that in psychotherapy remarkable physiological changes can take place. We have seen patients who for years have had many epileptic attacks each day cut back to one attack every three weeks with psychotherapy and no medication. We have seen the disappearance of a huge megalocolon. We have seen a patient who for 10 to 15 years was on insulin, and who, over a period of two years in psychotherapy, cut the 70 units down to zero. That same patient went back to her physician, who in his panic decided to reinstitute her original dose without consulting us. The effect of the dose was to throw the patient into insulin shock, where she stayed for 20 days until she expired. We have seen psychotherapy in a 45-year-old man produce an increase of two units in his hat size and two units in his shoe size over a period of two years, although every physician knows that bone structure does not increase after 18 years of age. This kind of evidence makes statements about psychotherapy being a process of "bettering communication" sound as feeble as the statement that love is just another word for sexual excitement.

What Is Love
in Psychotherapy?

To many nontherapists, the whole game of psychotherapy is thought of as too intense, too intimate, and too loving. For some psychotherapists there are the constant questions: "Am I being too seductive?" "Am I overidentified?" "Is my own pathology getting in the way?" "Should I be more objective, cooler, more distant?" "Will I make the patient worse rather than better?" These psychotherapists are in essence repeating the old cliche, "Love is not enough." Should it be instead, "There is not enough love?"

If we assume that psychotherapy is the process of loving used in the broadest sense, then what is *enough love?* What is love, for that matter, when it is used in this technical or professional sense? Let's try to form a classification of love.

The simplest level would be the level at which love is an experience of social fun, a sense of enjoyment at being with another person – playing, working, or fighting. It is an interpersonal communication game.

On a level below this, one could say that love is also a process of being more of oneself by doing for the other. Some psychotherapy might well fit into this category. The husband is loving when he is earning money for his family; the wife is loving when she is cooking the meals; and the psychotherapist is loving when he or she is listening attentively and with concern and caring. Sometimes this love may become distorted, as even biologically-based love can become. The do-good mother *acts* lovingly to substitute for being who she really is. A current joke about this topic describes the mother whose love for her two little chicks was such that when one got sick, she killed the well one to make chicken soup for the sick one! Some psychotherapists might suspect a colleague or two of having this quality in their work. Certainly, one could never suspect oneself of experiencing this kind of love . . . ?!

On a third level, love could be defined as the affective union between two persons resulting in a sense of self-fulfillment or self-fullness. This kind of love facilitates a loss of self-consciousness and the discovery of self-awareness. It includes a kind of increasing *union* and, therefore, increasing *individuation*. This kind of paradoxical change is characteristic of an expanding marriage.

On still another level, love could be considered an experience in which one is able to be more with oneself because of the presence of another who is with himself or herself. This is an old definition of friendship: one with whom you can be alone. That is, your own beingness is increased by the beingness of the other.

A biological level of completion might well be a still deeper way of defining love. I am a biological cripple. I am only one-half of what is needed to reproduce myself. I am incomplete; I have no breasts! I have no vagina! I cannot reproduce myself! Thus on a still deeper level, a biological completion could be defined or could be identified as love.

Are these classifications of love enough for the psychotherapist? Or is there still another level? Perhaps the level of identification is deeper in psychotherapy. In that experience, I sit across the desk and look at the person in front of me, and I see *myself*. This process is not just a matter of interpersonal union; it is a kind of *intrapsychic unification process* that takes place between the other and the self. I may look at the patient and see myself in a distant past; he may look like I looked when I was in high school. Or, I may look at him and see myself in the future. I may even look at him and see myself in the present. I may identify with him because we are similar in our styles of living, or I may look at him and resonate to his character structure because it has great similarity to my own. This kind of identification makes me more involved. This kind of loving, it seems to me, is more primitive than any of the others described above.

There is yet another kind of loving which is even more intense. If I cure a schizophrenic, I first must have some kind of identification with him. I assume that this identification has the quality of a profound transference. In effect, I am, inside of myself, very similar to his mother, and in my relating to him, I take her place in *his* inside experience. If this is true, then I must do it by double-binding him like she did: by producing a set of conflicting messages and an overriding pressure such that he cannot escape, so that he is locked in confusion, in denial of himself, and in a kind of horrible dependence on me. A distortion at this level might lead to an interminable impasse. If psychotherapy is successful with this kind of schizophrenic patient, however, it must be because the patient then responds to me by double-binding *me* in just the way he bound his own mother.

Thus we develop "the gruesome twosome," a kind of reciprocal relationship in which each one is capable of locking the other into a state of confusion, indecisiveness, and capitulation to his living. Again, assuming this psychotherapy goes on successfully, it is logical to presume that our relationship would be identical with the one the patient had with his mother. We know that in his relation to mother, if he is "driven sane," as Gregory Bateson says, mother frequently goes crazy. If he gets out of the state hospital, mother may well end up in the hospital. This is the kind of patient who proves that insanity is a two-person event. He would rather go crazy than let mother go crazy. Maybe this takes place between the therapist and patient as well. As they develop this symbiotic relationship, each then is able to make the other one crazy. Whenever one is crazy, then the other one is sane. When the patient is crazy in the hospital, mother is sane at home running the world. One of my colleagues was treating a schizophrenic patient whose mother was elected "Mother of the Year" for a large East Coast city!

In this state of reciprocal lock-step, the patient and I take turns at being in power. The difference is that, in contrast with his mother, I am not afraid of craziness. *I want it!* So when we get locked in tight, and I've taken the sane role and he's carrying the insane role, I then shift the situation by my own willingness, so that *I* become the crazy one and he is compelled to become the sane one. If this paradigm is actually true, then it may be said that at that point *we begin to be able to love each other*. Then each one of us is equally powerful; each one of us is equally free to be sane or insane, depending on our relationship to the other. My presumption is that, if the patient goes on to recover, he then is free to be first his crazy self and then his sane self, with less and less demand for the participation of the other. Thus, it is hoped, the system expands to involve others and becomes healthy.

Is there yet another level of love beyond this? Some contend that psychotherapy is not just a question of affective exchange but that it's possible to change the *physiology* of the body and even the *structure* of the body. My own background and training in medical school would make it all but impossible for me to even conceptualize the regrowth of the amputated leg that we were fantasying about earlier in this discussion. Is it possible that a kind of profound dedication and conviction about the other's worth and the other's basic substance is capable of producing physiological changes in the body? Could a psychotherapist activate the reticular-endothelial system? Could a psychotherapist reverse the pathology that produces *lupus erythematosus*? Is it even conceptually feasible to talk about reactivating the genetic components so that the organism can structurally rebuild itself? Many dermatologists carry a buckeye to wipe away warts. We are still suspicious that a reactivated cell may be the etiology of cancer, which is merely a distorted return to embryonic growth.

If it is possible that profound psychotherapeutic effects of this kind can be brought about, then what comes next? One day could we actually re-grow an amputated leg? Could we mobilize an arthritic joint which has been frozen for years? A psychotherapist would hardly dare say yes, but the biochemists do. Is it possible that we could reactivate an entire new body with new cells? It is not difficult for me to envision such an achievement via the pathway of chemistry some day, but it is difficult for me to envision it via the pathway of psychotherapy. And yet we know that even casual sexual experience can change the body's physiology. Perhaps all the body's physiology is available to change if enough of the therapist's life force (whatever that is) is available to demand or command or activate the life force of the patient—the victim, the disciple, the child of the therapist. Where do we go from here?

II
Marriage and the Family

Marriage:
Its Rocky Evolution to Integrity

The gradual process from being a college student who lives alone and plays with homosocial/heterosocial teaming to deciding to form a permanent team with a woman or a man is a complex one. Our culture places a massive premium on each individual's competence to operate as a lonely isolate, self-correcting for stress by living as a passive social robot. Dedicating oneself to contribute to the social structure by earning money, or making a reputation, or doing one's duty by the country or the company is a tragic way to live. The effort to tolerate the denial of self required in such dedication to being a non-person or a socioeconomic robot is not easy. The culture nudges us along by furnishing the anesthesia of appreciation, applause, and admiration. A kind of social image is constructed for anyone who succeeds. But in order to create this success, the person has denied his or her personhood to become a social mechanism who looks forward to the social idolization symbolized by becoming a millionaire, receiving a Nobel Prize, or finding political stardom.

Marriage (as differentiated from social slavery or isolate anesthetized success) is easiest to understand in terms of a metaphor. It is as though one has learned to play tennis and then decided that playing doubles is more fun. The court is bigger, the physical demand is less, and the need to be a hero to oneself has become less entrancing. One can play singles in the framework of a delusion system and be the international champion. Playing doubles creates a very different metaphor. The court is divided into two halves. Each individual is responsible for the balls which land in his/her court and for representing the twosome in each decision regarding what ball to go for and what ball to leave for the teammate.

These decisions are sometimes clearcut. You must receive the ball on the initial serve into your court, but from then on decisions are many times unclear. If the ball falls in a corner *near* your court but actually in *her* court, you can return that ball and she will appreciate it. If she returns a ball in your court in the corner next to her court, you'll appreciate it. If the ball lands on the line between the two courts, and she can return it with a forehand, or you could return it with a backhand, who makes the move? If you make the move, the crowd will admire your shot. If she makes the move, is she stealing a play for which you could have been applauded?

If she plays the net and misses the ball, was she really trying to make me look feeble? Is she getting back at me for the shot I took a while back? Did she think I was stealing it from her? Is she playing for the audience rather than for our team? Does she believe I'm playing for the audience? I'm really not. Would we have won this game if she had tried harder? Is she angry at me because I didn't try harder?

These endless, self-protection fantasies are also matched by a series of chance-taking decisions: Well, I tried to save that ball. I guess I looked terrible to the audience, but I suspect she wouldn't have gotten it if I hadn't. It's just a point we didn't make. . . . She didn't get that shot, but I would never have gotten it, and it was loving of her to try, even though she knew she wouldn't make it. . . . She seems tired. I think I'll take a few more of those shots that fall where either of us could make a try. As she gets a little more rested, things will go better. . . . I sure appreciated her taking that shot. I never could have gotten it. . . .

And, finally, the resolution of the dialectic: It certainly is fun playing with her. Whether we win or lose is less important than the fun of playing. I think we're getting better. That other team really has better players. Wasn't it wonderful that she took a chance on looking like a fool to protect me from failure? I guess she has decided in a kind of funny way that our playing as a team is more important than how she looks to anybody else, or even how she looks to me. We've gone through the entire set with neither of us trying to play solo, neither of us doubting the other person, each of us reveling in the belonging, the joy of thinking about the previous shot and anticipating the next shot, and the simple joy of our teaming.

Thus, solo playing and critiquing oneself in a fantasy team with one's own body are replaced by the joy of teaming. We are replacing the fantasy team of mother and father, or the biological team of familyhood, with the new team of marriage and the realization that the whole has become greater than the sum of the parts. *We* is more powerful than even the summation of the two individuals. Their wholeness has become secondary to the fulfillment of belonging to a team. The biological fact of *me*, the biopsychological fact of *me* has been replaced by the biopsychosocial combination of a team. Winning is the creation of a heaven on earth called children.

Once that teaming has become clear, the psychosocial belonging to her family of origin and his family of origin becomes an additional joy and a powerful implosion.

Game Plan for Marriage

In our culture the usual preparation for marriage is achieved via your gradual separation from the family and the process of living on your own in college or in an apartment in town. You occasionally rejoin the family and then reindividuate in your own solo life. There is a gradual search for a friendship network, a series of exploratory sexual liaisons, and eventually a "fix" on one person, with the accompanying fantasy that this blissful union will go on forever, and be forever more and more satisfying.

I have an alternative to this chanceful way of preparing for marriage that is more deliberate, hopefully more facilitative of successful completion, and of even greater constructive value. Given a successful graduation from the family, you then plan a series of *foster-child game plans* with yourself and your chosen teammate. The foster-child connotation involves a kind of recognition, shared or not shared with the teammate, that this is a temporary arrangement, that it is controlled by reality, that it is open for cancellation at any point, and that it is a simulation of the future with the remnants of past patterns openly accepted and freely utilized. This kind of game plan implies the need to "cool the mark." In this world of game-planning con games, this involves a recognition that whatever is going on now also needs to be structured to make the next step possible, that nothing is settled, everything is temporary, artificial, and open for change in any direction.

The second process in this preparation for marriage is what is known as the "bait and switch move." In interpersonal relationships, I suppose it would be easier to call it *flirtation* and *rejection*. This is a process of toying with other people in such a way that one continually increases their freedom to individuate, their freedom to back away, to deny the implicit license or freedom to go ahead. One of the best examples of this is a game played by identical twins who confuse the girlfriend of one by arriving, one after the other, with completely different poses.

The third step in this process of learning how to get ready for marriage involves a *game plan for a peer type move on the boyfriend's or girlfriend's family* to see whether the family can tolerate you as a peer. This might take some careful planning, but if you think of the usual tragedy of in-law relationships, the process of establishing a non-adoptive, peerlike contact with the possible in-laws is extremely valuable training. If this game plan is successful, it may set the model for winning in that struggle after marriage when the new spouse is supposed to be adopted by the in-law family as one of their *children*, and/or destroyed by the in-law family for having stolen their child.

The fourth step in this preparation for marriage game plan is the deliberate move on your family of origin and on the possible in-law-family-to-be, challenging *their* fantasy against *your* fantasy about the future. Elements of this fantasy about the new family you are anticipating to originate include geographical location, economic expectations, child raising issues and attitudes, and the inevitable competition between the two families of origin to see whose family is to be reproduced.

The final step in this game of preparation for marriage has to do with the basic concept of what marriage is *for*. Marriage is an effort to move out of being a member of a child generation and into being a member of the adult generation. Marriage itself is an effort to evolve a peership which constitutes a whole-person to whole-person relationship. Within this relationship there is a gradually increasing acceptance, tolerance, and even enjoyment of the craziness that exists in the partner's family, and of the never-ending status as an alien in the in-law family, attached but never quite *belonging*. Marriage becomes a lifetime process of adaptation and change in relationship to a foreign culture, not unlike moving to another country with another language, and learning how to adapt to and grow with the different metaphors, the different grammar, and the unfamiliar nonverbal communication of a new and strange culture.

If all this preparation is successful, the ultimate step is the decision to deliberately avoid short-circuiting the interaction between the two people who are building toward a marriage by a preemptory, premarital, sexual experience. It is frequently true and perhaps inevitable that premarital sex—sex without love or before love, sex as a game, sex as a sudden trial effort to fulfill mother nature's demand for children—becomes a process of the penis and vagina going off on a trip together, with no *people* along. This unfortunate occurrence raises the danger of a hysterical dissociation so that the two people never get there; the process of sexuality becomes dissociated from affect—it becomes a mechanical process that *separates* rather than unites. Marital peership is probably only possible if sexuality *follows* the whole-person to whole-person investment, rather than being used as a stopgap for the anxiety, panic, stage fright, and culture shock of joining someone who comes from a different family culture.

Styles of Marriage

The process of marriage is a peculiar and powerful dialectical process that swings across the individuation-belonging continuum. The strength of dyadic teaming can become so satisfying and so compelling that the temptation looms to desert individuation altogether and evolve a bilateral adoption in which each partner agrees to be parent to the other for the privilege of being child to the twosome.

The basis for success in this complex dialectic is a previous belonging and individuating from the family of origin. The capacity to belong in the family of origin and still dare individuation evolves slowly. It may be disrupted in many ways on many occasions without destruction, but each distortion in the process sets up a model for distortion in the marriage. If one's first experience with going off to college or work is a fortunate one, then the individual will dare more and more separateness. If he or she is reaccepted back into the fold after the venture into the outside world, then he/she is freer to become more and more intimate in relationship to the family of origin. The ultimate in separation from the family of origin is marrying to form a new family. This is an artificial separation, however, since it erroneously connotes a massive individuation from the family of origin.

The partner likewise must develop a freedom to belong without losing intimacy with the family of origin. Courtship, then, is not just a matter of becoming a team while also becoming freer to be individuals. It also entails the simultaneous complication of effecting new separations from each partner's family of origin. Marriage then ideally becomes a process involving two persons, each enacting a role of individuating and each enacting a role of belonging—while they both struggle towards a kind of peership that invokes the right of each to separate.

If one assumes that the marriage is an organism—the dyadic residual of two families of origin, or, if you will, the expression of two families' efforts to reproduce—then it ought to be possible to postulate a kind of evolution. First of all, we need to define the different kinds of marriages, assuming that each has an integrity, an identity, and a separate style.

In the first style of marriage, the partners are the two victims of an *in-law scapegoat game* in which each family sends out a scapegoat to reproduce itself. Both families assume that the other partner, the other half of the reproduction dyad, will simply disappear and the offspring will belong conveniently to *their* family. Parents cannot really appreciate some young person who comes along and steals their child, and although that sense of competition or feeling of paranoia can be covered and is frequently invisible, I assume it is always present as a dynamic factor. The culture shock between this husband and wife (or boyfriend and girlfriend) is always present, just like my farm upbringing is always present. Only gradually do the partners realize that they are involved in a set of triangles: his family, her family, and the couple; or the husband, the wife, and his family; or the wife, the husband, and her family. Although this need for adaptation has its stresses, it also has its rewards, just as the Japanese are proving as they adapt to the culture shock of teaming up with us in the United States!

In the second style of marriage we find what I call a *bilateral adoption contract*. He agrees to be her mother if she will be his mother. Of course, this is all covert. It means that each of them expects the other to respect his or her need for nurturing. This expectation is sometimes expressed by talking about how "she doesn't satisfy my needs," or "he doesn't satisfy my needs." To me, the inference involved in talking about *needs* is always that there is a generation gap, and there is the covert expectation of a two-generation system in which the speaker will be the child and the other partner will be the parental figure.

A third style of marriage occurs when there is a *bilateral pseudo-therapy project*. *She* is just the right woman for him, he infers or assumes, as soon as he gets her over her compulsiveness. And *he* will be the ideal man for her, she feels and may never know, as soon as she gets him over his drinking, or his preoccupation with golf, or whatever. This therapeutic process is really that of two dedicated amateurs trying to make-believe they are parental, and trying to get the other person to be infantile and respond to their tutelage. Like most therapeutic efforts in nonprofessional settings, the result is usually a bilateral impasse because of the bilateral transference role each of them carries! Pseudo-therapy may become a way of life, a psycho-therapy, or a struggle between one old person and another old person to create a peer relationship in which each of them is more and more an individual, and more and more a member of this new super-system called a marriage.

Behind the struggle of pseudo-therapy between the two partners is the latent fear of the two families. Usually this fear is not expressed, but it is my conviction that the panic is often present. *His* mother knew that this new wife didn't fit her son—she just didn't mention it. And *her* mother knew that this boy shouldn't really be trusted. Sometimes the intuitive, insightful mothers mention their musings to the fathers or even to their children, but many times these sentiments come out only in those flashes of shadow that take place in the middle of ongoing living. You must admit, it is difficult for parents to "back off" when some other kid has stolen their baby!

Behind this level of struggle is a subtler concept. Did father and mother have something to gain from their son's leaving home, or from their daughter's leaving home? They have the chance to get back to each other, as well as the danger of breaking up from each other. They also must face the fact that they see one another's struggle in a different way, and many times this difference produces a strain between them, just as raising children had strained them for the previous 18 or more years.

We used to say that this pseudo-therapy marriage problem, like all psychotherapy, lost its power and usefulness after 10 years. Then we said after 10 months . . . recently we talked about the growthful aspects of marriage as getting feeble after 10 weeks . . . or sometimes after 10 days! Then the problem is very clear: Will this couple dare to work out ways of psychological divorce and remarriage? Will they persevere long enough to discover that in this process of investing their individuation in the next bigger system, they can gain strength to reenergize their own individual selves? That the gradual evolution of more and more peerness fortunately diminishes the cross-generational transference in which they play therapist and patient, or parent and child, toward each other?

The fourth style of marriage is one of *symbiosis*, an unconscious-to-unconscious interlocking which takes place without either partner recognizing it. The symbiosis may be due to the fact of some symbolic stimulus—such as he walks like her father, or she wiggles her head like his mother—and neither one of them knows how this takes place, but it becomes a profound kind of lock-in for the other person.

Stages of Marriage

The evolution of a healthy marriage should have certain specific characteristics. I would postulate that the most important characteristic is that marriage is a kind of lifetime *whole-person to whole-person psychotherapy*—a change process in which partners have a responsibility or an opportunity to trade some of their individual rights, privileges, and capacities for the chance to belong to a *twosome* which is more powerful than either of them, and which each of them calls upon for the needed power to fight the social and cultural structure in which they live. This process happens in spite of the triangulation that each of them feels with all of their ex-relationships: not only with the parents and siblings in the biological sphere, but also with the many psychological and psychosocial coalitions they have experienced.

The first stage in this evolution of a marriage is the triangulation with the in-laws. He thinks he has married a woman. What he has really married, however, is another family. He has to struggle to convince himself that he has captured her from them, because the biological bind between her and her family is much more powerful than her psychosocial bond with him. The same, of course, happens the other way. She thinks she has captured him, but what she has really done is become a secondary-type daughter to his parents, who want to use her to reproduce their family but do not want to take responsibility for her as a member of their family.

The second stage in the evolution of this healthy marriage is the outreach for a supervision of the bilateral psychotherapy taking place between the partners. This outreach can range from a request by the couple to some friend or acquaintance for help in settling some of their struggles to the use of a professional in couples therapy—first to supervise the partners' efforts to be psychotherapists and patients to each other, and then, hopefully, to create the professional triangulation that produces a change in the marriage itself.

The third stage in this evolution is exploding the covert generation gap that exists between partners. An easy way to spot this stage is when one of them responds to the effort to help from the partner by saying "Yes, mother" in a sarcastic tone that denotes, "I will not accept you as somebody in an older generation—you are only a peer."

Once this has been successful, *the fourth stage involves some effort to deliberately unite the twosome by an effort at growth*: for example, getting a pet as a pre-baby trial; establishing her dog, his dog, *their* cat, *their* house, *their* car. Here, partners explore the issue: Can they take on something less than human but necessitating coordination in their relationship to it?

The fifth evolutionary stage occurs by rejoining the family of origin and reindividuating. If the marriage is successfully growing, she will be able to reenter her family of origin in an adult style, thereby becoming part of two families: her family of origin and her family of procreation. Likewise, he will be able to become a new kind of adult member in his family of origin, while remaining an individuating part of his family of procreation.

Assuming they have lived through the anxiety in this détente so far, *the sixth stage is what I've come to call a whole-person to whole-person relationship between the husband and wife.* This is a love independent of sexual stimulation or sexual attraction. It is hard to describe this stage. It is uniquely different from the original love affair, or even the therapeutic effort to change each other, or to renounce or modify the individual rights for the sake of belonging to a greater system (the marriage or the family of procreation).

The seventh stage in this evolution involves the willingness to triangulate for decision-making purposes. Here we find deliberate efforts by the partners to include other professionals in their decision-making, whether it is hiring a contractor to build a new home, or consulting with a pediatrician about their child, or seeking the help of a psychotherapist to make their marital teaming more successful, more flexible, and more powerful.

The eighth stage, as I envision it, is a peership set so firm that the partners can ebb and flow, accepting a kind of bilateral veto, because they have discovered that *he-ship* and *she-ship* does not equal *we-ness. I-ness* and *we-ness* are dialectically centered. One can only individuate and recombine in an endless process that always includes anxiety!

The ninth stage involves a kind of psychological divorce and remarriage. This is the massive whole-person to whole-person individuation from the twosome; it is a process of taking the psychologically life-threatening jump that makes for the increasingly powerful, increasingly broad steps in this dialectical swing. All-out individuation—the discovery of the joy and the pain of psychological divorce—is one of the ways of precipitating more maturity and carefully evaluating the dangers of breaking the decision to continue the life of one-ness and teaming.

The tenth stage in this process of evolving a healthy marriage is probably the most powerful one and frequently precipitated long before its culminating position in the orderly sequence I am proposing. *This is the arrival of the baby, and, of course, of baby number two, also.* The biological triangulation that automatically results from the birth of a new baby puts the greatest strain on the we-ness. It also offers the opportunity of making clear to the couple that their we-ness is the essential ingredient for the baby's freedom to define his or her own separateness as well as belongingness, rather than having it decided for him or her by the anxiety in each of the parents.

When the baby arrives, triangulation is generated on two levels. The two sets of new grandparents are faced with the problem of whose grandchild this is to be—his or hers? Who does he or she look like? Who does he or she act like? Which family's problems or assets does the baby have? All these become subtle or profoundly obvious competitive bits of the agony and ecstasy of family life.

Meantime, back on the farm, the mother and father are suddenly triangulated in a new way. Mother has this nine-month investment in her other self, and father is cheated out of this biological experience. Of course, the partners make profound psychological and social efforts to rectify this covert divorce and make the experience all it can be for each of them. But it should be clear that the unconditional positive regard that the baby offers its mother is only very slowly available for father, and the triangular problem of who is teaming with whom is endlessly reverberating through this new, two-generation family unit.

(Allow me a tangential thought. I have this fantasy that the first baby is automatically mother's mother: the person who provides the security that the new mother needs and that she previously got from her own mother. The pattern by which families carry out these undercover dynamics is very easy to overlook and also open to doubt. To carry my fantasy one step further, I assume that the second child is automatically viewed by the couple to be father's mother, so that he will feel secure and safe, as he did with his own mother. When there is a third baby, I assume that it is mother's effort to make sure that father keeps his heart in the family rather than letting it be seduced by money, golf, another woman, his job, or the TV. So far my only thought about the fourth baby is that it may have a chance to be a really free person, without symbolic overlay of the kind that passes on to the previous three babies a kind of loaded psychological imprinting.)

The final stage in the evolution of a marriage is the process of evolving a two-family alliance, the alliance of his family and her family of origin. This stage is fraught with many imitations and many preliminary as well as fragmentary efforts. It is always difficult and many times impossible to achieve this alliance on an emotional level, even though it can be imitated and postured socially and psychologically. Many times a kind of pseudo-alliance is present between one family and one of the individuals, or each of the individuals and the other family, but that is very different from the alliance of the two large groups.

Although the individuals who are married constitute a symbolic expression of their family of origin, it is a long step in learning how to unite these two independent, ethnically unique, biopsychosocial organisms called *families*. If that unification happens, then they become a community, each one respecting the other's right to be individual and at the same time joining in the process of a social and psychological unity. Throughout this process, the two families have been group psychotherapists to each other, learning *the tolerance for deviance, the power of unity*, and *the freedom to join and separate*—each of which is anxiety-laden but powerfully and rightfully due each family.

The Perinatal Problem of the Young Couple

The difficult fact that marriage requires the combining of two families is only surpassed by the struggle that surrounds pregnancy, delivery, and that early breastfeeding period up till one year, when the triangulation process in the young family mounts with greater and greater complexities. The wife, her mother, and the husband comprise the most obvious triangle. His mother-in-law may either become his mother, making a second complication, or simply remain a competitor—leaving the husband with the feeling that he can never really have his wife because she really belongs to her mother. Then there is his obvious need for more mothering from his wife, since he lost his mother when he took on this other woman. The wife is also the thief who stole that son from his mother. The relationship of the husband to his father and his father-in-law is usually much less significant, but in its own way, it may encourage him to tolerate that hopeless, mechanistic life into which men tend to escape to avoid the pain of human interaction.

The initial period of pride and masculine success evidenced by the wife's being pregnant is shortly followed by the sense of separation as the wife turns more and more to her affair with her inner person. The husband becomes the observer cuckolded in his most intimate adult role. The wife's desperate attempts to bring her husband in on the pregnancy, on her joy in her affair, are both exciting for him and, paradoxically, very painful. The more she tells him about the glories of her inner life with the infant, the more he becomes aware of how far outside he really is.

The ultimate moment in this triangulation occurs during the baby's birth. The excitement, the panic, and the reality of the birthing are quickly and painfully undercut by the sense that the husband is a "peeping Tom" at his partner's ultimate orgasm. He is fully involved with the discovery that their previous orgasms are as little or nothing, and that he will never be able to attain for himself this ultimate turn-on that she is experiencing. Further, as the baby begins to breastfeed, the mother is offered the golden opportunity to regress to her own infantile stage and experience the primary process that precedes language. Communication between the mother and infant is of such a primitive and profound character as to make contact between the husband and wife seem very shallow. More and more he is aware that he has been excommunicated biologically and relegated to the world of pychosocial relationships. Furthermore, her need and responsibility to regress in the service of her ego make it equally necessary for him to maintain the counterweight homeostatic quality of becoming her mother, symbolically. Even in this opportunity to compete vicariously for the opportunity of some regression, he is usually outdone by the arrival of the wife's mother, who participates in the perinatal experience, leaving him further outside.

One of the obvious responses to this very difficult situation is for him to deny all of his deprivation and for her to deny much of her primitive satisfaction in the hope of maintaining some semblance of the previous intimacy between the two of them. She is really not a black widow spider; she does not kill him. Yet in many psychological ways, this is a good metaphor for the situation as it exists on a covert level. Having discovered that his wife has psychologically turned her back on him during her pregnancy, the husband frequently finds himself vulnerable to falling into an emotional alliance with either the struggle for money and power in the outside world or with some other female. Turning his back on her in retaliation for her turning her back on him usually turns out to be a very painful process, however, because pride triggers an ongoing competition in the family for warmth and humanness.

There is more! The discovery of the profound interaction available to his wife via her body-to-body relationship with the infant makes the fetish of his worshiping his penis and his physical strength seem very feeble; his impotence is now not a feeling but a *fact*. He is very aware that his ability to arouse his wife is very tiny in comparison with the infant's at the birth, not to mention the infant's continuing ability to completely absorb her attention and affections via breastfeeding and the utterly intimate communication that passes between them throughout the day. The dejected husband may then try to augment the mothering component in his experience with his wife or, more likely, he may become sexually impotent in depressed, futile hopelessness about his humanity.

One common resolution is to instigate an actual legal divorce to demonstrate and reinforce the emotional divorce that has already taken place. The legal divorce offers the couple a massive, lifetime protection. *He* can blame the rest of his psychopathology and his unhappy life on her for leaving him, and *she* can blame all the pain of her own stress on him for leaving her. She has the additional factor of falling in love with the child who represents him; she thus may pathologize that ongoing relationship as well. Another sad by-product of the divorce is the emotional fallout that characterizes it. Both partners become bitter about human relationships in general, so that all subsequent heterosexual relationships will be distorted by their assumptions that "all women are the same; all men are the same." Each becomes more manipulative, more cynical, more distant, and more convinced that the only successful intimacy is with the self.

With all this covert horror, isn't it amazing that Mother Nature makes it all workable?

Marital Feuds

It seems increasingly clear to me that pathology in individuals, whether it is physical or psychological in nature, is most often an effort to change that family as a whole. Marriage is merely one evidence of this kind of pathology. *She* comes from a family that is too close and is becoming gradually aware of it; *he* comes from a family that is too distant and is becoming aware of it. These two representatives of their families get married with the hope that each one can learn something about what the other is so good at. Once marriage has taken place, the two individuals become more concerned with loyalty to their families of origin, and so there begins this feud. *She* wants to have their families close; *he* wants to have their families distant; and the two families do not speak to each other because of this difference in lifestyle. The marriage then finds itself in big trouble as the two partners struggle simultaneously to bring therapeutic changes into their families of origin *and* to be loyal to their families of origin. *He* tries to prove to his wife that being separate is more valuable, and *she* tries to prove to her husband that being closer is more valuable.

What to do about such a situation includes two aspects: one preventive and the other therapeutic. The therapeutic aspect involves the need to bring in both families of origin in order to do anything about the nuclear family. It is much better to start with three generations if you hope to make any real changes in the marriage and the relationship of the husband and wife to the children. It is the preventive aspect, however, that is becoming more and more interesting to me. It involves the possibility of bringing in both sets of parents of the families of origin *before* the marriage takes place so that it is clear that they are trying to structure their families around this new marriage, and that the marriage is between the two *families* rather than between the two *people*. Thus, the feud between the two families is at least out in the open.

Why doesn't the bride or the groom actually do something about changing his or her own family? First of all, they both have been programmed from infancy to recognize that life and death depend upon family loyalty. If you don't stay loyal to your family, you won't be breastfed. If you bite the breast, you'll starve to death. As years go by, the pattern is less profound, but by that time the patterns have been solidly established. Loyalty to the family is really a way of acknowledging yourself: You *are* the family, you *are* the personification of it. To deny the family is to deny your personhood, your body. To fight the family demands a separate structure, a freedom from the family's world, and that is almost impossible to attain. It is just like saying: How could you stop being a person and become an ape?

The inference, then, is that if you get yourself in trouble by developing a psychosis or a neurosis, it is covertly an effort to help your family accomplish one of its aims: to change. You are trying to be the ghost, the messiah, the therapist, and help the family accomplish its end. Of course, as soon as you do this, family members turn against you because they have already decided that this is the best for which they can hope.

The Exquisite Accuracy
of Partnership

Marriage is absurd. It is growthful to the extent that it is countercultural. It is an experience which threatens one's being and wrenches one down to the roots. Like hypnosis, marriage is an altered state of consciousness. The deeper one goes, the more possible it is for things to happen. One note of caution: If you can't stand loneliness, do not marry.

Most people categorize: "She's a bitchy female and that poor guy, I feel so sorry for him." Or, "He's a cold bastard and that poor woman." I feel my first discoveries in this area are universal: *The match between partners is absolutely accurate*. It is accurate not only in how one partner complements another in the present, but also in how each partner views the other in terms of growth in the relationship. The choice of a partner takes into consideration the marital seesaw: the adaptability of the other person to your depressions or to your sadism. Don't believe anyone who says his marriage was a business arrangement, or "I was drunk." That ten-billion-unit computer that each of us has in our head matches exactly the other computer we lock into.

Let me give an example. You see an alcoholic who is a very little boy, and he is so hungry. He is married to this competent woman, loving and caring. You ask yourself: *How did she get stuck with that character?* He is a four-year-old who is still on his bottle, and she looks like an adult. Stick around for a while like I do and work with them for an extended period: It turns out that she, too, is a four-year-old! She is mother's little girl still taking care of little baby brother. You don't discover this right away, but watch her when she gets to be 45; she looks 65. She has remained a *function* all of her life; she has never become a *person*. She is not really mothering him; she is *pseudo*-mothering him. She is the taxi driver. She runs the damn town. She makes enough money to pay for his whiskey, she takes care of the five kids. But as a person, she is a non-person. She is a function. She is an endless series of roles. He is a baby, she is a function, and there are no people involved!

The more I work with couples, the more I am convinced that, emotionally, the husband and wife are the same age. If he is a 12-year-old absorbed in Boy Scouts, hunting, or whatever it is that defines his little-boy fun life, then she is the same age, even if she looks older. Or it could be the other way around. If she is still a six-year-old oedipal, pseudo-sexy little girl, then he is the same age.

One of the assumptions I make is that aggression is always the same on both sides. His wife is constantly raising hell with him, giving him endless beatings, so he gets your sympathy. But watch carefully. It may be as simple as a "Yes, dear," whereby he displays that little stiletto that he slips between her ribs. Suddenly she feels guilty, and he has just taken off her left leg. The difference is merely one of style: One way is overt; the other is covert. She is pounding him with a rubber hammer, and he is underhanded. But *the aggression is equal on both sides*.

Love is equal, too. She says: "We've got to stay married. I'm really fond of him. I still love him."

He says: "I'm fed up. I've had all I can take of her. She can have the kids. She can have the money. I just want out."

Don't believe either story. See what happens if the situation is reversed. If one day she says, "You know, I think a separation is a good idea; I met this guy the other day and I think maybe he and I would get . . . ," then all of a sudden *he* is the one who calls up and says, "Hey, Doc, how about a two-hour appointment?" *The love on both sides is equal*. Partners merely take turns with who is going to insist on the love and who is going to protest against it.

The Marital Seesaw

I began to wonder, if the factors of emotional age, aggression, and love are all equal, what about the double-binding that occurs in marriage? What about the verbal message that says one thing and the nonverbal message that says something else? What about all the manipulating?

He is a con artist who has been screwing everybody in the range of 50 miles; you feel she is a sincere, concerned person who hasn't been running around. But they are actually involved in a funny kind of "lock-in." Take the example in the previous section in which the wife is in love with the new baby. The husband is too immature to handle it, so he falls in love with money, or with a new job, or with his secretary. Once the baby is three years old or so, she gets tired with the whole mothering scene and starts to go after him. But now he's not so sure of her. It is fun to have her chase him, but he is still going to run around. She then goes back to the kids. Wife and husband continue this dance of who is going to get back at whom the most effectively. This behavior is natural and commonly results in marital crises.

The manipulation is also equal. She says, "You have no right to run around because the kids need you." She really means that she needs the kids and wishes she could get him, too! *The manipulation on both sides is the same*.

I believe the love is always bilateral in an established relationship. (It may not be so in an affair, but I suspect that it could be.) When Don Juan is told that he can get to heaven if he finds a woman who truly loves him, he feels they all love him. As he checks things out—as he meets one after another of the women he has slept with who love him—he gradually realizes that they were conning him at the same time that he was conning them.

The love is always equal. One partner proclaims it, the other denies it, and it is equal. The same is true with hate. He says, "I hate your guts." She is quiet and reserved. But the anger is equal—one expresses it more openly while the other is more concealing.

I saw a woman once who had had six years of individual treatment. She left her husband because he beat her up. I refused to see her individually because she already had a good therapist. I worked with her and her 11-year-old son relative to the oedipal stress that occurs during adolescence. I worked with them each summer for five or six summers. She kept coming back—a kind of backwards way of becoming a patient again.

One day she finally said, "I want to bring in my parents." Great! So she showed up with one parent who lived 100 miles away. Why not the other one? She said her father was very busy and she didn't think I needed to have him there anyway. I said, "Boy, are you in trouble. I'm going to charge you for the session and I'm not going to see you. I'm sorry about your mom having made this trip. But, you know, even though it is a lousy trick on mom, it is a worse one on dad. Because I think he is important. So go get him, or give the whole thing up."

The three of them arrived for the next session, and guess what happened? The 38-year-old daughter and the 60-year-old father ended up in a physical fight. They got through with it and dad said, "You know, this is so ridiculous. She is always accusing me of incestuous feelings. We're always having these crazy fights. I think it's absurd."

I ask, "Do you think it has to do with her ex-husband?"

She answers, "I haven't seen that so-and-so for 19 years. I have nothing to do with him, and I'll never see him again!"

I say, "Sparks, eh? It sounds for real. Call him and tell him I need him. You've been fussing around with me for years and it doesn't sound like it is about you and your parents. It sounds like it is about you and your ex."

She says, "Well, he won't come. He's been married and divorced."

I say, "So call him."

She calls him and he says, "Sure, I'll come. When do we meet?"

"Wednesday," she says.

"Good, I'll come Monday."

He arrives on Monday and she invites him into the apartment with herself and her 19-year-old son. Before Wednesday, she has beaten him up—19 years after she left him for beating her up.

They spent four interviews each day for the next four days wrestling with my question, "Hey, why don't you guys get remarried? For God's sake, if you mean this much to each other, why the heck are you staying separate? This way you can fight every day, and you can take Sunday off."

They were still very uncertain. It was clear that the reason he had divorced his second wife was because he was still locked into his first marriage. A year later they were still telephoning frantically back and forth about whether to get together. They spent a week together and decided they couldn't make it into a marriage. It is now four years that they have been on the seesaw. I got a call two or three months ago from her saying, "Well, you know, I arranged to lose my job."

I said, "Well, maybe you're just going to go back and get him again."

She is finally individuating in a whole new sense. Whether he will be able to match her individuation and they'll make it three years from now, I don't know. You do what you can do, and life has to do the rest.

The Affair:
Infidelity is Bilateral

It is five years since Tom and Kathy got married, and the thermostat is cooling. She doesn't turn him on quite so much because he is sick of her acting like his mother. He doesn't turn her on so much because she is sick of his being like her father or, more likely, her mother. The relationship is beginning to break. They are getting into one of the serial impasses of marriage.

They begin to exchange covert cues. He is reading the newspaper one morning and says, "Say, did you see this crazy thing? You know, this guy and this woman . . ." A week later she says, "I was talking to that guy down the road, and do you know what they are going to do? There is a neighbor of theirs and . . . " The couple begins to set up these stories about how valuable it is to have an affair.

Soon they have arranged that one of them is going to have an affair and that the other one is not going to take notice. Then, when they arrange that she will find a condom in his pocket, all of a sudden it blows up and the fat is in the fire.

When partners say to me, "We're both having affairs and it is okay with each of us, but we're wondering about our marriage," then I say, "Well, both of you, both of the affair partners, and both of the spouses of the affair partners must all come in, and together we will all work on it." It is amazing how helpful that suggestion is.

To one couple I said, "I'll be glad to help either way. Either you stop all the screwing around and just have emotional intercourse with each other, or else you bring the whole gang in. I will accept either way, but I am not going to accept things the way you are presenting them." Then I added, "You have those two psychotherapists (affairs) out there, and you know *I* don't like infidelity."

Later I got a letter from the couple: "We can't stand therapy; it is too much and too expensive." Two months later there was a second letter saying, "Thanks so much for helping us. Things are going much better. The therapy meant a great deal to us."

It was the "they" who decided on the affairs; "they" planned the affairs for therapeutic purposes. Amateur therapists were better than nothing. When they began to get desperate about their marriage, they finally came to see someone in the health profession to see if he might be better than amateurs. There is still some question about that!

Suicide of the Marriage

Why is it that some people cannot stay married? To pose this question to someone who has been married for 50 years sets up the possibility of multiple answers. However, I'm afraid it is one of those questions where one can never choose two sides. I have one basic answer. Every few years, I seem to be married to a new wife. People who stay married don't just stay married; they move from being united, to individuating, and then remarrying or reuniting. That is, *the same process takes place over time that takes place each day or hour, even within the first week of marriage.*

The reasons why people do not stay married are complex and involve many factors. The most obvious factor in our current time period is the evolution of the cultural values of both sexual freedom and marital freedom. It is as though all decisions are reversible. This illusionary premise promotes every young child's fantasy. "There must be somebody who fits my needs exactly—mother didn't, father didn't, my previous partner didn't." Or, as one famous movie star said, "This eighth wife is just the one I've been looking for all these years!"

Another factor that activates the disruption of a marriage is the transmission of marital struggles between his and her parents into the current generation. The wife may be in full rebellion against her mother, who had capitulated to *her* mother and so will not capitulate to anyone. Our culture is now dedicated to independence and has evolved a belligerent defiance to any control system. Denigrated by a confused parental control system and trained to fight against it, partners continue to fight against the controls and restrictions that must underlie any marriage. No partnership can be free, each loses individuation by uniting, just as each loses isolation by uniting. Actually, growth in marriage is like growth in the individual. As I have said, it is a process of endless dialectical alternations between *union*, with the danger of *enslavement*, and *individuation*, with the danger of *isolation*. There is no resolution of this endless process, this alternation between belongingness and separateness.

It is probable that some marriages become impossible to sustain because one or both partners become panicky, lest they fail in their individual efforts to climb the ladder of community success. The inability to stay married may also stem from trouble between the two families or origin. A childhood imprint of the husband-wife war between the parental figures pressures the young married couple to repeat the scene, even though they may have hated it and have every intention to *not* repeat it.

Also, there are marriages that begin with a delusion of attaining adulthood by teaming to avoid the painful insecurity of adolescence. It is not easy for the marriage to continue if these two 16-year-old teenagers get united so that they can become one 32-year-old and thus make it in the big bad world. The modern hard-sell for sexual adventurism also makes it difficult for couples to settle down into the responsibilities and pressures that develop around the establishment of any partnership—and marriage is nothing if not a partnership.

Finally, it is probable that a good many marriages are entered into before the young adult has successfully divorced his parents and established his right to be an individual. Trying to belong to a new family when one has not really dared to be separate from one's family of origin is apt to promote a phobia. Each spouse expects to be adopted by the good parent-partner. Individuation and rejoining is a stepwise way to change this paradox, but it is painful and endless. Psychological divorce and remarriage moves to peership, but the arthritis-like ache of every step needs more than aspirin, and alcohol doesn't solve it. Even psychotherapy is no panacea.

Divorce is on the rise, not only of the first marriage, but many times of the second, third, or fourth marriage. With it comes the concurrent blending of real fathers, stepfathers, foster fathers, adopted fathers and, now that things are less clear in male and female roles, the blending of stepmothers, stepfathers, and even new combinations including, for example, a homosexual partner who functions as mother or father. The question of what is happening is still in the hands of the researchers, but theoretical discussions are alive and varied.

If we assume, as I do, that the pathology of marriage for the past 40 or 50 years involves the delusion that marriage is a process by which two individuals become one, disappearing into a *we*, then we can understand how this pathology has resulted in the massive repression of individual needs. Many times both the husband and wife turned into the function of father and mother without even becoming *persons*. With the decline in religious capitulation to the sacredness of marriage and the concomitant rise in the drive for individuation, divorce has become one way of breaking out of the binding quality, the enslavement that results when two individuals submerge their identities and become non-persons for the sake of symbiotic togetherness in the complementarity that is marriage.

Once the delusion that marriage was sacred was fragmented, the process of developing a life of isolation became one of the substitutes for marriage as enslavement. The marriage was broken up by the man's running away or the woman's running away, by one or the other committing suicide, or by living back-to-back in deep and carefully disguised bitterness. As soon as it was clear that this kind of isolation was socially and culturally acceptable, it became more and more possible for people who had married to solve the problem of individuating by getting a divorce. Unfortunately, the residuals of their enslavement did not disappear. The affectional investments they had made in each other were not cancelable, and their freedom to invest themselves in another partner was hedged with suspicion and paranoid feelings about any marital relationship. The attempted resolution of this bind by living with someone without contracting to become intimate but merely using the union as a sexual game was only partially satisfactory. And, frustratingly, the effort to increase that satisfaction by marriage frequently resulted in a disruption of the illusion of freedom that was maintained during the long-term sexual affair.

In essence, then, we have moved culturally from the struggle over a delusion that we-ness was sacred to a delusion that I-ness is sacred. Actually, the process of learning how to love and how to become part of a *we* without destroying yourself is a long-term project. It begins with learning how to love yourself and then learning how to love someone like you, and moves on to the courage to love someone different from you, to learning how to tolerate the vulnerability and struggle over the problem of how to be all you are, which must include a significant other. Thus marriage becomes not a bilateral adoption in which two 16-year-olds unite to make one 32-year-old, but a real team process—a Ph.D. in human relationships in which one contracts to become more and more totally related to another individual so that one can find the total expression of one's whole self. As Martin Büber says, this total expression of the whole self is only possible in a free relationship to another individual. In contracting not to escape from the struggle, one finds more and more of one's own strength and more and more of oneself. Thus, in the dialectical fashion, *I* become more and more of who *I am* by becoming more and more a part of who *we are*.

The Family Infrastructure:
A City and a Wheel

Talking about the family and understanding it is like talking about a city and trying to understand it. The city looks very clearcut and available. Some buildings are higher, some are lower, some are older, some are newer, some are constructed straight, some uniquely designed, some eccentric, some obviously unused. One can go inside the buildings and study the interior design: Some of the doors are locked, some are open; some of the windows are broken. It all seems very simple.

However, if you talk with the city engineer, you gain a whole new picture of the city's true composition. Usually described as the "infrastructure," it externally involves the streets, the sidewalks, the manhole covers, the bridges, the traffic patterns, the varying qualities of street repair. Internally, under the surface, there is the sewer system which has evolved over a hundred years or so, with its varying designs superimposed on each other via sewage outlets and disposal systems, branches of electric cables in various stages of repair and disrepair, gas lines branching and rusting, water lines and hydrants for fire-fighting, and hot water systems for heating large buildings. The design, construction and repair of all these subterranean infrastructures are almost as complex as the architecture and construction that takes place above the surface. There are sub-basements, and sub-basements to sub-basements, down one, two, or three floors—with all the complexities and all the needs for variation to accommodate these structures as well as furnish the foundations for the structures on the surface. The reverberations from these infrastructures are powerful, even though the actual facts of the infrastructures are largely unknown to the usual observer.

Thinking about this metaphor produces massive inferences about the life

99

of the family. It may be helpful to use the metaphor of the personal unconscious or even the cultural unconscious to describe the state-of-affairs that the therapist confronts when he moves into a family. This state-of-affairs is analogous to that encountered by the engineer from a nearby city who moves into a new city and must learn to understand its infrastructure. The metaphor is even more relevant if you think about the suburbs, the fact that they also influence the operation of the city even though they are outside its limits, even though they both contribute to and take from the city as such. In a similar way the extended family with its peripheral social and business networks both contribute to and detract from the family's mythology that has been transmitted for generations. This mythology is comprised of a myriad of psychosocial factors: the family's response to illness, the family's traditional response to death, to birth, and to its attachment to another family by way of marriage, occupation, or geography (neighbors); the family's relationship to intimate community groups, to the large community groups, to the political scene, to handling strangers; the family's handling of stress in its many and variable patterns, of shame, of secrets, and of decision-making; the degree and method of repression, the freedom to talk about intimate matters or to hide intimate matters, verbal communication as a way of enjoying one another or as a pattern that is untouchable (i.e., the New England retreat from words versus the Jewish involvement with words); the relationship of the family to issues of religion and money.

Talking about the structure of the family is difficult to do because of the multiple factors involved. Perhaps I could use another metaphor. Imagine a large wagon wheel. A family that I saw in therapy called this a picture of their family. The hub—the center structure that attaches the wheel to the wagon—they called the mother. The spokes that ran between the hub and the rim of the wheel they pictured as the children, separating the hub from the rim which they called the father, but holding the two together and forming an essential part of this three-component entity. It is fascinating to think of the extended family as a two-wheel vehicle or a four-wheel vehicle, which could be called the family community or the community of families.

The metaphorical implications are very intriguing. The support, the intimacy, the closeness of the mother and the children—the mother's connection to the extended family via emotional bonds, physical biology, and psychological intimacy—are in a relational position very different from the protective rim (the father) that connects the family to the reality of the earth, the outside world. Given this kind of picture, it is easy to understand how families fall apart under stress. One of the spokes of the wheel becomes loose, falls out, or is broken, and the whole wheel becomes unstable. As more than one spoke falls apart or somehow breaks down, the instability of the wheel is much increased. However, if the peer relationship (to extend the metaphor) between the hub and the rim and the spokes can be evolved, it is possible for the wheel to go on turning without any one part becoming enslaved by the fact of this relationship or of the other parts and their dynamics.

The Tangled Web We Weave

The relationship between the family and the social network (be it a friendship network, a neighborhood network, or an occupational network) needs greater exposure and explication. Most critical to this exposure is the big lie that "we share an identical world view." Behind this lie is the fact of the family's subjugation by the culture and by the laws, not to mention the fear of punishment and the danger of the temptation to rebellion. Still farther back in the scene are the residuals of the family hypnosis, the indoctrination of community living, of school, of work, the forced language we learn with all its double entendres of communication and all the nonverbal reinforcements, and the denial and undercutting of our overt interpersonal interactions involving give and take. Threaded into this relationship of the family system to the larger system is the pain of work and an overall indoctrination of subservience to community demands, reinforced by the threat of psychosocial isolation.

One of our responses to this tangled web is our pseudo adaptation to the *they* and the *we*: the public relations smile of conformity; the overt contract arrangements that are then violated or covertly undercut; the anesthesia that ensues as a result of the pseudo hero worship of the athlete, the guru, the religious savant; or the seduction of the reward system, be it financial, political, or professional.

Leon Fierman wrote about Dr. Hellmuth Kaiser in a book called *Effective Psychotherapy*. He was searching for the universal human symptom, and he arrived at a conclusion which sounds very correct to me. The universal human symptom is the universal delusion of fusion: the concept that if you can reunite with your mother, with God, with a wife who serves as a constant source of additional power—in other words, if you sacrifice your individuation for the certainty of belonging to a larger system—then your isolation, your aloneness, your panic will be relieved.

Uncovering the *universal family secret* is an equally worthwhile effort. What does each family hold underneath as a covert, hidden haunt—the ghost in the closet? I would assume that this could best be answered by citing a personal notation from Milton H. Miller, who was endlessly repeating the question, "*Who is the they?*" There must be a *they* who are doing things, a *they* who are not doing things, a *they* who are against us, a *they* who are for us. *They* implies that there is some mysterious group, couple, culture, country, family, neighbor, but it is never quite clear who is implied, or who is identified as the mysterious, powerful, haunting *other*— the outside force that haunts us. Is *they* the family of the in-laws? *They*, for her, is her husband's family. *They*, for him, is his wife's family. Does the *they* include his mother's family, his father's family, her mother's family, her father's family, his colleagues at work? All of these elements represent the ominous haunts that hang in the background of the family, haunts that are never really clarified, or when they are clarified, give rise to further complications that remain unspecified!

If I move in such and such a way, will *they* be more apt to support me? If I don't do something, will *they* back me? The endless process of identifying the *they* is also carefully tied in to the endless problem of determining should/shouldn't behaviors. I should do so and so; I should be so and so; I should do this or that; I should not do; I should not be; I should be; *they* want me to be; *they* want me to not be. A long series of possibilities is opened as soon as one thinks seriously about this unknown *they*.

Indeed, one of the most powerful influences on the family and its living is the fact of the cultural belief system. We are all culture bound, and the culture bind changes from generation to generation and from decade to decade. The culture bind of the early twenties, thirties, and forties was the disappearance of the individual into the marriage. *They* became a symbiotic *we*. This was a result of the religious dedication which arose out of the pilgrim ethos and the escape from the political enslavement of the Old World. As it became increasingly crystalized, the symbiosis was beautifully depicted by the painting of two farmers, husband and wife, with a pitchfork between them, called "American Gothic." The anger, bitterness, and repression of their slavery were all too graphically reproduced.

This American culture bind then underwent drastic transformation via the abnormal loyalties that followed the depression and the need for national unity to prevent starvation, the isolationism that prefaced World War

II, the unity in self-protection during World War II, and the glories of world power that followed the devastations in Europe and Japan. The 1960s emerged as the "me generation": a rebellion against the fantasies of world domination as they were expressed in the Viet Nam War, and the paranoia about the next world war with Russia. Actually, it really wasn't a "me generation." It was an "anti-us generation"—a kind of metaphorical expression of the psychoanalytic delusion that enough self-understanding, enough self-expression would produce maturity, happiness, and a beautiful life.

A by-product of the "anti-us generation" was the social play of the sexual revolution, when penises and vaginas went off on trips together. Mostly, there were no people along, only the question of whether the game of sex would ever develop into whole-person-to-whole-person love. Soon enough, the biological power of reproduction took over, so that the obstetrical wards that were empty through the early part of the 1970s began to be replenished. By 1977, the family had begun to be authenticated once again by the culture. There still remained as a vestige from the sixties the compet-ing pressure for each person to be an individual and to deny the deep validity of the family. Now, the isolationism of individuation has produced a kind of backlash expressed in a frantic search for health, exercise, and medical care. Technical efforts to live forever put a great deal of pressure on the culture to supply the security, wisdom, and power that previously emanated from the family but had been lost in the adventurous sixties.

Staying Alive as a Member of a Family

Treating 15 to 25 families a week for these past 20 years has produced a peculiar kind of understanding in me, perhaps in the way the Indian learned to understand the woods, or the farmer learns to understand the land. My learning was mostly nonverbal, and yet I was endlessly under pressure to convince the residents in training of the value of the family in their work with emotionally or physically disturbed individuals. Let me say that my deductions or conclusions or observations are very relative, open to all sorts of doubt, and I offer them only in hopes that they will be useful in your own personal theory-building.

There are three kinds of families. First, there is the *biopsychosocial family* where the "blood is thicker than water" truism has tremendous power. When I look in the faces of our six children, I inevitably connect them with my face, and my wife's face, and our 50 years of marriage, and no one else has that kind of power with us. Of course, the power is at one point agony and the next point ecstasy, but the power is unmatched in either case.

A second kind of family is the *psychosocial family*. This includes adoptive families, couples who fall in love, people who are profoundly attached to each other in the psychological sense and in the social sense of living together, working together, playing together. I am not underestimating the power of this group of families, because love can be a tremendously powerful force. But just as the psychological world of our daily living is less compelling than the immediacy of the physical condition of our bodies, the psychological world of the loving family is less powerful than the biopsychosocial family. There are, of course, mixtures of these two kinds of families—what I call the *his, hers and theirs family*. There is the second marriage, the psychological family of the high school love affair, or long-term human relationships which contain more and more psychological investment and therefore become more and more powerful.

The third kind of family is the *social family*. This family is held together by the bond of common interest and pursuit and is seen in professional football teams, skating duos, and all the many groups, communes, teams, and organizations. Here the term *family* is used only to denote the generation gaps between the older and the younger, the experienced and the beginner, or the group of peers.

It is also becoming increasingly clear to me that there are three kinds of genes. The *cultural genetic legacy* from one generation to another is a profound and powerful but largely disguised effect that becomes clear to us when we talk about cultural groups such as Irish, Iranian, Caucasian, Black, Oriental, and so on. There is also a psychological inheritance within each family in the form of the transfer of family culture—be it the work ethic, the freedom to be angry, the freedom to be intimate, or the converse of these—these are all part of the *psychological genetic inheritance*. It is also easy to sense that there are *social genes*: the senior members of a community in New England transfer social rules and a sense of responsibility to the junior members in the same way that the culture of the California family is transferred from parent to child, from friend to friend. We usually do not notice these patterns because they are so pervasive that we do not bother to distinguish them. They are like waves in the ocean—they ebb and flow continuously and without our awareness.

The Eight Dialectics
of the Healthy Family

The process of family living, just like the process of social living, creates stress. How the stress is resolved, how it is moved from intrapsychic to interpersonal, and how the interpersonal is resolved bear similarities to negotiations among the family of nations. Indeed, the process of family living usually ends up like the United Nations has ended up: as an important process of massive double-talk accompanied by very little understanding of the power moves that would be helpful, and little or no power to enforce the moves that people do perceive. The extended family is obviously a series of family integrations: his family and her family, his mother's family, his father's family, her mother's family, her father's family. All have their influence on the family's accumulated living patterns, and the methods for resolving the differences (both cultural and experiential) have been passed down from generation to generation on each of the four or sixteen sides.

Defining the healthy family involves an initial understanding of the process of growth. Growth in the individual occurs by increasing the integration that exists between intuitive and cognitive components of the person and the establishment of a sense of whole uniting these two discrepant territories. This is also true for the family.

Perhaps growth in families is more easily understood in terms of a dialectical struggle at several levels. The most significant dialectic is that found in the opposition/synthesis of *belonging* and *individuating*. I have pointed out how individuation, when carried to its extended and evolved limit, was thought to produce a kind of wholeness in the person, which then made for maturity. This brand of maturity, however, turns into a kind of isolationism brought on by the denial of any need for belonging. At the other end of the continuum is a way of trying to escape the threat of belonging, called *enmeshment* by Salvador Minuchin. The individual who lives at home with his family into adulthood is enslaved by this belonging-ness and is sacrificing all of his individuation.

The extrapolation of this polarity can be found in the dialectic: The freer a person is to individuate, the freer he is to recombine in a more cooperative, interactional, and satisfying sense of togetherness with members of his family of origin, his family of procreation, and his community of colleagues and peers. Once he is free to move beyond enmeshment and toward individuation, he gains new strength and competence as a person. He is freer to belong while maintaining his individual status, individual function, and individual freedom to rejoin and to separate at will.

A second dialectic which carries the same dilemma of all dialectics—the kind of see-saw that is not resolvable but constantly expandable—is the dialectic between *cognition* and *intuition* commonly clichéd as left-brain, right-brain. It is clearly recognized that some people are more intuitive and less cognitive; other people are more cognitive and less intuitive. But the concept of a dialectic shows how an increase in each side is preferable to defining the two components as opposing entities.

Our third dialectic is that between *roles* and *personhood*. Our lives are filled with *roles*: the job role, the roles assigned in our family as parent or child, mother or father; and the roles assigned to us as members of social groups. All of these slots are defined and, in essence, the person fulfills his roles more or less adequately by choosing some and modifying others to the degree possible. Dialectically related to this is the fact of *personhood*. I can be a role, but if I am integrated, I also constitute a person, with a life as such. The fact that this personhood, this presence, this centeredness, is very difficult to attain and is only relative because roles are always impinging on our life, does not negate the fact of this personhood. It merely exposes the problem of resolving the struggle between personhood and role.

A fourth dialectic involves *control* and *impulse*. The process of control impinged on us by our community (be it the family or the larger communi-ty) is something that we more or less accept. However, the ultimate accep-tance of this control by the community amounts to a kind of social death. The individual becomes nothing more than a robot operating in the service of the social structure and having no personhood. "Social death" is a relative label and is frequently diagnosed as rigidity, political sophistication, social conformity or nicety, or just plain drudgery. The other side of this dialectic is impulsivity: the demand for space, the demand for personal freedom, the demand for the right to follow one's own bent. Carried to the ultimate, this becomes the impulse to kill or the impulse to dominate the other person, the other community, the other part of the system, in which one is a member. The resolution of this problem is impossible! We all live in a balance between control and impulse, and this dialectic then has the same process: The more one controls, the more one can satisfy one's impulses, and the more one has impulses, the more one needs control. There is no resolution; there is merely a balance and a dialectic process.

The fifth of these dialectics is that of *public relations* and *personal relations*. Public relations involves a deliberate role manipulation in which the person is endeavoring to modify the group by his own careful assignment of roles to himself and to the others around him. Politicians are famous for their capacity in public relations, and so are salespeople and advertisers. The other side of this dialectic is personal relations: the intimacy of interrelationships with one's spouse and with one's parents, or the intimacy of a partnership or of a working triad. It is as though one is transcending all roles and becoming a whole in relationship to another whole. The ideal marriage, of course, is a process in which two peers are equally role-free in their relationship to each other. But the ordinary process of living contains an endless dialectic between personal relations and public relations, with a mixture of both present at all times.

Our sixth dialectic is that between *love* and *hate*. As soon as the relationship of the system heats up, either because of love or anger, one is struck with the impossibility of resolving the set by moving full-tilt toward either hatred and killing or loving and dedication. *Symbiosis*, a word describing a bilateral parasite quality, is characteristic of both love and hate. There is no way of resolving this dilemma, either. The dialectic is a balance between lovingness and hatred, where the lovingness or hatred produces a kind of two-person craziness. (One-person craziness is isolation.) The attraction, the impulse towards union, is not resolvable. The freedom, the growth in this dialectic as in the others, has to do with greater freedom for each person to express the opposite.

The seventh dialectic is that between *craziness* and *trickiness* or, if you will, a high level of individuation and a high level of adaptation. Craziness is a process of nonrestrained expression. Trickiness is an expression of massive adaptive capacity, and involves a kind of a two-person craziness—the trickster and the tricked. The balance between these is set, and as either one increases, it makes possible an increase in the other. If craziness is freedom then freedom is crazy.

The eighth dialectic is that between *stability* and *change*, or if you will, between entropy—the gradual breakdown of the whole—and negentropy—the growthful component within the breakdown of the whole. The balance between entropy and negentropy is nicely represented by the growth of plants as the fertilizer and the water in the soil are chemically broken down to supply the necessary food.

Beyond Oedipus:
What Every Child Deserves

I believe that the first baby is always incestuous; this baby is the actuality of the little girl's fantasy of having a baby with her daddy. It is very terrifying, even though the woman may never consciously realize it. Most of us never know. I lived for 65 years and never knew I wanted to marry my mother until she died. Actually, I don't believe my own statement. I think I wanted to marry my mother from the time I was a little boy. I can remember kissing my mother good-bye at the age of 13 and realizing that her body was stiff. I don't think I ever kissed her that way again. The unconscious dynamics in the family as a whole were funneling down to me, as they do to everyone.

How to get at those dynamics is another matter. I don't think you can get at them by education; I don't think you can get at them by detective work; I don't think you can get at them by theoretical pre-planning. I think that *if* you get at them, it is because *you* go crazy, and the family goes crazy with you. That is, you go into your insides and that gives the other family members the freedom to go into their insides, and then maybe things change.

In psychiatry we talked about the Oedipal triangle for so long that it occurred to my rebellious inner self that we should find a new way to talk about the parent-child relationship. What would help a child grow up to have a sense of security, an exploratory courageousness, and an ethical sense of values? It is easy to postulate what would be most valuable: a set of parents, each of whom has evolved through a psychological divorce and remarriage in his or her family of origin. That is, both mother and father have separated from their own mother and father, have established independent lives, have gone back and reconnected with their parents as adults, have separated again and reconnected again, so that they have the freedom to belong and to individuate from their families of origin. When both partners have had this experience of divorce and remarriage in their families of origin, the nuclear marriage becomes a genuine move into belonging to a larger system, the twosome of marriage. It becomes a subtle decision to carry out the psychotherapy that marriage consists of knowing that the psychotherapy will go on for life, and that there will be an endless process of whole-person to whole-person interaction. Once this connection has been well-made, and the child arrives at that point but not earlier, then the child belongs to the *system*.

In the beginning, the baby has a life-and-death connection with the breastfeeding mother that no father can match at any time in any way. This process, which might well be called *biopsychological hypnosis*, means that the child is very slowly going to evolve the understanding that the breast is not part of his body, that mother is not part of his body, and then live in the awareness that his relationship to mother is the first time she has known this love since she had it with her mother, and that it is a kind of intimacy and we-ness that will never exist with any other person.

This real world of infant-mother has been grossly distorted by the fantasies of the Oedipal struggle. I should like to replay this struggle and add that the next move is the freedom of the father to be nurturant toward the baby, and to have mother support this, enjoy it, and participate in it. What then evolves is the simultaneous attachment of the child to the *relationship*: The baby now belongs to *them* more thoroughly than to *her*. *This necessitates the child's discovery that they are more important to each other than he is to either of them*. This shift produces an entirely new orientation, since the mother-child bond and the father-child bond are both "as if": The child makes believe — and the mother plays with the belief, and the father plays with the belief — that this twosome is an adult kind of twosome; that the little boy is, indeed, his mother's make-believe second husband, that the little girl is father's make-believe second wife, as if the two of them can parent the other adult in this triangle of growth.

More important, as the first three or four or five years go by, the child is increasingly free to become attached to the relationship in the most primitive way. His security, his safety, his nurturance come from the *team* — from time to time represented by both or either of the two adults — but essentially from the *we-ness* that is evolving as father and mother become a team. Uniquely, this process of belonging to a system means that the child is free to move away from the system, to be adventurous, to be a discoverer, a creator, free to make a pioneering move to visit the family next door, free to love his puppy, free to like his teacher. All of these experiences constitute "as-if" relationships: playful efforts to move into the social structure, to be on his own with a clear recognition that his parents are glad to have him go. At the same time, the child knows that he belongs to his parents any time he wants to come back and feel secure and safe. He knows that he can play at how to make it in the big, bad world by the play with mother and the play with father, neither of which threatens the relationship between mother and father. The agony and ecstasy of marriage are matched by the agony and ecstasy of the child's exploring the world farther and farther away from his parents, with a ready return guaranteed whenever the exploring leads to insecurity.

Behind or beneath this dynamic process is the Oedipal scene, but this time the agony and ecstasy of the psychological incest are understood to be "as-if"; there is no threat to mother and her world, or father and his world, or the world of the twosome. The private relationships of father-mother-child are thus available in a uniquely different way from the public relationships of father and his work, mother and her work, the child and his explorations, and the family and its relationship to other families in the community in which it exists. The Oedipal horror thus becomes a glory by staying in the "as-if" game for learning and for establishing the freedom for regression in the service of the individual ego and the family reunion.

III

Doing Therapy with Families

I Don't Believe in People —
I Just Believe in Families

The culture, and particularly the medical model, is predicated upon the physical body as a self-contained unit. This one system is regarded as a unit, not as a part of the hierarchy of systems that goes from subatomic particles on up to the cosmic system. The universe is an infinite stepladder of new systems with reverberations up and down the ladder, with each system having its unique properties and its unique contributions to the systems above it and below it.

Until about 1944 the human body was regarded by the medical profession as a series of discrete entities: The various organs — the heart, the blood vessels, the intestinal tract, the kidneys, the liver — all were seen as self-contained, non-interacting units. In 1944, the first medical textbook that contained the concept of "systems" was published (this was the *Cecil and Loeb Textbook of Medicine*). Vague references were made to how the endocrine system, the thyroid, pituitary, and adrenals all interacted. Now there developed a growing understanding of the cardiovascular pulmonary system, the cardiorespiratory system, the central nervous system, as an integrated unit.

In like manner, the arrival of the Freudian revolution in the early 1900s produced an intensive study of the intrapsychic world of the individual's dreams and fantasies. The whole process of living unconsciously, below the level of awareness, was still assigned solely to the individual. Gradually, the psyche as a system was integrated with the body as a system. Then there developed an understanding of the hierarchial relationship between bodies and between persons. Today we talk about the marital system, the child-parent system, the nuclear family unit, the multigenerational family unit, and even the interface between the family and the community of families.

Nevertheless, it becomes very difficult to switch our thinking from the smaller systems to the larger system. My own opportunity to do so (really, it was a coercion) was catalyzed by a fortunate academic offer to work full-time teaching and practicing *family* psychotherapy only. So for 20 years, I was cheated of the tunnel vision that involves watching the single individual and was assaulted by the multiple input from families as a whole.

It became increasingly clear to me that the family as such is an *organism*, with all that is implied by the use of such a term. I found myself intrigued by the assumption that *there is no such thing as a person*, that *a person is merely the fragment of a family*. This line of thinking led to the next deduction: that a couple is really not a family. A couple is merely two in-laws who happen to be living together in a psychosocial contract. The arrival of the first baby, which can be called a concretized orgasm, produces a completely different framework of orientation, stress relationships, and triangular combinations that weren't present before the birth. The new baby disrupts the triangles that have been established among him and her and his parents, and her and him and her parents. This led to the obvious inference that marriage is not really a combination of two persons; rather, it is the product of two families who send out a scapegoat to reproduce themselves. Then the struggle for a lifetime begins: whether they are going to reproduce *his* family or *her* family—a war which is never settled. It sometimes resolves in détente, and it sometimes resolves in bloody warfare and a zero-sum-game including divorce, remarriage, and all the other possible variants.

Individual Versus Family Therapy: *Apples and Oranges*

The effort in the therapy setting is to establish the most efficient and effective role process, the most efficient and effective pattern of operation for the psychotherapist, with the assumption that the patient or family is a constant. The patient deals out of his whole person, whatever the deviations or distortions of that whole person are. In individual therapy the design of the therapeutic relationship, the pattern of its operation, will emerge in a natural way. In family therapy the design must be pre-planned. In essence, family therapy is a political process in which the therapist is in a role similar to that of a director of an orchestra or a coach of a baseball team.

In individual therapy the power is essentially with the individual patient, who may or may not be ready, willing, or able to participate in a therapeutic alliance at an adequate level. In family therapy the power is clearly with the *system*. The family is a professional group who has lived through many years together, with many generations of established cultural patterns that are highly responsive to stress. Most of these patterns are hidden from the therapist as well as from the individual members of the family itself. The therapist must be careful in his use of what power he does have and in the effort to establish a therapeutic alliance in which he not only carries some power, but is not co-opted, overtly or covertly, by the family.

The relationship in individual therapy is person to person; the relationship in family therapy is system to system — two organisms which contain individuals. Individuals may try to speak for the system, but they are part of the system and within its power. The dynamics of therapy in the individual are in the person of the therapist. The dynamics in family therapy are not within the therapeutic system; they are within the family system itself or with the combination of family and therapist. The role continuity of the therapeutic system is its greatest, most dynamic force.

Whereas in individual therapy the beginning phase is determined by the patient, in family therapy, the onset of treatment is clearly up to the therapist. His or her capacity to structure the "blind date" — the introductory phase — is critical to any subsequent usefulness (more on this blind date later). In the mid-phase of individual therapy the power and initiative are still up to the patient; in family therapy the middle phase is one in which the therapist is free to be his complete creative personhood, both as an individual and as a system modeling for the family the qualities of individual initiative, system operation, and adequacy. The ending phase in individual therapy is a highly symbolic, powerful experience which carries a tremendous amount of weight. The ending phase in family therapy is nonsymbolic and is almost incidental.

Contaminants from the outside world (other persons, reality factors) may grossly impact individual therapy, whereas outside realities in general have fairly limited effect on the family as a system. In individual therapy the therapist's role is critical throughout the duration of psychotherapy. In family psychotherapy the therapist's role begins at a very critical level and becomes minimal very soon. The family, in essence, takes over the psychotherapy in a very early stage and will continue to direct it unless otherwise impeded. Individual psychotherapy is tender and easily damaged for some time after the termination; it can be greatly altered by the processes of living. Change in the family system is in the *infrastructure* and is therefore far less permeable; the process of change tends to go on within that infrastructure and below the level of awareness of either the family or the therapist.

In individual therapy the first interview is tentative; it may even be feeble, bilaterally paranoid, and full of shyness. The first visit in family therapy is critical, power-loaded, and probably sets the structure for the success or failure of the ongoing experience. In individual psychotherapy, the arrival of a consultant or a visitor—whether on the family side, on the patient's side or on the therapist's side—grossly contaminates the psychotherapy, many times precipitating triangular problems and/or weakening the illusion of transference. In family psychotherapy, visitors—whether the consultant to the therapist's system, or members of the extended family, or friends of the family—are always helpful to the therapeutic process. In individual therapy there is an illusion of a subculture: Everything is different in "here"; the rules are different, you can talk about anything you want to, and there will not be any retaliation. This illusion is called *transference* and is very important. Family therapy *is* an actual subculture. No one outside the family belongs to that family, but the therapeutic system and the family system become a community, a second subculture.

Individual psychotherapy essentially deals with the past-tense, at least in most types of individual psychotherapy. Family psychotherapy, in the sense that it is dealing with the infrastructure, is always dealing with the past *and* the future *and* the present. The past determines the family dynamics, the future is always in the cross-generational projections, and the present is in the relationship between the family system and the therapeutic system. The challenge for the individual therapist is how to get in and stay in—what some therapists have called "acting in" (the opposite of "acting out"), which is a process of intensifying the relationship to bring about greater effect. In family therapy the essential process is how to stay *out* and visit *in*—how to be political in regard to the two subcultures. This entails being able to join the two systems, but it also entails protecting the therapeutic system from being projected upon, entangled, and co-opted by the more powerful family system.

The Origins and Evolution
of Family Dysfunction

In talking about family therapy we consistently confuse the origins or etiology of pain and impotence, the evolution and symptoms of expression of the pain, and the effort to help the family make changes. I would like to separate these three factors and talk about them in different frameworks.

Origins

Dysfunction in the family seems to evolve from concealed and ulcerating situational experiences: marriage, the arrival of a new baby, serious illness, grandfather's death and the ensuing crisis over the will; grandmother's death and the rupture of dependency by her children; the experience of poverty or wealth; geographical isolation and dissociation among family members; the in-law feud that evolves over a series of small events. In essence, the origin of the pathology (the etiologic precipitant) can be found in the breakup of the family of origin's infrastructure—its personal mythology, the *sense* of identification, the *fact* of identification, the evolution of family patterns of behavior, misbehavior, or intrapsychic mythologies. Many times the origin of the pain and impotence in the dysfunctional family is reinforced by nonprofessional therapists—by "good advice" from a neighbor or non-blood relative or someone in the professional fields who misunderstands his or her role and acts like a dedicated amateur by giving sage advice which only violates the family's inherited cultural patterns. Or, the dysfunction might be reinforced by interaction with a drinking partner, the pseudo therapy of an affair, or the retreat to non-experience.

119

Evolution

The evolution of family pain and impotence is fostered by covert gossip—
the dyadic or even triadic input of social paranoia in which one individual
offers a rumor or a theory that is expanded by a second or third party. For
example, the husband and wife, who represent two different families of
origin, evolve a second-generational psychological divorce because they are
both only in-laws to their spouse's family of origin. They then begin to
enlist the children in a third-generation cold war—a war that has much
paranoia underneath it. Ideally, the infrastructure of the two differing
patterns of living represented by the two families of origin would have
melded into a new one with the marriage. Instead, what typically evolves is
a kind of in-law battle.

As this pain and impotence intensifies, there is the establishment of
leaders and followers. A label is attached to one of the family members,
who becomes the family's scapegoat. (Actually, the scapegoat really should
be called a "family fragment" rather than being talked about as a person.)
Usually, we label the scapegoat person as "bad," "mad," or "sad." However, it
seems clear to me that this individual begins to team with a co-partner, and
a psychological infidelity to the family emerges. These two have a psychosocial affair which protects them from the family's power, and protects
them from the ragged edges of isolationism, but is itself a pathological
entity in the family as a whole.

This family fragment, now a dyad, is apt to be combined in certain
specific ways. A "bad fragment" combines with a "mad fragment." A mad
person unites with a sad person, or a sad person (fragment) combines with a
bad person. Apparently the only psychological separation that exists between two family fragments, besides the intrapsychic defense system, is the
fact that one of them is apt to be overt and the other is apt to be covert.
(Husband and wife also tend to combine around the overt-covert differen-
tial).

There are many types of this pattern in which the co-dependency of
these two people manages to produce security and peace. It is a resolution
or, if you will, a constructive negentropic extra beyond the overt scapegoat,
who is so labeled without any awareness of the co-dependency. The most
specific of these has been recognized for some time as the alcoholic and the
enabler or co-dependent spouse. It is easy to assume (or at least to theorize)
that similar combinations take place between the depressive scapegoat and
the phobic partner, the hysterical scapegoat and the impotent spouse, the

socially acting-out partner and the asocial retreater, the crazy person teamed with the sociopath. This teaming is additionally reinforced and bonded by the dyad's failure in the scapegoat role of being the family therapist, and then come the scars that result from the failure. Additional power can be given to the team via the enlistment of a third person (someone within the family set, a non-professional, or even the professional therapist) who does not recognize that he is dealing with a *team* and instead treats it as though it were an individual.

Anti-entropy (Negentropy)

The positive component in this negative entropic process that we have been talking about is the growth that occurs in the midst of decay—similar to the growth that follows a forest fire. The family begins to make efforts to prevent the ongoing entropic destruction: Family members may decide not to isolate themselves from one another; they may begin to face the pain and the impotence with each other; they may prepare to tolerate the suffering that takes place in times of change, rather than finding a way to counteract it with alcohol, drugs, or by moving across the country to avoid the stress. They may triangulate in a foster parent—the pastor, the social worker, or Great-Aunt Minnie; they may gossip to a professional or a social therapist and move towards either the suppression of gossip within the family or the deliberate effort to be more open with each other. Or they may return the pain to the intrapsychic space where it rests, covertly producing hypertension, asthma, or other kinds of physiological or psychological pathology.

Establishing the Context
for Family Therapy

The most essential precursor for psychotherapy—the "anesthesia" for it—is the personal reverberation experienced by the therapist in response to his/her introjection of the family's pain. If the therapist cannot reverberate or empathize with this pain, he/she is not set up to do good psychotherapy. Assuming this reverberation is occurring, the therapist can utilize the following approaches (many of these points are elaborated in this and other sections of the book).

1. The therapist can demand bigger "unit decisions" than are offered. The twosome who come for therapy, or the white knight who asks for help for the scapegoats, dares not enlist the whole family. This enlistment must be done by the therapist, who pushes for a greater investment on the part of the family members than they are able or daring enough to offer.

2. The therapist must establish his "I position" of power for handling the structure of the professional interaction. He must pre-plan time and place and space. He must not accept the requested therapeutic role until he has defined his control in these key areas. This is an administrative task: clarifying the number of people involved, the place for meeting, the time for meeting, and the therapist's simple availability.

3. The therapist must produce a structure of power to handle the power in the family. (Hint: the therapist can gain great power if he can play with the inferences of those historical bits that are offered as bribes for caretaking.)

4. As the therapy begins the therapist must learn how to negate the family splinter groups.

5. The therapist should be free to add creative options to the changes the family members begin to evolve as they define their "I position," which the therapist has forced them to develop by refusing to enact their fantasied grandiose gift of power.

6. The therapist needs to make clear that he does not belong to the family. He does this best by making "meta-moves." These meta-moves include his initial reverberation with the family that produces the anesthesia, then his individuation from the family, which proves he is a separate person, followed by his rejoining to increase members' courage in moving further in their definition of family wholeness and family reconstruction.

7. The therapist should offer a model not only of joining and individuating, but also of openness. He does this by sharing bits of his own personhood, his relation to his family of origin, while being careful to preserve the privacy rights of his nuclear family.

8. The therapist needs to make special efforts to catalyze new triangulations and new subgroups within the family.

9. It is critical that the caring therapist stimulates bits of the family wholeness that emerge during the family members' time together in the therapeutic session.

10. The therapist must be very careful to respect each family's ethnic sub-community. The cultural system of each family is unique, and the therapist does not belong to either of the families represented.

11. The therapist is responsible for exposing and stimulating the approaching reality of the bilateral empty nest syndrome: Both therapist and patient (couple or family) will be lonesome without the other.

12. The therapist should offer a therapeutic "family reunion" on call.

We then separate the four languages of family therapy: the language of pain and impotence that family members employ on arrival; the language of inference that the therapist utilizes in structuring the family process in its initiation; the language of options which the therapist utilizes in the middle of therapy to help the family evolve freedom to be irrational and personal; and finally, the language of separation with its sharing of pain and its recognition that parting is such sweet sorrow. The nuances of these different languages will become clearer as we proceed.

As I look back over the years, it seems very clear that many of the ponderously difficult beginnings and the sad outcomes of working with families resulted from my failure to struggle with the *context* before I started the psychotherapy. It is very clear to me that the better the context, the better the process. I believe that *process* is critically more important than *progress*, because one never knows what the process is going to lead to, and progress can be an illusion; progress in one territory may open up a can of worms in another territory that nobody knew existed.

The family massively outranks and outpowers the individual therapist and frequently a team of therapists. Therefore, it becomes very critical to establish the setting and the pattern for the family therapy. It is best to do this before the therapy begins. Whomever makes the initial contact with the clinic or the individual family therapist is the person who is most in danger of destroying the therapy before it begins. This is accomplished by trying to manipulate the family into change in the way that he or she perceives it, which automatically sets up a rebellion in the family. The family members want to make their own decisions, and the person who calls is frequently one of the family manipulators. So if the therapist takes this telephone call, he must be careful to preserve the dignity and independence of the family as a whole, and of the other members as individuals or dyads.

Handling the Request
for a Blind Date

I rarely accept the initial request. Mama calls up and says, "My doctor says my asthma is emotional and I have to come and see you."

"Well, fine. Bring your hubby and the kids and come on in."

"I haven't told my husband about this."

"Well, sorry. I think you ought to and then call me back."

"But he doesn't believe in psychiatry."

"Well, if he doesn't believe in psychiatry, you and he ought to fight that out before you come in and see me, because I don't want to be blamed for your getting a divorce. So talk to him, and if he has any questions, have him call me."

"I'm not going to talk to him."

"Well, okay."

"So you won't see me?"

"No."

"Why not?"

"Well, I don't believe in people—I just believe in families."

They usually call back and say, "Hey, you know what? He's coming! He didn't mind a bit."

If you can tolerate a longer version, let me give you a realistic composite example. Mother calls and tells me she is having a problem with her toddler. I say, "Well, how about bringing the baby's father?"

The imaginary patient responds, "Oh no, that son-of-a-bitch, I haven't talked to him in months. He beat me for years, and I will have nothing to do with him!"

"Well," I answer, "I don't know what we're going to do. I'm just unwilling to be your child's new father."

"Well, I just want a *psychotherapist*."

"Yes, I know, but I was telling you how I think about it."

"Well, I don't care how you think about it. I just want some help."

"Well, I'm sorry."

She persists, "Well, what am I going to do?"

And so do I, "I don't know."

"Well, you're supposed to help me!"

"No," I respond, "you just *think* I'm supposed to help you. I would like to help you, but I won't help you the way you would like me to help, which is to be the baby's father."

"I don't want you to be the baby's father!"

"I don't believe you."

"I'm not lying to you."

"I didn't say you were lying to me. I just said I didn't believe you."

Now she is angry: "You have no right to say that!"

"I just said it."

"Well, you're wrong."

I continue, "That's all right. I don't mind being wrong. I'll just tell you my belief because that's what you're calling for, and that's what I'm here for: to tell you what I believe."

"Well, I don't want to hear it."

"Then hang up."

"But I want some help."

"OK, get that man."

She protests, "I don't even know where he is."

"Well, where are his mother and father?"

"I don't like them either."

"Well, I'm not here to be your child's grandmother."

"Hey man, you're crazy!"

"I know, I've been told that before."

"But what should I *do*?"

"Well, I don't know, what do you want to do?"

"I want to see you!"

"Sorry, you're going to have to work out some new plan."

"If I get my ex-husband's mother and father, would you see me then?"

"How about *your* mother and father as well?"

"My mother and father? I haven't spoken to my mother in years!"

"Neither have I."

"I don't know, I don't understand you."

"I don't understand me either. Let's see if we can get a therapist to help one another."

She continues, "I should get my mother and father to come and talk with you about me and my son?"

"Sure."

"Every time we come?"

"I don't know, we haven't gotten there the first time yet."

"Well, I'll talk to them. My mother has been wanting me to talk for years, and I usually send her a Christmas card."

"Does she send you one?"

"Oh, she always sends me a present, but I think it's a fake."

"Do you send it back to her?"

"No."

"Why not? If they're fake presents, she should keep them."

"I never thought about that. Well, now, I don't know how to do this."

"Why don't you call your ex-husband. He's not an ex-father you know, he's just an ex-husband. You can't be an ex-father, it doesn't work. If you can call this ex-husband and tell him that you talked to me and I said I wouldn't see you without him. . . . "

She interrupts, "What if he's re-married?"

"Well, might as well get his wife, too."

"I don't want to meet her!"

"That's your problem. I would like to meet her, and I think if I'm going to help you, I have to make the rules for how I do it."

"Your rules are crazy. What'll I do next?"

"Well, you can have any of those people call me. I'd be glad to talk to them."

"You mean, you'll talk to my mother?"

"Sure, I'm in favor of mothers. I think they're important. I had one of my own."

"Well, OK, I guess. Thanks."

The first requirement in establishing a healthy context for family therapy is to take charge of the initial referral, the initial telephone call. The response to that phone call should be: "Why me? How did you happen to call me? Who told you to call me? What was your objective in calling me?" This kind of questioning establishes an *interpersonal set* and interrupts the caller's automatic tendency to plead his or her cause while you listen patiently. You are establishing your strength, which is what the caller needs and what you need in order to create a healthy context for ongoing therapy. People call for therapy out of their pain, their impotence, and their hope that you will resolve the pain and make them potent in their living. So your strength is necessary, and *you must be clear that their pain is something you postpone participating in until after you have established a healthy context.*

I try to think of this initial telephone call as analogous to a boy calling a strange girl for a blind date. Male therapists make this initial phone call very difficult; they simply do not understand the complexities that girls have been taught to protect themselves from the casual telephone offer for a date. Girls—and, I assume, female therapists—are much wiser in this way. They know that the important thing is to preserve the initial power, because at a subsequent moment the power may be more equally balanced. This dynamic is also very true for the therapist. He should protect himself in every way possible during this telephone call, not at the time the caller wants it, nor in the way the caller wants it, but in the way *he* wants it. The typical girl or woman being called for a date would make it clear that she was not available "off the cuff," that the couple's first meeting might be over coffee at the office with her girlfriend, or that it might be nice if they met with the man or woman who suggested the call. This daytime meeting would be a way of checking out the situation and trying to judge ahead of time how much of the natural paranoia is valid and how much potential danger is hidden by a careful con job.

In adapting this transaction to the family therapy situation, it is very important that the therapist establish his or her power. As I have said, family members are calling because they are impotent and/or in pain; they have decided that the situation is so desperate and their efforts have so failed that they want to (must) get help from a stranger. This is a massive decision. It is best to check out the basis for the call. The therapist can gain a great deal in this process by using the language of inference, by inferring whether the person who called was sent by the family, how many of the family have known about it and anticipated and okayed the call, how many do not know about it, and how the caller was expecting to handle his or her own paranoia. The therapist should assume that these people have had previous therapy and ask for details of when, how it worked, and why it wasn't appropriate for them to go back to the same therapist again. In addition, be careful to disabuse them of any magical expectations that they have picked up before the call. It may even be useful to request letters of intent, one from each family member, specifying what they want the family to get out of this experience and what they themselves hope to get.

The initial problem ordinarily involves an individual; the problem needs to be utilized as a lever for moving to a broader context regarding the chief complaint. If the chief complaint is an interpersonal one—"My husband wants a divorce," "One of my children is in trouble"—broadening the context is an obvious response. The person's language of pain automatically should move you into a language of inference.

"Have you talked to your husband about calling me? Have you talked to your children about calling me?"

You can even move to the next step of making sure that the husband is the father of the children, or that this is the first marriage, or that the living set is what you expect it to be (actually, it may be very different). Once you raise the initial level of inference by making the problem an interpersonal one, you are ready to move to a further extension of the context.

"Have you talked to your father and mother about this problem, or one of your brothers and sisters?"

This sets the pattern for having an initial conference with the extended family.

"Has your husband talked to his parents about the possibility of divorce? Is your husband having an affair? Are you having an affair? Is this your first marriage?"

This initial negotiation is most effective if it moves through the whole process of establishing the context before any plan for a second meeting or even a second telephone call is discussed. Included in the context of the initial chief complaint and your response to it is the question of who participated in the decision to make the phone call.

"If you talked to your husband, did he think it was a good idea to call me? Do you usually negotiate family problems without talking to him? And will he be agreeable, or does he feel left out?"

This kind of simple context planning establishes your relationship with the entire family and prevents you from appearing to be a co-conspirator operating in cahoots with the caller, behind the back of the family. All families are involved in small group struggles, and the temptation to utilize the therapist as a co-conspirator in the covert struggle is strong. Once you have established the idea that the other people are also part of this phone call, you can extend the context indefinitely.

"What do your husband's parents think about the problem of divorce? Whom has he talked to about it? How did he help you get to the decision to call me? How would he respond to my idea that every therapy ought to begin with a family conference that includes everyone who really cares, and maybe some of the people who don't care or whose care is expressed in hostility?"

Taking Charge of The First Interview

The second step in this process is the interview itself. The blind date interview is really a bilateral check-out process in which both members are paranoid and have fantasies and assumptions that should be cleared. The therapist should take the lead in this first interview and begin it with the social outsider—usually the father, the father's father, the previous spouse, or a stepchild or adopted child. The purpose of the therapist's leading during the first interview is to prove to the family that there is strength available. If one does not take this initial power move, the therapy frequently breaks down into a bilateral struggle over who is in charge of what happens. Then the family members prove that *you* are impotent, just as they have proven before they arrived that *they* are impotent in bringing about change in their morale and power as a whole. And the family's power as a whole is the basic understructure toward which the therapy should be heading. The family should be able to reorganize *itself*. Someone else's tricking the family into change does not relieve the impotence, even if it relieves the pain.

Grandfather should be asked first about how it was with grandmother and her parents, how it was with grandmother and her son, with grandmother and her daughter. Then, in a very methodical way, you can go on to ask father how it was between his siblings and their mother, how it was between his siblings and their father, how it was between the siblings of the father and the siblings of the mother, and then, finally, how it was with his wife and each of the children. Next, ask the wife how it is between her husband and each of the children. The children can be asked how it is between other siblings, and how it is between other siblings and their father and their mother. This kind of dyadic diagnosis prevents rationalization, excuse-making, whining, projection, and all of the many things that make history-taking so impossible.

In the extended family, one should be careful to include those people who are *negatively related*: the father who hasn't spoken to his daughter (the caller) in 10 years, or the uncle who double-crossed her father and toward whom she is bitter still; and, of course, previous spouses, the girlfriend her husband is having an affair with, or the boyfriend with whom she is having an affair. Bringing in extended family members on this initial contact does not make them paranoid. It merely makes *you* strong and makes them more aware of how involved the problem is. If you bring up all these additional relationships later, *then* it makes them paranoid!

On many occasions it is very important to involve the friendship network. People tend to have confidantes—amateur therapists whom they've been talking to, confiding in, crying with—and it is very useful to include these folks as well. This friendship network also includes the in-laws, those people who are apt to be on the other side of the family subgroup cold war. His mother, who frequently is the enemy, needs to be brought in so that the husband has a better chance of establishing a healthy context for the nuclear family by virtue of his mother's at least agreeing to sit with the wife she has been angry at and the grandchildren she has been forbidden to visit. In addition, the friendship network may include the pastor, her best girlfriend, and maybe even his business partner. The context of the work scene is also part of the friendship network—his work scene, her work scene, the children's work scene (whether it is babysitting, school, or day care).

This kind of an approach is important and must be learned. Fundamentally, that learning must come from *listening to oneself*. Nothing is unimportant. Nothing that emerges is merely real. All experiences of the self are symbolic and therefore significant. This is a conceptual exercise for its own sake, and is a way of augmenting one's wholeness and one's capacity for further expansion. Essentially, it means that *there is no truth. There are only approaches to the truth*. It is the *process* of therapy that is important, not the *progress*. All concerns with progress are ways of double thinking and inevitably produce a role-like effort to manipulate. It is also true in daily living that it is the process that is important, not the progress. The effort to evaluate oneself, to critique one's changing, to critique one's evaluation, is a syllogistic mistake because it is not possible to stand outside oneself.

The experience we are aiming for is one of being repeatedly surprised at oneself. Secondarily, we are aiming to *avoid* the listening mode of educational hypnosis—that altered state of consciousness in which we accumulate data with the hope that someday we can use it in another manipulation similar to the one that induced this knowledge. *The effort, therefore, is to activate interpersonal evolution, and secondly, to actively protest and offer alternatives to all experience.* Finally, we are aiming to find the courage to look for feedback from other persons, to seek *their* perceptions, and then to assume a hysterical dissociation between their percepts and one's own, so that together they may make a binocular vision of an assumed reality.

Adding the Right Brain
to Family Psychotherapy

In her delightful and very important book, *Drawing on the Right Side of the Brain*, Betty Edwards postulates that one of the problems in our growth is that, in order to catalog the massive amount of information we are fed, we develop a kind of shorthand memory, most conspicuously apparent in the way we draw faces. We follow a model that developed when we were eight or ten years of age, and never change it. Is this model also true for social interaction? We develop a model of verbal shorthand—"Hello," "Goodbye," and "How are you today?" and learn to connote large components of information via very simple social stereotypes.

Sadly, this trend creates a tremendous handicap in the field of psychotherapy. It is all but impossible to develop the kind of changes in social rules and communication rules that help a patient expand his socially constricted and pathologically protected interpersonal system. Family therapy is even more tenacious in this regard because families develop a kind of socialization shorthand to inculcate patterns and an infrastructure of symbolic internal fantasies, most of which are generations old and well below the level of awareness.

The psychotherapist needs to teach the family how to free associate, how to be creative, how to move away from social stereotypes. The psychotherapist can best accomplish this by himself modeling these modes. One of the simplest ways of doing this is to adapt the rule of thumb developed long ago by the psychoanalysts: The therapist also may share all the unimportant bits and fragments which float through his head during the interview. Interestingly, the danger inherent in the therapist's exposing himself to the family is much less than the danger in exposing himself to an individual patient.

In the initial contact with family members, you must vibrate with a personal caring for their pain and a personal identification with their arduous efforts to self-correct. They are not coming to you out of curiosity. During the first interview you need to develop an intimacy and the right to be part of a new therapeutic family. Then, many new options become available.

One of these options is sharing some fragments of yourself that may embolden family members to share fragments of their inner worlds. These include fragments of your fantasy life as it occurs in the here-and-now, as well as fragments of your free association world as it erupts during the interview.

This sharing can be dangerous, of course, so you do need to have some kind of clinical protection. But, in general, I believe that creative bits are never irrelevant, and unless there is some clinical reason for not sharing them, the therapist owes himself and the family this example of momentary intimacy, momentary self-exposure. *The creative world of the right brain can thereby be added to the rational, professional components of any good psychotherapy.*

Uniquely enough, the therapist promoting creativity by modeling it becomes a richer presence, if the relationship is well-established. When my wife, as co-therapist, once complained about stiffness in her neck, for three-quarters of an hour the family members proceeded to talk only about their body experiences, as though this were a new rule. In the same imitative manner, my office is a playroom. If I start to play, the family will become interested in my puzzles or in my game playing and this lessens the family stress, as family members become less anxious about being anxious, and begin to see their struggles as more clinical, or even as creative.

You need to deal with the fact of the family unconscious. The best way to do that is to be as blatantly direct as you can, and the time to start is before the first interview. Unfortunately, we are hindered by our training in this regard. We are trained to believe that empathy is the only thing that is really important, that caring makes the difference. In my view, the predominant directive of our training is: "Offer anybody who comes into the office your right breast, and if they bite that one, you put it back in and you give them the other one."

With families *you need to speak directly from your own unconscious.*

For instance, I say to a man halfway through the first interview, "You know, you look like a cold fish to me."

He replies, indignantly, "What do you mean, I look like a cold fish?"

"Well, I don't know, that's just what came to my mind."

"Well, that's a hell of a thing to say."

I continue, "It's worse than that. It may be that it has nothing to do with you. It may be that you look like a patient I saw last year, or that you remind me of my uncle, but if the pathology is in me, you need to be careful because you musn't trust me. If the pathology is in you, then we have more problems, but I just wanted you to know the data."

I tell the man the data with all humility and with no sense that I know an answer, merely that I'm offering him the problem.

Changing the Family Means Pain

The more you lay it on the table, the better.

The mother called up and said, "You know, that first interview was very difficult. My son Joe came home and cried half the afternoon, and little Mary couldn't sleep because she had bad dreams. So I'm not going to bring them in."

I said, "Well, maybe that's a good thing and maybe we ought to give the whole thing up."

"Oh no," she said, "the rest of us still want to come."

I said, "I'm sorry, but I can't work that way."

"You mean, you're going to make those little children be exposed to all that?"

"Not only that, but it's going to get worse. If you think you can change this family without pain, you shouldn't have come in the first place. It's just like taking out the appendix. There's no way to do it without cutting a hole in the belly. And if you aren't willing to take the pain and hurt from this and lay awake and walk the floor, then don't bother. Go on the way you have. Maybe you'll make it all right. Things change. I don't think I have the secret of life. And I get tougher and meaner. I'm going to be tougher the more you guys come in."

One of my assumptions is that there is no altruism. I explain to the family. "I'm not interested in you guys. I really don't care much about you. I'm hoping that in seeing you I'll get some more for myself. I'm all for growing, and I figure if I can get something from you guys, then it will be worth seeing you. So don't get the idea that I'm goodhearted and altruistic, because it isn't true."

I want to get rid of the myths they have about me, that I'm going to be the loving mother that their mother wasn't, or that I'm the magician that cures diabetes in one shot.

When the Problem Seems Too Big: Turn Your Back

A great many families coming for psychotherapy are so powerful that the therapist cannot win the battle for structure. The family is unable to envision the therapist as the expert, as the powerhouse they need. They cannot accept him. This poses a dilemma for the therapist. Many therapists feel the only answer to this problem is to palliate the situation, to assert friendly hopes, or offer the same kind of advice the next-door neighbor would offer. Public relations-wise, this is very smart; malpractice-wise, it may be quite safe; but psychotherapeutically, it is frequently a failure.

There is one countermove which is "surgical" in essence, and takes a certain amount of adroitness on the part of the therapist, just as does the four-minute appendix operation on the part of the surgeon. This is the tactic whereby the therapist takes control of the family members and their needs *by turning his back on them*. It is like turning your back on a good-looking girl who is lonely, or not kissing a girl on a first date even though you want to. It makes the next move *their* responsibility. It is very similar to the approach René Spitz recommends with affect-hungry infants: You must be very careful and back up to them and give them your hand, then take it away, then give it to them again. Taking control by sharing your sense of futility and confessing your impotence may be the most powerful way of working. It is frightening for the family to have the professional from whom they are seeking help say he doesn't think there is much hope. On the other hand, if the family members choose to stay in therapy, they realize that they're going to have to put all the effort they can into the situation to make anything happen. You are being realistic and honest. It is similar to the situation in which a husband and wife who have been drinking for ten years come to a psychotherapist saying, "We'd like to get over our alcoholism." Any therapist who takes that statement at face value is doomed!

The Family and the "Critical Mass"

Mother had been seen previously with divorced father, his new wife, and their child over the problem of her 14-year-old's failing grades and indifference to school. This was the father's third marriage; he was supporting a previous wife, this current mother and her four children, and now his third wife. The mother's passivity and querulous rationalizations had helped her to escape therapy after two or three interviews last time, a year earlier. This time she came in because the twins had gotten in trouble with the law. One of them had broken into a house and stolen $40 worth of liquor, and the other had participated with some friends in repeatedly throwing several bicycles off the top of a low building. Both boys had been caught by the police.

Mother's attitude was one of passive curiosity and comfortable nonchalance. The only real affect she demonstrated in the first 20 minutes of the interview was in regard to why the other son, who was being accused of being the lookout, had not escaped before the police came. The boys smilingly told the bare facts of what had happened and everybody sat around playing dead, including the older sister who was married and was smiling sweetly throughout the whole session, as were mother and the two sons. Of course, father and the delinquent of last year did not show. After 20 minutes we suggested that everything looked like it was in fine shape and nobody really needed any help, so why didn't they leave? And they did, with no particular trouble.

In essence, we told the family that it was all right for them to continue fighting with the law, that it was all right if the boys got into a delinquent institution (that might give the mother a chance to find a new husband), and that it was all right for them to throw the bicycles off the roof—it might even have been better if mother were standing under and they landed on her head! We were helping them face some more of life by declaring ourselves impotent and suggesting in an offhanded way that, if they really wanted to do something about it, they might come back again, but that we weren't willing to make an appointment now because it didn't look like they had much need for us.

One factor that probably contributed significantly to the deadness of the session was the fact that the "critical mass" was not present for any real "heat" to start generating. One way in which therapists often delude themselves with their ideas of grandiosity is in believing that they can supply the heat and the affect that missing members in the family must provide themselves. Therefore, in letting the family go we also freed its members to rearrange themselves and gave them the opportunity to bring back the necessary critical mass to make something happen in the session.

The David and Goliath Syndrome

One Sunday forenoon I was working in my front yard when a car suddenly stopped and backed up. Out jumped a 16-year-old boy who said hello in a funny kind of little-boy voice, and then was surprised that I recognized him as the 10-year-old whom I had seen with his family five years earlier. He was my first in a long series of battles over a child's delusion of grandeur. In this case, the 10-year-old was the sophisticated son of a faculty member. He exposed a psychodynamic diagnosis of each family member during the first interview, but bitterly insisted that no one was to make a diagnosis of him. After six or eight interviews I gradually proved that I did not look up to him, as the rest of the family did, just because of his brains. He then physically assaulted me in the middle of the interview, and we fought for half an hour. Each time he felt I was winning, he would back away; I'd let him go, and then he'd come punching back at me, until he finally became convinced he couldn't defeat me physically.

The next week he returned with the story that he had fought his father during the week and, to his amazement, it turned out that he couldn't beat his father either. He had never known before that he couldn't beat his father.

Now this 16-year-old had become warm and very loving. We gossiped about his four-year-old romance that had broken up recently. His new romance and his new girl had made him cut his hair from 18 inches to approximately 10! As we parted, ten minutes later, we shook hands. He hung onto my hand very tightly, as though the remnant of our relationship was very much alive. It was very alive for me, also. He talked about wanting to come back someday and talk more, and I invited him to visit in the office; but, of course he won't. I'll be re-repressed where I belong. He has real parents. The pilot plant needs to be dismantled.

Family Therapy
in an Institutional Setting

Many people who work in institutions assume that family therapy is unavailable to them unless it is sponsored and authenticated and provided a sense of administration by the head of the institution or the direct supervisors. This is not necessarily true. For example, if you're working at an institution, a clinic, a hospital, or a halfway house, you can use the initial anxiety of the person you see to help him or her turn that anxiety into "group accumulation" rather than symptom relief.

Mother comes in saying her son is delinquent, or on drugs, or is looking very withdrawn. Instead of trying to talk with her about her problem, you talk with her about your need to have her accumulate a group. His father should be there if he loves his son. You're unwilling to try to make a substitute effort at being the father because you feel that not only will alienate the father but will also be artificial, and the son will know better. So she'll get the father, and *his* mother and father, and *her* mother and father, and the other siblings, and you can go on.

As you move through the list of possible people, she may hit upon somebody who won't come but who would be an important person, or somebody who would be glad to come but whom she has never asked. Then you direct the anxiety of her symptom into a creative effort to make her more involved in establishing a therapeutic alliance. Be careful not to be diverted from your effort to bring in everybody possible by her panic or by her effort to solve it by telling you the father has not been seen in 10 years.

"But you could find him through his mother and have him call me. I'll help explain to him how important he is to his son's recovery."

You redirect her anxiety with your own feeling of impotence. You infer from her presentation all the other possible symptoms which she will not mention. You don't have to play detective; you just have to push for the size group that can make a change in the setting that she is worried about.

If you need to deal with a supervisor, one of the simplest ways to circumvent resistance to your plan is to get him to help you with an experiment and supervise your first effort at family therapy, or your first effort at changing the administrative structure.

Assuming that you are successful at arranging a meeting of your family group, your first focus is to get a thorough history of where the family members have been before they came to you. Do not try to help them until you know their background, because they will be in charge of the psychotherapy if you aren't careful. They have more power than you have. You're an imitation—you're in a role, and they're not. They are playing for real. This history-taking should be three-generational and should include the history of all the family stresses (divorce, serious illness, unemployment, deaths), as well as all their efforts to change (change by moving, by changing jobs, by remarriage, by amateur psychotherapy or professional psychotherapy, pastor, neighbor, etc.).

One of your most important efforts in this history-taking is to detumesce the scapegoat. Family members will deny that there is any scarlet letter, that there is any accusation surrounding the patient. You must be careful not to let them talk about him. You want to get acquainted with the *family*—not their lead player, not their front, their face-saving imitation of stress. Most of all, you need to search for an assumed covert stress. Out of your own fantasy, and bearing no relationship to any fact they have presented to you thus far, you can ask questions about death, rage, suicide, murder, incest, issues of triangulation, the in-laws, the previous spouses, and so forth. You also need to ask about their experiences with other helpers in order to protect yourself from falling prey to an iatrogenic fear that a helper will make them worse. You should check for sibling rivalry in their father's family and in the mother's family; sibling rivalry between the children; the phobia of craziness, always present in one or more members of any family; the question of battle fatigue in mother; the question of the children being replicas of someone in the previous generation (the first son looks like mother's brother or father's sister). You should face with them your doubts about why they are really in therapy, in hopes that they may be able to openly participate. Then there are the questions of whether there were other pregnancies that didn't turn out well, abortions, miscarriages, serious accidents in the family.

As you move further along during this initial history-taking, you need to get a sense of the whole. Is this family aware of themselves as *the Smiths*? Are they the real Smiths? Do they have a sense of the generation separation? Is it clear to the parents that they do not belong to the children's generation, and clear to the children that they do not belong to the parents' generation? Can you define a rotating scapegoat? Are there other people in the family whom the members can feel free to try and scapegoat? Is there a fear of physical illness? Is there a fear of Alzheimer's disease? Is there any covert alcoholism? These are the kinds of questions you need to ask with the clear anticipation that the family will conceal the answers unless you ask very carefully. Is there a question of psychological abuse? Does mother think father is too harsh? Does father think mother is too soft?

This kind of history-taking is very acceptable to any institutional setting. In fact, it is the kind of thing they like! Once you have established a respectful effort to have the family members tell their story, you need to clearly communicate to them your respect for their unique family style.

You do not expect them to be like any other family, and you hope to help them become more like the family they are, and freer to respect themselves. You will be endeavoring to be a foster parent, a temporary grandparent, a temporary uncle, or a temporary rehabilitation trainer. Your plans are to try to help them become a more powerful group and to work out a way of resolving their anxiety about the patient and their anxiety about their family's unique competence.

You need to be clear with them where you stand in relation to the institution: that you have certain rules, that the institution is in charge of you and what you do in terms of your time, in terms of your patterns of operation, but that you'll let them know so the two of you can make a team in responding to the hospital's demand. You also need to give them some sense of your respect for the family's ongoing qualities: for the timeless fact of three and more generations in the past, and the generations to come, and the history of their health as well as their fear about this particular period of illness. It is sometimes fun to tease the three-year-old daughter or the seven-year-old daughter about how many children she is going to have, whether she is going to have boys or girls, what kind of a husband she would like to find. As you talk in this manner, you help family members feel free to talk about the future in a new way.

Battle Plan for a
Three-Generational Family Reunion

Much of the progress in psychotherapy has been serendipitous. Professionals do not tend to be innovative until pushed by the caring and creativity of their patients. Thus evolved my moving into couples work because of my insecurity in treating individuals, and thus evolved my moving into work with families as a way of breaking out of the impasses with couples. The latest move has been into discovering what one person can do to bring about the reunion of an entire family.

It was accidental in 1975 that I was invited to be the catalyst for a reunion of a family with 31 members, all of whom had split apart into two opposing factions. Most of the family lived in a fairly small town in the midwest. For 15 years, the third generation of one-half of the family had not been allowed to talk to the third generation of the other half of the family—across this town of 50,000 people. One day, a middle generation psychotherapist and a middle generation physician got fed up with the feud, called me, and I met with these 31 people all day long for five days. All I had to do was ask, "How can I help?" and one of the family members said to another, "Where were you last Christmas? You didn't come to my house!" Somebody else spoke up, "Why didn't you speak to my father?" Within 30 seconds, the place was pandemonium.

A year or two later I began to construct such an extended family system. I had no office, I was not really interested in taking on families for a series of weekly conferences, and the nuclear family had become more boring to me. So when confronted by a family's symptoms, I now began to organize family reunions that included the third generation, the uncles and aunts, the previous spouses, the new boyfriend or girlfriend, the boss, even the neighbor.

As the time of my retirement began, it became more and more obvious to me that this approach could be an exciting way of meeting with an extended family group. I structured the time into three-day sessions consisting of four hours of therapy a day, with the requirement that all participants live together during these three days. One of the most fascinating things I discovered was the fact that the three-day, nondirective family reunion conference seemed to be self-terminating. It seemed as though once the interpersonal stresses began to change, the family members themselves took over. The family change process then continued by long-distance telephone, by subgroup conferences, and so forth. The feedback we got from the family reunions encompassed some of the pain that had developed during and after the reunion, but in most cases the long-term results were positive: The family, once it had taken over the power, moved naturally toward self-correction and a healthier pattern of interaction.

In an extended family, you can change any *one* element or factor and it will catalyze a change throughout the system. All you have to do is sit there. You are the person who is moderating this chaos and, inch by inch, the chaos begins to resolve itself, begins to get somewhere that it wasn't before you were part of it. You are the outsider, you are the catalyst that doesn't really take part, but somehow your presence precipitates the system into changing its dynamics.

The parents, the children and the two sets of grandparents constitute the three-generational unit. They produce an amalgam of two lifestyles: One set of grandparents and their loyal son or daughter and the other set of grandparents and their indoctrinated son or daughter—all are present in the same room for eight to twelve hours. The intervening periods produce a forced socializing. Because they live in the same spa, so to speak, a special kind of interaction is produced. It is as though the therapy implodes the extended family, adding the symptoms of the husband and his parents to the symptoms of the wife and her parents.

These two augmented lifestyles are in quite direct contact during the hours of infiltration by the therapeutic team. The team opens bits and pieces of family stress and individual family lifestyle as expressed through the two parents and through the children. Every extended family is well-schooled in defending its own lifestyle and in living out its own pattern of homeostasis, but the addition and the interlocking of the two lifestyles produces a new stress. The fact that this all happens in a precipitous fashion over a period of two or three days augments the freedom to reverberate from it over a period of weeks, and also facilitates a tolerance during the intense experience itself.

In the same sense that society is the parent of each family, the extended family is the parent of the couple, just as the couple are the parents of the children. The family reunion is a very graphic and powerful setting in which to live for even three days. It is even difficult for the therapeutic team to talk about generation gaps and role reversals in which the therapist becomes the patient and the patient becomes the therapist — even though we all know about episodes where the patient has taken on a new boyfriend to protect the therapist from his sexual feelings, which we do not recognize as transference but instead call "pathological peer relationships."

One of the characteristics of family therapy is that the greater the number of people, the less need there is for a professional therapist. As I have said, our role as therapists in the three-generational family reunion is to catalyze the interaction within the unit of treatment and to provide a time and place for coming together; it's not even necessary for us to moderate. The anesthesia is our caringness and our reverberation to the family's pain, both stated and unstated, observed and assumed. Because of the anxiety and the pre-planning that have gone into the meeting in each person's head, as well as between the members of the group, the meeting is already loaded with secret agendas. The anxiety already present in each person and among the family members makes the issue only one of who is going to have enough courage to get started. The therapist can feel free to structure the situation by giving some idea of what systems theory is about and by destructuring everyone's fantasies about what the therapist will contribute.

Once the family reunion has begun to move, usually with the senior people speaking their feelings about the family situation, the battle is on, and ordinarily the therapist need only sit still and watch. Many times there is so much stress that he will not be able to add any perspective — the situation is too hot for him to belong to it. The use of the traditional multiple impact approach is probably not worthwhile, since the family reunion has its own dynamics; and probably the meeting will be difficult to put together more than once because of time, and space, and schedules. It is possible, however, to use one, two, or three days of full-time interaction and accomplish remarkable releases of affect, discovery of new realities, detriangulation of some of the family structurings, remobilization of groups that were previously intimate, as well as detumescencing some of the wars that have been going on in the family overtly or covertly for several generations.

The cost to the family is stress, blood-letting, and the surfacing of residual ghosts. The most significant of these may be the ghosts. Hopefully, if the reunion is useful, the ghosts will return to help in the curative process as well as the anesthesia. The cost in money varies, depending upon the situation, but is contracted before the beginning of the reunion. A more difficult "cost" is our demand for several days of no coalitions, no scheming, and no social psychotherapy within the family unit. Each individual must maintain his or her own internal dialogue and not share it with anyone else.

The role of the two therapists can best be stated in a metaphor.

"Dr. Whitaker is the choreographer, Mrs. Whitaker the librettist, and you, the family members, are the cast of dancers for this particular ballet. No psychotherapy is offered without the presence of all family members available or attainable. Dr. Whitaker's background includes 49 years of practicing child psychiatry, adult psychiatry, and psychiatry with psychotics; 30 years of teaching trainees in psychiatry; and 20 years of family psychotherapy only. Mrs. Whitaker's background is 49 years of raising her husband and six other children, with that profound participation in the family dance which included live-in members of the two previous generations. Simultaneously they are a team, and their 49 years of teaming makes a completely different unit of action than either of them as individuals."

I assume the stress within a family is the result of profound biological, serious psychological, significant sociological, and important situational experiences. The time we spend together as a suprafamily should leave the family members free to think, to listen, to talk and to take notes. I assume that all family living includes a dialectical oscillation between *teaming* and *individuating*, with no freedom to solve the stress by moving into massive individuation (which only leads to isolation) or massive teaming (which only leads to enslavement, stultification, and psychological death).

The process of our work hours is a pilot project, a micro-system of family living in this suprafamily that now includes Mrs. Whitaker and myself as a team of strangers. Our team's initial effort will be to construct an abstract portrait of the family in the style of a mobile. Our second intent will be to operate as a reflective, multidirectional "mirror house." We assume all family members are addicts of their biological family and live in a state of hypnotic residuals from the past. Metaphorically, the family is like our federal government and the individuals are like the individual states.

We begin with a history, a portrait of the family over time, making a serious effort to avoid any questions of *why*, and being careful to prevent any individual from talking about himself. The oldest members of the family should begin.

We ask of the first generation:

- Will you describe in very brief form your in-laws as they were during your child-bearing years?
- Will you describe your parents as they were when you were 10?
- Will you describe your parental teaming during the first 10 years of child-raising?
- Will you describe your children, not as individuals, but as they related to each other, from the age of five to fifteen?
- Will you describe your spouse's progress towards death—either physical death or the death of the marriage?

Then, turning to the second generation:

- Will you describe the relationship between each of the other siblings in your family—i.e., your brother and your sister, your brother and your other brother, your sister and your other sister, and so forth?
- Will you describe the relationship between your mother and her in-laws? Between your father and his in-laws?
- Will you describe the relationship between your father and mother and the change you saw in them throughout the years of your growing up?

Finally, members of the third generation are addressed:

- Each person shall describe the relationship between any two of your siblings, your parents, and the change that took place over time in that relationship.
- Describe the relationship between your father and his in-laws and your mother and her in-laws.

Even those with very limited experience in treating nuclear families (defined as a two-generation unit) will recognize that the family reunion is not a variant of group therapy. This is psychotherapy of a different organism. It is composed of a series of individuals and a series of subgroups which are subjugated to the family as a whole. That whole does not include just two generations. It includes all the biologically related members and subgroups, their dynamics as subgroups, and the introjected historical family style, which can be traced back for generations.

The objective of such a conference seems to be the resolution of rifts in the family subgroups and, almost as important, the discovery of who the other family members are—their lifestyles and their standard codes of operating—as well as the integrative experience of uniting oneself. Some may ask the question of whether this reunion effort is simply one of reorganizing the old-time families. I have no intention of trying to recreate that world. My intention is one of establishing channels of communication that are sustaining and supportive. Just the fact that one can call on the members of one's blood connections for help, feedback or chitchat makes a great deal of difference to a person who is isolated in a socially manipulating, cold-feeling, urban community.

It is a strange fact that many of the family therapy experiences I've had these 25 years have come out of the failure of individual therapy. But very few of the people who were in family therapy have gone on to individual therapy! It is also interesting and mysterious to me that the family reunions do not seem to lead into family therapy or individual therapy. It is as though they are an entity unto themselves and serve the therapeutic need of the people involved, rather than acting as a preliminary to something more intrapsychic or more stimulating for the nuclear family.

The concept of reempowering the family members to be their own therapists is a massive structural "re-think" for me. Only within the last few years has it become clear to me that *the objective of family therapy is to put the family back in charge of its own change process rather than to make change happen*. The family as an organism is perfectly capable of reconstructing itself, in the same sense that it was capable of developing the chaos that it brings to the therapist. The power needs of the therapist occur in the beginning of therapy; once he has taken the power away from the family, he can force it to take it back. The family members will then do what needs to be done with that power to reorganize the symptoms and the stress with which they arrived.

This is really another way of talking about the old, old concept of transference neurosis as a way of getting rid of the crippling neurosis that individual therapy was endeavoring to cure.

Out of the Ashes
of the World's Greatest Lie

More recently I have used the family reunion format to do something about the world's greatest lie: "I didn't marry your blankity-blank family." As I have said many times, I believe that marriage is *not* a process that takes place between two individuals, but a contract that takes place between the *two families*. Whether the families are explicitly involved, explicitly aware, or explicitly permitting of this union makes little difference. I recently suggested to a groom-to-be that he bring together his family and the family of his wife-to-be for a conference *before* the marriage, so that the two families would get to know each other *before* they developed the standard hostility about the woman or man who stole their son or daughter. Thus, they could sidestep the typical inauguration of 30 years of indignant aversion to each other.

To everybody's surprise, the family gathered on the day before the wedding ceremony, 18 strong, for a two-hour videotaped conference. The outcome was surprisingly satisfactory to everybody, including myself. I tried to "goose the system" by suggesting that I was interested in the bride and groom getting to know something more about each other by having a deliberate conference with the families in which they could get some picture of how the spouse had been trained and the kind of family he/she had learned to live in. I warned the young couple that marriage very quickly became a bilateral pseudo-therapy competition: each of them patient and each of them therapist to the other. Marriage is also a struggle over who sets up this new family in the model of his or her family of origin. This is the old family loyalty struggle.

The two-hour exchange netted family philosophies, family lifestyle stories, a few family myths, and some discussion about why one family was oriented towards keeping peace and the other family was oriented towards fighting it out. The atmosphere was congenial and loose in spite of the fact that the two parents of one spouse-to-be had not met since they said good-bye in divorce court some years earlier. Subsequent to the conference, the two sets of parents read as one voice a statement designed by the couple in which they (the parents) relinquished control and turned over their son and daughter to this, their new life.

It seems possible that this could become a new kind of ritual in which our behavioral sciences, now the new religion, take responsibility for trying to facilitate the divorce from the family of origin and the marriage to an in-law family. This should set up an extended membership in a now, two family-of-origin league. If ritual is one of the means by which people are bonded to each other, this ritual might serve to bond two families.

IV

The Process of Psychotherapy

A Panoramic View
of Psychotherapy

Psychotherapy is Parenting

If there is any one metaphor that is most consistently reliable in talking about psychotherapy—whether it is with the individual or couple or family—it is the concept of *parenting*. Parenting involves both the problem of caring and the problem of functioning. That is, one has to be not only a person who is concerned with the well-being of the "other," but also a person who is willing to put aside some of his own personhood in order to function in the best interest of the other. In the same sense that an adult cannot go "all out" in fighting with a child, one cannot be *only* a person while doing psychotherapy. *One has to discipline his personhood.*

The purpose of our parenting is to allow the patient to be free to become more and more of himself, to discover new limits to his own operation, new freedom for anger, new freedom for intimacy, new freedom for self-centeredness. This freedom arises from the fact that the therapist (that is, the parent) is handling the situation, is supplying the security, is providing the comfort. Thus, the patient can alter the social rules, the control systems, that are operating in his day-to-day world.

The isolation required of the therapeutic setting allows for a kind of craziness without the isolation that makes ordinary crazy experiences so frightening. It is craziness with a valid boundary supplied by the professional other. One of the reasons that marriage is such a help in producing good parenthood is that it involves a preliminary security bond. This establishes a baseline for the freedom to care more fully for the child. If it is true that the basic symptom behind all human growth is the delusion/illusion—the fantasy that if we can combine with another we will not have to suffer the pain

151

of our own aloneness—then psychotherapy is a process for escaping from our first prison, that is, the family of origin. We discover that it is possible to find other security, which, although temporary and artificial, is still adequate. If we succeed in the effort to find independence and strength, we can rejoin our family of origin as a peer rather than a prisoner.

Once one talks about parenting, it becomes easier to understand how to survive psychotherapy. If you are the patient, capitalize on your freedom. If you are the therapist, remember that your discipline, not just your caring, is the essence of your usefulness. There are many fringe benefits to psychotherapy. One of them is the gradual dissolution of the fantasy life that has curtailed our own willingness to be all that we can be. The fantasy fear of the future, the fantasy horror of past tragedy, the nightmare of crises past and future, the cost of survival, and the interest on our investment—all make the "cost" go up as we become less and less free to be a whole person. This mortgage on our person is also liable to inflation. Cultural influences alter our social structure and create pressure on us towards a bull market and then toward a bear market. It isn't easy to audit one's net worth, or to balance out one's emotional debts and emotional assets, or to insure one's future security.

The residuals of psychotherapy when it is effective or even when it is useful, like the residuals of parenting success, are many and varied. One of the most important ones is freedom from the past: freedom from the haunting fear that "it" will happen again. Other by-products of good psychotherapy are the freedom to resonate to the needs of another; the freedom for increasing availability to one's significant other; the discovery that there really is a *we*, that there really is a *they*, and that there really is an *I* (the act that we put on in social scenes does not need to be a constant contorting pressure); and the development of a presence—that quality of "good vibes" that separates the adequate, competent, coping person from the *whole* person. Finally, the effects of psychotherapy should make it possible for one to get therapeutic gains from daily living while evolving a continually expanding personhood.

What Exactly Is Therapy?

The word *therapy* has acquired very confusing meanings. For instance, many things are therapeutic but probably should not be called *therapy*. Therapy is itself a deliberate role (like parenthood), while *therapeutic* means a growth-inducing or integrative movement. A therapeutic experience can include such events and processes as a visiting nurse in the country, or the whole system of education and adaptation training whereby you are deliberately encouraged and supported in your effort to learn how to walk when you're partially crippled or to learn how to learn when you're feeling very uneducated. Some experiences are boring, stultifying, dominating. Any experience may *become* therapeutic. Most war experiences are destructive, but some people come back from having been in a war and exposed to great horrors and dangers with a tremendously increased, integrative personhood.

Abreaction can be therapeutic: the expression of one's feeling in a behavior such as beating on pillows, screaming at somebody you care for, or screaming at somebody you're angry at. The process of regression, of becoming childlike can be therapeutic: whether it is in the state of fun or in the state of dependency—being cuddled, being admired, being free to be dependent, to be accepted. Likewise, the process of *joining* can be therapeutic: dating, participating in team sports or discussion groups, belonging to a social club. The process of hypnosis, an altered state of consciousness brought about either deliberately or accidentally, may be very therapeutic. The whole process of being therapeutic may be enhanced or happen by itself in what has been called *transference*: Some situation arises, and you attach to it the significance of previous powerful relationships with your parents or siblings.

We should be clear that what is *therapeutic* does not necessarily involve the experience itself; it involves the significance the individual attaches to it. A very minor experience can be therapeutic, and a very major experience can fail to be therapeutic—that is, fail to produce integration, more oneness, more personhood. All psychotherapy is oriented towards increasing personhood, increasing oneness, integration, self-esteem. Many times, of course, it does that and many times it fails to do that.

Another category of being therapeutic comes about via nonprofessional psychotherapy. Basically, this involves the presence of an important person. For me, it was my grandfather when I was five; he was a model of wholeness. It also can be a group experience in a church, an occupational or social group, or a team membership. Either way, it is a process whereby a person or a group sees you in a fuller sense than you see yourself and encourages you by that supportive fantasy or projection to be more of who you are.

A further way of talking about the therapeutic experience is to talk about it as one of those painful or difficult things that happen in life: the experience of being physically mugged, of failing in school, of psychological rejection by a group or by peers; a sense of social ostracism; surviving drugs or courtship or marriage or pregnancy or raising a child; or the death of someone significant (or even the death of someone insignificant) in which your participation is massive. These situational stresses or opportunities, if you will, foist upon you a kind of nonprofessional psychotherapy that can include all kinds of life experiences, small or large: artistic work, the experience of poverty, physical illness, accidents, serious work, participation in Mother Nature, a reckless moment in which you are "born again," a massive, long-term education, the experience of a pet, the cause-and-effect breakthrough of a no-seatbelt wreck, or the death of a passenger in a car you are driving. All of these experiences can provide nonprofessional psychotherapy. Some of these may be deliberate; some may be purely accidental. Some may be jointly organized and carried out with another person at your initiative; you may create the opportunity to go "one down" so that you can learn to be more of who you are.

Unfortunately, therapy may continue for many years with great effort and with great sincerity on both sides, yet still fail to produce the kind of breakthrough we all seek. The therapeutic experience itself is a deliberate process carried on between a person called the client (patient or customer) who is deliberately going one down, taking the chance that the other person, a relative stranger, will be able to help him find more of himself. This other person, the therapist, is in a role: he is artificially, deliberately making an effort to help the other person (client, patient, customer) be more of himself. He achieves this by becoming attentive, responsive, and directive of the patient's effort to be more of who he is: to be more open, to be stronger, to be deliberately dependent, to be dangerously open, to take initiative in ways he has never been able to before, to have the courage to abrogate all roles, and to find more of his personhood. The process of setting up this therapeutic alliance is quite technical and quite artificial. The process of carrying it out is dangerously intimate, and may result in anything from a chaotic failure to a smaller or greater success.

Before the arrival of professional psychotherapy, therapeutic experiences were catalyzed by the experience of stress in the person whose anxiety level was high, together with the presence of a giving, nurturing professional or socially available older or more tolerant individual. Shamans, rabbis, priests, and any individual who slips into the role of being a social therapist—all function therapeutically in this manner. Professional therapy, however, is different from these particular kinds of therapeutic experiences. The decision on the part of the stressed individual to "enter therapy" forces him to deliberately "bend the knee"—regress in the service of hoped-for change and ask for help from another.

Life itself can also be therapeutic. As I mentioned, losing a job, inheriting money, the death of a spouse or intimate friend, recovery from a serious illness or life-threatening episode—all may be, if they become symbolic, therapeutically effective. (By "symbolic" I mean that the experience takes on special meaning and becomes the kernel for a reorganization of the individual's lifestyle.) There need not be any deliberate quality or conscious intentionality in all of this, unless one includes such actions as the man who does a poor job so that he will be fired as a way of retaliating against his spouse, or as a way of challenging the boss for greater closeness.

Most conspicuous among these nonprofessional therapeutic experiences are self-help groups. Alcoholics Anonymous is a notable example, and it adequately bridges the difference between *therapeutic* and *therapy*. The individual in an AA meeting is pressured into confessing his infantile need and thus asking for help from the group, who serves as the suprasystem or the parental role. This same process also takes place in fraternity and sorority houses, as well as in many work groups, labor unions, fraternal orders, and golf clubs.

Professional psychotherapy is unique in that it is deliberate, structured, and the therapist is a paid professional. The dignity of the dependent request is countered by the reverse role in which the patient is fathering the therapist by giving him money. Assuming that this return to childlike dependency is respected by the therapist, the transference phenomenon begins a change—or, if you will, the artificial role is assumed by the therapist. There ensues a direct emotional regression. It is a temporary state and serves as the anesthesia for the therapist to gradually increase his/her demand that the patient take full responsibility for his living and his decisions, including even the decision to return for another interview. In essence, the therapist has become a foster parent; he is artificial, playing a role. He is not being himself in a social sense so that the patient (individual or family) can be free to struggle within for greater strength, greater freedom, and greater enjoyment.

Just as there are two kinds of anxiety—*negative anxiety*, which ultimately becomes the fear of going crazy or the fear of death, and *positive anxiety*, which is the fear that one will not live up to one's competence (as in stage fright)—so, too, are there two kinds of psychotherapy. Traditionally, psychotherapy has been viewed as the process of excising "the bad": getting rid of pain, getting rid of pathological stress, getting rid of internalized haunts like the unwillingness to accept father's death or the unwillingness to face the aloneness with which each of us is stuck.

Psychotherapy can be seen in a completely different frame, however. It can be viewed as the process of inducing or creating greater mental health. Mental health may be augmented by a joyful experience with the therapist in which the patient goes away feeling that he is respected, esteemed, and revered as a person. The concept that the patient is a peer, the concept that the patient has contributed something to the therapist and his growth, the concept that the patient will always be near and dear to the therapist, the concept that the therapist could lovingly enjoy the patient's pathology (the patient's slips of the tongue or ear) the concept that the therapist revels in the patient's personhood, even reveling in his own defeat by the patient—all these are contributions to the patient's increasing mental health and, as such are valuable components of psychotherapy.

High among these contributions is the willingness to face and even enjoy the experience of aloneness, the sense of one's own integrity, one's own personhood, one's identity, one's unity with oneself, one's trust and participation in one's own *livingness*, the freedom to enjoy one's own creativity and spontaneity, be it good, bad, or indifferent. All of this is a sense of *deep participation in one's own physical self*—one's body, its operation, and even it defects. All of these are healthful, growthful, self-actualizing and potentiating experiences which can be created, expanded, or colored red during psychotherapy.

This is one of the great assets of couples or family therapy: It enables the members increasingly to experience the healthful components in their relationship instead of merely hurting one another with the painful relationship components.

One of the healthful components in psychotherapy is the capacity to transcend the loving process itself, to be able to view with warmth and delight the ironies, the disorientations, and the disturbances. The healthful components the therapist can offer are expanded when he can be free to laugh at her and at himself with her, and do it lovingly. Thereby she may get the sense of the absurdity in her purposeful, painfully organized drive for attainments of one kind or another. This facetiousness, this capacity to laugh at life, can be a great health-producing component of the psychotherapy process.

Orientations in Psychotherapy

One way of talking about psychotherapy is to talk about the different general orientations. I should like to suggest three.

First is that of symptom relief. The patient or family comes in a state of emotional starvation, like the child who has been rendered weak, insecure, and unable to operate because of lack of nourishment, lack of strength, lack of developmental opportunities. The obvious response to this kind of symptom is the comforting nurturance of a foster mother. The closeness, the teaming, is so much like that of a school teacher who can encourage the child to read, to study, to learn, to create, and to be more and more interested in learning. One of the problems with this orientation, however, is the gradual evolution of a "mother knows best" syndrome: The therapist offers tricks that make things change, but this results in the patient's loss of freedom to take initiative. This means that the patient or family becomes more dependent and gradually evolves more and more self-doubt, thus leaving the foster parent in a temporarily wonderful phase of being God-like. Then the foster parent/therapist is confronted with the problem of how to get out of that predicament—which is not unlike the problem of the child leaving home when emotional age and emotional starvation are still major problems.

A second method or orientation in psychotherapy is a life-reconstructing pattern. This approach used to be centered around the proffering of insights, understanding, analysis, and effort to prove that the therapist knows a better way for living. In the sense that the patient's pain and impotence make him insecure, this learning of new techniques for living can be very valuable. The problem is, again, that the temptation for greater dependency is so prominent and the loss of initiative is so tempting that the patient becomes like the adolescent: alternately needing and fighting for dependency, and alternately rebelling against the loss of selfhood, the loss of his own creativity.

A third pattern is called re-empowering the patient (or re-empowering the family). In this approach the adult is feeling weak and wanting to belong, has been overcome by failure, wants to team, to be put in charge of himself, but does not realize how to make such things happen. Hence the therapist is much like the father: demanding, believing, exhorting that it is possible for the patient to attain adaptation to stress by greater efforts. The role of the therapist in this motif requires a peculiar kind of nonsupportive demand for power, like the football coach who pushes the players to increase their aerobic tolerance, and encourages their full use of self, their spontaneity, and their initiative. The therapist must take the power away from patients and demand control of a restricted segment of their lives—in essence, how long they exercise, what kind of exercise they choose, and the time and place. If this method is successful, and the patient does not give up "playing ball," the development of strength becomes something that is satisfying to him or her. There is, however, a preliminary period in which the "coach" must force the "player" to take the power back: the therapist must force the patient to define his own kind of game, his own kind of participation, to choose the role in which he can be most successful, gain most enjoyment, and most easily invest. Then the coach's role—the therapist's role—becomes more and more one of cheering for the patient and enjoying his or her dreams and progress.

In any of these orientations to psychotherapy, the "meta problem" is one of how the therapist can learn to perfect the process of his therapeutic role without becoming enslaved by either the dependency of the patients or the fantasy of his own power. The danger of being a therapist is like the danger of being a mother: It is almost impossible to switch roles and become a peer with someone who has once been the child!

Learning the techniques of family therapy via experience (since they cannot be taught) requires the fact of responsibility, the fact of peer critique, and the recognition that the team of peers is more powerful than the individual—in essence, that two minds are better than one. There is a similarity between psychotherapy training and learning about acting. It takes a tremendous amount of practice, critique, rehearsal, and disciplined tryouts to become a good actor—or, for that matter, a good skater, a good skier, a good team player, a good therapist and, in fantasyland, a good marital spouse. Perfecting the role of psychotherapist requires the unlikely blending of *personhood* and *rolehood*. It should be understood that the role is trainable whereas the person's growth into personhood is a different, much slower, and much more painful process. Changing your operation in the role is much easier than changing the operation in your life. Being an actor is much easier than being a patient.

The Secret Life of Assumptions

All psychotherapy is based upon a set of assumptions. One of the assumptions that is usually not articulated is that all of us, without exception, are schizophrenic during our sleeping hours. Our dreams are nonrational; they are couched in symbols that are different from our daytime language, and they are quite unacceptable to the culture-bound living patterns of our daily hours. If one assumes that it is possible to deal with this underground world within the psychotherapeutic interview, it produces a completely different orientation on the part of the therapist during that hour. To deliberately try to share one's craziness, one's dream life, one's unacceptable inner self with the family requires an intimate relationship as well as a willingness to be regarded with suspicion. The therapist must tolerate inner confusion and, at the same time, precipitate confusion within the family— all of which can be tolerated only from a strong foundation of intimacy.

There is a crazy understructure that I believe is characteristic of every family. The family myths, the family rituals, the family stress episodes all have the quality of the psychotic dream-life that each of us lives every night. We live in our underground—or, to say it another way, *our psychotic self lives us*. The conscious life is merely an epicurrent of the unconscious process that controls our living. The truly essential parts of the therapeutic process are the searched-for moments of freedom, of creativity, of tolerance for or actual joy in the creative, nonrational aspects of the family's life together. The therapist's interaction with the family produces an entirely new and unique operation by facilitating a new kind of intimacy that encompasses lovingness, freedom for anger, healthy competition, and a whole-person to whole-person peership.

Teaching psychotherapy to trainees for 40 years has made it very clear to me that every patient arrives for the first interview with a series of covert, unformulated, but very binding assumptions. These are assumptions about the therapist, assumptions about the process, and assumptions about the dangers, which I will simply summarize here.

Patients assume that what has happened to their friend, relative, neighbor, or favorite movie star can and will happen to them. This assumption swings in both positive and negative directions. Patients may dream of a wonderful breakthrough moment of change that will alter their entire lives, or they may wallow in the threat of all those terrible things that *could* happen: that someone in their family will become ill, or that they will be rendered helpless by some kind of malicious maneuvering, or that the comfort and security they yearn for will be offered and then withdrawn. They also fear that their own best efforts, which obviously have repeatedly failed, will cause the therapist to degrade them. They fear that their worst fantasies will turn out to be true, that their guilt will be augmented, and that they will be subjected to a humiliating exposure or to a mysterious kind of hypnosis over which they will have no control.

Even more serious in my learnings has been the discovery that therapists know very little about the assumptions they bring to the treatment process. They assume that patients arrive in their offices with an open, hungry acceptance of them that makes their feeling of impotence disappear; they assume that they will feel like a remarkable discovery to these people who are asking for their help; they are trapped by the fantasy that their knowledge can be transferred to patients and that their understanding of themselves will change patients even though their understanding has not changed them! More serious is the assumption that the deliberate, conscious verbal interaction taking place on the overt level is the essence of what is happening and the basis for the dreamed-about recovery. Behind that assumption and essentially unseen by therapists are their own beliefs that more knowledge will produce any desired result, that people can *will* their lives into being different, and that they as therapists can *will* patients into willing to change. More profound still is the recognition that beneath all of these layers is a set of transference vectors that influences the ongoing process of therapy more than *any* overt factor.

When you see individuals for the first interview, their implicit contract (of which they are completely unaware and certainly do not verbalize, and which the therapist ordinarily doesn't know about) is that you will be the good mother and agree with them that their bad mothers have produced all their problems. Implicitly you have accepted their transference and agreed to be this wanted super-mom who will give them the security, power, and simultaneous independence *from* their family as well as a full measure of belonging *to* their family that they have been dreaming about since they were in grade school. Given this implicit transference phenomenon, which is partially created in fantasy before the beginning of the first interview, any move on your part becomes a double-cross. Your request to bring in the spouse for the second interview, to bring in the parents or the children, is a shocking rupture in the implicit fantasy projection the patient has formulated. The patient's attempt to postpone this variation in the therapeutic process until the therapist has become more established in the relationship is typical and carries the paranoid inference that the contract was never an acceptable one, and the therapist has just been maneuvering in every way from the beginning. Even if your request to change the process is accepted by the patient, it seems like blackmail—and like blackmail, it sets up the stage for a repeat performance and a double-cross at a different, deeper, and more painful level.

The answer to this pitfall is to set up the initial blind-date contract with all sorts of protection for yourself as the therapist: No therapy is begun until it is clear where the lines of responsibility will be drawn, until the fantasy of transference euphoria is ruptured. Furthermore, the offer to proceed with the therapy is tentative and the freedom to withdraw after the first interview is maintained with great care and clarity. It should never be assumed that the therapist is involved in an ongoing therapeutic relationship just because the first interview seemed to go well.

At the core of this whole phenomenon hovers the fact that this current relationship will be structured by patients in exactly the same compulsive, repetitive manner that characterized all their previous efforts to get help. The therapist only succeeds if he can be sure they break out of that deadlock, with its implied and pre-set termination in failure.

Evolving and Maintaining the Generation Gap

Whenever a patient asks for help, there is an automatic inference of regression. The patient can ask for this help in a number of ways. If he is infantile, the attitude is one of "Please, Mama, kiss it and make it better." If he is in a child-like mode, the request will come in the form of, "Daddy, please do it. I'm too weak and you're strong." If he is a teenage level, the communication will amount to: "Let's get together and do something I can't do alone." Or, if by chance the patient is even older, the message may sound more like: "Please help me get over defeating myself"; or "Please help me get over being too successful."

The therapist is then offered the opportunity of establishing a generation gap by putting himself in the role of foster parent or temporary adult to this temporary child. When the generation gap is kept alive and unchallenged, the patient is structured to regress to the full limit of his capacity and to revel in his belongingness and his nourishing relationship with the therapist. He then gradually develops the freedom to institute his own belief system, his own freedom to parent himself, and his growing readiness to leave the foster home and establish a real-life home that is his own.

The simplest beginning of establishing this identity is administrative in nature: Who shall be at the interview, how long it should last, what will happen in the interview — all of those reality decisions which are part of the business of professional psychotherapy.

The secondary means of establishing the generation gap is to avoid responding to the patient's communication with a peer-level response. All responses by the therapist should be in the frame of parental language. This language could also be called the language of inference.

Thirdly, maintaining the generation gap implies and, in fact, *demands* that the therapist *not* share with the patient any dubious, unclear, or unresolved issues. The therapist should always maintain the sense of final authority, while at the same time allowing the patient the privilege of agreeing, disagreeing, or having opinions of his own. In addition, the therapist should insist that the patient make all decisions without his partic- ipation. The therapist's function is only to help the patient think about the decisions, even though it is inevitable that the patient will take inferences and form decisions based on them. If the patient shares his inferences, the therapist should attempt to frustrate them.

The Phases of Psychotherapy

The process of psychotherapy can be divided into a series of phases: the pre-therapy phase, the first interview, the early mid-phase, the central work phase, the full alliance, the impasse, the augmented impasse, and the ending phase.

Pre-therapy. The pre-therapy phase is sometimes unavoidably absent alto- gether. The person is brought in by an intake or triage procedure that does not involve you. You thus have no preliminary way of assaying or becoming involved. The decision has been made. The process then becomes one of immediately sharing the frustration, the dangers, and the alternatives to failure on both sides of the alliance, with a clarity that the alliance itself is distorted, artificial, and in serious danger of complete uselessness.

Assume there is a pre-therapy phase in the form of a telephone call. The person expresses the need for relief from pain and impotence, and the therapist's problem is to infer the possibilities from what is offered. It is feasible to gently request a history of life: of nonprofessional psychotherapy, of the use of alcohol as therapy, of the family as a therapy resource, and of previous experience in professional therapy. It is not invasive on your part to elicit the horror story, the ultimate sense of failure, and the degree of hopelessness.

The process of this pre-treatment phase is an assay of pathology, an assay of hope, a definition of the business of psychotherapy, a definition of the financial responsibility, an establishment of the time scheduling, and the maintenance of control over the decision to move forward. It is as though the caller is asking for venture capital. Do you want to offer your resources without any certainty of return? Your process should involve a delay of all decision-making, a denial of referral to someone else, and a barrage of questions: *Why now? Why this? Who else? Why me?* You move back and forth between limited understanding and a clear separation process.

The distortions in this pre-therapy phase involve such qualities as sincerity, acceptance, empathy, a co-transference, and the emergence in the therapist of a resonance to what is being offered rather than assay and analytic thinking about it. Further distortion comes from offering a sample of therapy, a sample of nurturance, or a failure to discover the queen in the woodwork—a rich aunt, an illegitimate pregnancy, a legal involvement, a negative transference. If the therapist is resonating to what is being offered, he is automatically in trouble; if he is unaware of this resonance, he is in deeper trouble!

The blind date. The second phase of psychotherapy I call the blind date. As I have mentioned, it is an interview in which each person is and should be paranoid. The therapist should be more paranoid than the patient, since he or she is in control of the interview. The therapist is the female in this blind date and the one who is in danger of becoming pregnant. This is a technical phase, the phase of deliberate planning. This is also the phase during which the psychological prostitute structure is differentiated from genuine love in much the same way that Melina Mercouri differentiated the new sailor from the old sailor in that famous scene in which she said to the old sailor, "Never on Sunday."

The process of this first interview, this blind date, involves a trial of labor in the sense of letting the pain of the uterine contractions evolve into more and more serious preliminaries to the actual delivery. This trial of labor involves time together and a careful diagnostic screening of what happens during the hour: the evolution of a preliminary co-transference game with a protective denial of the future, the move past the non-honesty offered, handling the "you will fail" ploy, playing scapegoat yourself, educating the patient about the process of the foster parent role. Therapy education can also include (perhaps *should* include) the offer of transference and the matching of it with the avoidance of co-transference as the therapist's problem via his fear of it. In essence, this process is setting the stage for the therapist's successful co-transference and his freedom to be crazy.

The distortions begin with rupturing the contract for that first interview. One of the family members doesn't come, the time is distorted, the responsibility is distorted, and so on. A classic example is the patient who, at the end of the first interview when he is asked to pay, says "Oh, I assumed this was free. Everybody who does psychotherapy offers a free first interview." The therapist has distorted the process by offering a parental welfare gift, a kind of turkey on Thanksgiving.

Another distortion can come from the therapist's fear of failure and his consequent offer of reassurance or anesthesia or hope. Then there is the distortion that comes from the therapist's own inner guilt for not responding as fully as the patient needs or requests and the distortion that arises via a demand from the community, the person who gave you the referral. The community's expectation of your magic can distort this early phase most easily. In walks your aunt's favorite neighbor, your mother's high school chum, or a referral by your favorite colleague so that you carry a double burden (though this can be modified by sharing it and warning the patient of the dangers it involves). This phase is also an opportunity to succeed by failing and to face the therapist's fear of failure with the patient.

Mid-phase. The early part of the mid-phase—the second date, if you will—is a process of pre-alliance, a rehearsal for psychotherapy, a co-transference trial, an opportunity to block the intrafamily psychotherapy that one is trying to replace, the opportunity to expose the family symbiosis and to talk about rotating the scapegoat, or even playing the scapegoat as a trial process. The distortion of this early mid-phase can come from the anesthesia of reassurance, an assay of the future, a covert delusion by the therapist, the resonance of his empathy, and the danger of gossip.

Central work phase. The central work phase is basically a process of listening, of developing an alliance in which the family takes more and more responsibility for initiating each move, each process, each interview. This phase requires breaking the culture bind in language, behavior, and openness, and breaking the time bind so that the psychotherapy is not delusionally assumed to be either short-term or long-term. It is an opportunity to break or augment the path of transferences, to break the present transferences—your own and theirs—so that it becomes clear that this is not a lifetime adoptive parenting role you are assuming but rather a time-limited foster parent project. It is also a time to play at being crazy, to clarify that this relationship is not love, and to make clear that you are not peers and will never be peers.

The distortions in this central work phase occur via the therapist's anxiety, forgetting to team with another therapist, letting the family control the therapy, or trying to control their lives because your life comes out of a different culture. Their life has a cultural integrity which must be respected or it will be further distorted.

Full alliance phase. In the full alliance phase, the therapist should be in the process of *following*, of expanding horizontally with what is going on in the present, and expanding vertically by way of exploring the past and the future. He should be expanding into the third generation, the fourth generation. He should begin to share his fantasies, his dreams, his horrors. The possible distortions in this phase of full alliance involve the dangers of role reversal: of role rupture by being co-opted and adopted by the family, or co-opting family members and adopting *them*—in essence, making the psychotherapy into an adoption project rather than a foster project.

Impasse. The impasse which comes out of a preliminary full alliance can be worked at by sharing a fragment of yourself, sharing bits of your own therapy (including the idea that you have forgotten your therapist), sharing your fear of failure, sharing the fear of your empty nest, facing the fact that you are only in a role, facing the fact of your imminent death as a therapist and as a person. The distortions in this impasse resolution effort occur through avoiding help or the need for help, exposure of your own family, dealing with your pride, and being distorted by your "take-home growth" from this therapy in the form of what they are doing for you.

Augmented impasse. The augmented impasse includes bringing in the extended family as a consultant to help with the problem of your failure as the therapist. A colleague may help as a consultant. However, you cannot change your responsibility for any failure as a therapist, because *the family* never fails. Only the therapist fails. The colleague's job is to help with the process of psychotherapy—not diagnosis, not seduction. He is consulting to you, not to the family.

This phase can also include an ex-patient as consultant, or a family friend, the local pastor, the neighbor, the boss or secretary, the infidelity partner, or any others who are intimate or significant to the family. The therapist must share his failure, must face his impotence, and must accept the family's implicit decision to end therapy. The distortions come from the therapist's not accepting help, from exposing the family rather than himself, and from hiding his failure out of shame or guilt feelings.

Ending. The ending phase is a process in which the family's participation is subtle and critical. Their message may be, "Enough already," "Things are better," "Things are worse," or the exposure of outside transferences with or without the stories: that is, "I almost forgot to come," "My job is going better," "My boss is a wonderful guy," "I'm falling in love with my wife." Essentially, they are saying that life is more important than psychotherapy.

The distortions that can occur during the ending phase include the family members' offer of new symptoms, their denial of change, the bribe of their fear of anxiety returning, a symbolic dropout ("Joe didn't come this morning because he had a football game"), the presentation of a pseudo-symptom, a symptom in the therapist, the discovery or the presence of concealed hostility in the therapist or the family, the lack of humility in the therapist, or the pride of the therapist in being humble. When ending is successful, there evolves the arrangement for a future alliance (if needed), a discussion of the lining of the therapist's empty nest, his request for direct therapeutic help from the family members, his learning from their case and the sharing of his real-life fragments in terms of persons, his work, new cases, the money, and his inner video replay of their joint experience together. Finally, ending includes the therapist's dream of greatness and his dream of craziness, and his sharing with them of Plato's famous summary of the dialogues, "Practice Dying."

The Impasse

Much of the criticism of psychotherapy is in one way or another related to the problem of impasse. One day we say psychotherapy is no good because the patients get nothing out of it—that is, nothing *moves*. Another day we say psychotherapy is bad because it goes on forever. Most patients come to a therapist because of an impasse in their daily living. Somehow, they have been stalemated. (If the stalemate lasts a long time, we call them "rigid" or "burned out.") They also come because they are either *beginning* to break out, *hoping* to break out, or *determined* to break out of their impasse with life. Psychotherapy is a microcosm of life. When psychotherapy does not succeed, it frequently is due to the unpleasant reality that it has become a stalemate, a kind of cold war that locks therapist and patient in a fixed state.

The impasse problem is by no means restricted to the field of psychotherapy. There is a cultural impasse in the United States now between its black and white citizens. Neither is able to move in, and the tension of the lock-step state is more and more frightening. The world agonizes daily over an impasse between parents and children. (I'll bet even cavemen faced the one between parents and adolescents.) Nowadays most marriages pass through serial impasses or end in divorce. The ten-year syndrome and the seven-year itch are both metaphors of this kind of lock-step between two individuals, or groups of people, or states of being.

There is something about the impasse that is like a bilateral symmetrical dance. Neither of the individuals is able to change the rules of the dance; neither one can switch to being creative. This "dance" is a kind of mutual disrespect. Somehow the process becomes, as they say about a love affair, "bigger than both of us." We know about dead marriages in which the partners sit, each in his/her individual rocking chair positioned back to back, she reading *True Romances* and he reading *Playboy*. Al Scheflen described such a couple as the "gruesome twosome."

Sometimes the impasse is three-cornered. For instance, Father H. was a fat, soft, petulant, "seven-year-old" prone to temper tantrums. He was a blustering tyrant, but there was no chill in his emotional storm. Mother H. was a tight-lipped fury with every muscle locked, ready to spring, yet all was hidden under her idealistic, gentle, agreeable mother image. Impassed with each of these and with their partnership was the 16-year-old son. His lash-back sneer of disdain, his teetering on the edge of delinquency, was combined with a derisive and degrading attitude toward father and a sarcastic, pseudo-sweet snarl for mother. In this case, the impasse had a peculiar quality. No combination of two was stable in this unit. As soon as father and mother got together, they would break up, and father and son would get together in a fight, or mother and son would get together to discipline father. Thus, the triangular impasse revolved around a constant instability which was in itself very stable.

In the therapeutic setting of a one-to-one relationship, the impasse develops after therapy is underway and after the transference has been established in both directions. The therapist and the patient sell each other on an image and agree to conceal their personhood behind these images. Once this has taken place, there is a kind of mutual enjoyment of the state, and the dance goes on and on. The systems theorist would say that the units of which the system is composed are under control and the system tends to maintain itself in a steady state.

Assuming that we want to do something constructive about the impasse on a deliberate level, the therapist is wisest to deal with it as a problem in prevention. Many aspects of psychotherapy can be set up to prevent an impasse. The early establishment of a deliberate, contrived role structure for the therapist undoubtedly prevents subsequent impasses, or at least tends to if it is well done. If the therapist is in charge of everything that happens in his "hospital operating room," the patient is not apt to tie him up in a bilateral unchanging role. Once this deliberate therapeutic structure is established, the therapist is freer to respect the unique, custom-made living style of the patient and to not invade his life but only his feelings and his personhood. Prevention of impasse probably is also aided by any secondary commentary—that is, an objective discussion of the transference. Then, when the existential and peer relationship typical of healthy, late-phase psychotherapy develops, it is not contrived.

It is not new to say that negative affects must certainly be expressed to prevent impasse. Assuming that the impasse is based in the secretive character of the one-to-one relationship that characterizes most psychotherapy, it follows that the use of a consultant early in therapy tends to break up this lock-step. The same result is frequently obtained by bringing in other family members or even extended family members and sharing with them the lock-up in the therapeutic relationship by asking them to participate in the relationship.

In the conduct of psychotherapy, any freedom for the creative flow of communication tends to prevent a game-playing lock. Freedom on the part of the therapist to leave the scene emotionally, or even physically, also helps. If the therapist dares vary his own role stance, he creates a happening, and such a happening makes it very difficult to get into a fixed impasse set.

One obvious way of breaking up an impasse is having a war. When the cold war stalemate is disrupted by a hot war, this changes everything. The war may be started (and frequently is) and won by the patient. He/she ends treatment, walks out, or in some other way breaks up the relationship. Better it should be the therapist who starts the war so that it can be verbal, affective, and made part of the ongoing process. This takes a kind of freedom in the therapist to "hang loose," because once the patient has him uptight, it becomes very difficult to reheat the cold relationship. However, a deliberate effort to make the impasse a joint problem is aided, as I mentioned above, by the humiliation of bringing in somebody from the outside.

At the risk of sounding "far out," I would like to postulate how the schizophrenic patient grows in psychotherapy. If the schizophrenic does develop a transference, it is because the therapist is like his mother: his mother was a double-binding person, and so is the therapist. They establish a relationship in which the therapist double-binds the patient, and the patient is able to double-bind the therapist. Gradually this bind becomes tighter and tighter, until each of them is locked in step with the other, and neither is in charge of any change. Indeed, neither is capable of more than minute bits of change. This is exactly the state of imbalance the patient had with his mother. We know that when such a patient gets well by some fortuitous and still unknown means and leaves the hospital, frequently mother herself comes into the hospital or goes crazy in some other way. Assuming that this is also true in psychotherapy, our patient dares not get better for fear his therapist would go crazy. On the other hand, the therapist entered into this relationship deliberately, and I assume that at least *my* objective is to find some more of my own craziness. So at the point at which my patient and I are impassed in a kind of figure eight reciprocal double-bind, I elect to experience some more of my own craziness (my growing edge), supported by the homeostasis of that relationship.

When I do "go crazy," the patient has no recourse but to be the "counter-schiz" to my schizophrenia. We are in a pseudo impasse, and each of us is capable of forcing the other. But I as the therapist want to be "crazy," and he as the patient is thereby forced to be "sane." Once this reciprocal movement is established, the oscillations become wider and wider (assuming all goes well), until we are farther and farther separate. Then one other factor has to be added to "dance." Once the freedom to oscillate is residual in each of us, we are free to love each other, and this is the kind of love that revels in the other's gain, not just in one's own gain. With such love, the movement apart—or rather, the movement into life on the part of each of us—takes place gradually and with appreciation for the life and openness of the other. The love lasts forever, but the freedom is constantly increasing.

Could it be that no impasse in a relationship means that no love is developing? So why not go on and break up the impasse with one psychotic after another? I'll tell you why! My society fights my craziness. Each time I have to defy this pressure for social lock-step, I get scared!

Some Benefits
of Professional Psychotherapy

What benefits does professional psychotherapy offer with its deliberate quality and its hopefully greater freedom for being? Obviously, the first benefit it offers is a relief of symptoms. But this relief is both an asset and a base for further stress. If one relieves psychosomatic symptoms, one is apt to precipitate a psychotic episode. If one relieves the psychotic episode, it is apt to precipitate depression or a manic attack. And if one relieves the symptom of depression or a manic episode, one may precipitate neurotic symptoms. So the relief of symptoms is a two-edged sword.

The second benefit that professional psychotherapy offers is the relief of repression. The catch here is that being psychosocially dead may help one adapt to the culture bind or the exigencies of one's living situation, whereas relief of that repression may result in acute anxiety or a bevy of neurotic symptoms.

The third by-product of good psychotherapy is an increased creative freedom that opens a new expression of self and releases the intuition of what we now call the right brain.

The fourth is an increased integration, a developing oneness between the intuitive right brain and the analytic, socially-trained left brain.

Finally, the fifth benefit is an increased capacity to encourage the positive anxiety of risk-taking—to precipitate oneself into situations of stress for the sheer joy of adapting to or integrating a new country, a new human experience, or a new life setting with different and greater stress.

I shall use myself as an illustration. One of the benefits I gained from professional therapy was learning to be a patient at the "drop of a hat." Many opportunities allow this one-downmanship—that is, chance-taking

170

with another person or another setting in the hopes of belonging, integrating, or individuating from this new set. After being the patient in psychotherapy, there were many other one-down therapeutic experiences to be had in the profession. My career is comprised of these: the ten years of doing co-therapy with individual schizophrenics and teaching medical school; the ten years of private practice with the same group who had been teaching with me in the medical school; the 20 years of practicing and teaching family therapy only; these past several years of retirement with the increasing freedom to think about therapy and to evolve an integrated understanding of the therapeutic process.

Throughout all these experiences, that drop-of-the-hat freedom to be the patient has been expanded. Now it becomes almost automatic in any workshop. I become the patient to the audience when I am lecturing or demonstrating. The very careful separation of therapist role and real life only happens before and after the professional hours. That is the counterweight. I am not the patient or therapist at dinner, or at a cocktail party, or watching television at home.

It is important to recognize that anything therapeutic, including professional psychotherapy, necessitates a kind of psychological intimacy. In addition, therapy necessitates a psychological generation gap—what Freud called "regression in the service of the ego"—so that the person who is changing can be engaged in a freedom ordinarily very similar to play, i.e., *responsiveness without responsibility*. The other partner in this psychological intimacy, the parent person (better known as foster parent), is taking the responsibility for control, for adaptation, and for protection.

A metaphor of this process is the experience of participating in a game of competitive quality without competition. For my wife and me, ping-pong without scoring has become a process of intense play with no double thinking. The absence of double thinking means greater integration, and this kind of muscular free association is one of the ways of describing the process. It is similar to the psychological intimacy of the therapeutic process. The patient has no need for double thinking because the therapist is accepting the responsibility for his or her role restriction and the double thinking that makes for responsibility.

Psychotherapy Addicts

On the flip side of benefits from professional psychotherapy we have its pitfalls.

The current cultural demand dictates that if there is anything wrong within yourself or between you and any other person, you should find a therapist and practice interpersonal living in that laboratory until you have learned how to better relate to him, or to yourself, or to whomever is causing you stress. Unfortunately, very little attention is given to the pattern of bringing about change by what the old philosophers called "taking thought." This may be related to the fact that, increasingly, thought and intellectual or reasonable thinking are identified with the limitations of logic and with a rational "thing-oriented" process. Actually, the old philosophers many times used the term to denote an experience of *one's self*. In his book, *Self Renewal: The Individual and the Innovative Society*, John Gardner of the Carnegie Foundation talks about self-renewal as the essence of self-development. He uses this theme to help us learn from those people who continue growing all their lives, and those people who become increasingly stale and finally die on the vine. These people, Gardner points out, are like the old prospectors who gave up on a gold mine: They have abandoned their own "gold mine" of growth, change, and education.

It has been my sad experience to observe the withering of a number of creative, innovative people because they began to worship the school, the idea, the invention, the orientation which was significant to them. As Sherwood Anderson said in *Winesburg, Ohio*, "Any truth taken to worship makes the person a grotesque."

One of the ways of dying is to become an addict of psychotherapy – an addict of interpersonal relating, whether it is in one-to-one therapy or family therapy. It is as though the process of *examining* life becomes a substitute for *living*. In essence, the individual becomes preoccupied with his own navel; he becomes less and less available to other encounters and even to his own creativity. With some patients who come to me after having gone through several psychotherapists, or having moved from another territory so that I am the next guru, I have found it possible to suggest that instead of trying to get to know *me*, they put themselves in an isolated corner for 40 days and see if they can find *themselves*. I suggest that they avoid the TV, the radio, books, friends, entertainment, education and diversions of all kinds, and instead simply live in relationship to *themselves*; that they make the relationship a process of meditation, a process of body awareness, and a process of rumination. The mere fact of turning their backs on the usual fragmenting experiences of our interpersonally crowded worlds many times brings about a calming, quieting, and strengthening experience. One patient said it was the first time she had discovered that she didn't need her boyfriend, her mother, or her psychotherapist!

Many times the interpersonal relationship that does not work has involved a process of giving oneself away, of uniting with another person much like two 16-year-olds who become close friends so that, in their union, they become one 32-year-old. It has not become clear to them that when they use somebody else to strengthen themselves, they are simultaneously being used by the other person. This type of relationship becomes a bilateral lie: "If you will let me be 'Number One' in your life, I'll let you be the most important person in my life." Factually, of course, *I'm* the most important person in my life, and no one else can take that place, even though I may give that illusion and even believe the illusion myself. I am the only person in my skin and, although I can decide to give my life to someone else for a proscribed period of time or even for all my life, that does not make that person the most important person in *fact*, only in *fantasy*.

One of the distortions of psychotherapy is that, because the therapist lives in an illusion that he or she is more important to the therapist for this hour than anything else, the patient many times makes the illusion into a delusion. He really believes that the game they are playing is for real, that the therapist has become a non-person for his sake and, therefore, he should be a non-person for the therapist's sake. Thus, they end up with a very painful, empty giving. It is my presumption that the counterforce for this is the discovery of one's *self*.

Process, Not Progress

One of the most tantalizing things about helpfulness in a cross-generational effort to be useful (whether it is via parenting, teaching, or psychotherapy) is the temptation to step into a kind of double thinking process in which one is involved with the pornography of the past (a peculiar kind of morbid curiosity about what made things get to where they are) and, even worse, the fantasy of the future. If I move correctly, will that change the world? What would make for progress? What would make for a better setting, a better experience, a better future?

I think this perspective is a serious mistake, because the more one double thinks, the less one is a person. The more one is preoccupied with a fantasy, the less free one is to be in the world of here-and-now, and the less one is available to himself, to his teammate, and/or to this patient or family or victim or client or customer or foster child.

The counter to this kind of double thinking is a preoccupation with becoming more and more expert in the process of acting the role of a foster parent, enacting the role of a professional psychotherapist—even to the point of sharing with the patient the peculiar kind of artificial absurdity of this make-believe parent we call a foster parent. This is usually achieved in some measure by means of the artificial process of timing the beginning of the hour and the ending of the hour. Many times, in the middle of the hour, the patient and the therapist are both making believe that this is a kind of magical world that can go on forever. The therapist makes believe that the patient is utilizing the transference experience for tremendous character change, and that he (the therapist) is not an actor but rather the adoptive parent or even the biological parent of this person or family in pain.

The challenge for the therapist is to evolve the kind of courage that makes it possible for him to perfect the details of the therapeutic process, thereby making it feasible for the patient, who is not in a role (he is a real person trying to be more of who he is), to experiment with new kinds of freedom and new kinds of opportunity in this foster parent effort to reconstruct the struggles of his real-life growing.

Levels of Communication
in Psychotherapy

All psychotherapy develops a spontaneous level of communication. In the highly intellectual graduate student, the level is usually one of fine English, carefully developed abstracts of information, and highly constructed theories. But good psychotherapy must involve deeper levels of communication in order to bring about change. With some particularly square persons, this requires an almost impossible effort. One way to break out of this constricting level into something more personal is to communicate the therapist's inner experiences, arising out of his boredom, out of his free associations, out of his fantasy life, or out of his body responses. The sudden association to some part of his outside life—a library book he failed to return, a gimmick he wants to get fixed in his water faucet at home, the fact that he doesn't like his wife's new hat—anything which pops into his head should be communicated to the patient.

In moving to the level of free association or of incidental information, the therapist precipitates the patient into moving to that level as well. The therapist may be moving to the level at which the patient is already operating and thus almost forces the patient to move into a different level of communication. The therapist can also communicate creative fantasies that suddenly flit through his head. Sometimes these are like nighttime dreams of a diffuse, unrelated, or nonrational character; yet, they should be communicated as such. If the therapist suddenly has the urge to belch, has intestinal cramps or the impulse to fart, experiences tingling in his right leg or twitching in his left eye or itching behind his right ear, he should share these with the patient. Declaring himself unable to understand his experience is sometimes a kind of anesthesia for the shock effect on the patient, but it is not easy for the patient to then avoid responding in the same metaphor.

It must be clear that the therapist also needs to have some kind of control over his communication. There are things that flit across any therapist's mind which are inappropriate to express (for social, clinical, or professional reasons), and those should be withheld. It is important to understand that the anesthesia for this kind of therapeutic operation is the therapist's own caring feelings about the patient. One final note of caution: It is not appropriate to do this kind of free associative communication during the first interview, or until you are really concerned with the patient. Otherwise, this kind of intervention amounts to bald manipulation, and perhaps even malpractice.

The Languages of Psychotherapy

Countries have different languages; professions have different languages. The profession of sailing has many terms that are completely foreign to our usual social language. Specialized language characterizes music, painting, the stock market, trucking, crime, and politics. The language of psychotherapy has emerged partially from the territories of sociology, psychology, anthropology, and medicine. In the field of medicine, requests for help have evolved a specific language in response. If you go to a physician and say, "I have a cough," he immediately thinks of 10 possible reasons for the cough: a cold, a chronic infection of the upper respiratory system or the lower respiratory system, tuberculosis, cancer, and so forth. In an analogous manner, a series of technical terms has emerged in the profession of psychotherapy. Having some understanding of the linguistics, the grammar, and the dictionary of these terms makes it considerably easier to think about the process of psychotherapy.

A primary component of the overall language of psychotherapy is the sub-set of the language of the patient. This language is mostly internalized, but under sufficient pressure it becomes clear that the patient is talking about *pain* and *impotence*. "I am suffering, and I can't do anything about it." This lament may be carefully disguised and subtly presented, but however it is camouflaged, essentially it is a way of trying to make contact with someone who may be able to provide some help.

A second component in the language of psychotherapy I call the "language of inference." From what is overtly presented, I infer what may be covert, implicit, frightening, manipulative, or learned.

Behind every communication, whether verbal or nonverbal, there is a series of inferences. A simple "no" can infer "I don't mean maybe," "Ask me again and I'll change it," or "Ask me again and I won't change it," or "I demand that you listen to what I say and believe it." These inferences become a whole language, and many times psychotherapy is the process of evolving a language of inferences. Both patient and therapist have three sets of available knowledge: the *known*, the *knowable* (that is, with effort, pain, time, care and concentration, one can make some unknown into a known), and the *unknowable* (that part which will never be known, can never be known; in some mythological literature it is called the "face of God," while in our professional connotations it is called the "unconscious").

One of the assets of the psychotherapist is his capacity to deal in the language of inference, thus making for the patient a momentary transition from the known to areas of the unknowable. Although these areas may be accepted as unknown at the present time, they may become known. This is sometimes called "speaking the unspeakable"; it is sometimes called "schizophrenese"; it is sometimes called "craziness." It is most valuably utilized as an indirect communication that is a kind of whimsical, half-humorous communication by the therapist to himself, but said out loud so that the patient can hear it. (The language of inference is probably best utilized if it is restricted to the therapeutic scene and not used outside that special, protected subculture.)

The language of inference also can be communicated nonverbally. One way for the therapist to talk straight and the patient to listen more directly is to utilize a diversionary method such as the use of toys, puzzles, or anything that makes it obvious that the therapist is not preoccupied or panicked by the patient's story. In essence, the problem is how to break through the patient's pre-interview delusion that the therapist will be totally available, completely competent, and magical in his power. A therapist is also a person.

The patient who has been to a whole series of therapists has picked up words that have held significance for each preceding therapist and is then able to utilize those words in trying to make more powerful contact with the next therapist. The language of pain and impotence may thereby be covered, amplified, or modified by the patient's learnings about how to manipulate the therapist, which the therapist must learn to infer.

There is yet another component in the language of psychotherapy which I have come to call the "language of options." In the process of thinking about and talking about the patient's efforts to change, alternatives from her experience and options that she has not thought about now emerge. The patient says, "I can't stand living with my husband, and I am unwilling to get divorced." The therapist then can offer all sorts of options, many of which the patient may have thought of but could not tolerate thinking about, such as going back to live with her parents, adopting a child to make their living different, going to work, or quitting work, or moving to a different community. These options help to expand the patient's thinking, relieve her pain, and perhaps give her the freedom from guilt and shame that allows a new willingness to think more openly about her situation as a whole. In essence, the patient is offering the limitations of her programmed thought processes, to which the therapist adds extensions and expansions.

There is still another component of the language of psychotherapy that I call the "language of irrelevance." Irrelevant thoughts, irrelevant statements, free-associative fantasies, contributions that appear to have no connection with anything may suddenly take on significance, usefulness, and great value. It is as though there is an undercurrent capacity to respond that we do not ordinarily utilize—connections which we make with what is going on in the relationship that we don't know about, do not understand, and frequently lose because we dare not contribute. To anyone who has done group psychotherapy, it is quite clear that conversational contributions by one member to the group are always useful to one or another of the members, and possibly to all of them. Interestingly, what seems to have no relevance to one member may be very significant to another member— many times to the complete amazement of those people who do not respond to the contribution.

The process of establishing a successful relationship involves the freedom to contribute irrelevancies to the ongoing dialogue. Within this irrelevant category are not only free associations and bits of language which arise seemingly from nowhere, but also the emotional aspects of the therapist's ongoing experience. The sudden twinge of anger, an unidentifiable connection of this situation with previous situations, apparently unwarranted suspicions, the sudden onset of a headache or an intestinal spasm, the momentary loss of memory—all, however seemingly irrelevant, may be making a contribution to the patient's expanding personhood.

Finally, I would like to suggest an altogether new language: the *language of transformation*. Each family should be regarded as we regard another nation. Family members have a sacred culture of their own which has evolved over the years; they have a history involving generations of progress; and they are the result of the final combination of the two last generations, which has produced the nuclear family with which we are currently dealing. The request for therapy is based upon a split within the family. The exigencies of living, birth, marriage, death, sickness, and stress of all kinds and varieties can produce a situation in which the family is virtually paralyzed—paralyzed by the stress between the subgroups in the family, paralyzed by sources of stress from the "outside" cultural world, or paralyzed by an evolving pathological method of resolving stress either by using a scapegoat or by avoiding the full mobilization of their family powers to produce change. The therapy setting offers the therapist a chance to help family members mobilize their power. But preliminary and crucial to that mobilization is the sacred respect—in Carl Rogers' words, the unconditional positive regard—which the therapist must have for the family members. As they offer their pain, and the therapist responds with his inferences and his options, he must be grounded in the conviction that they possess a unique culture and in his insistence that that culture is the only one he will help them to inherit and mobilize.

Critical to helping people change and important in families where that change is hard to induce is the freedom to create a double message. The usual message is one comprised of words, but words are not the only means of communication. Vocal tones, facial expression, and body movements all create a secondary level of communication. The first level is connected to reason and rational thought and is endlessly complex. Part of the usefulness of the double message is to avoid the double think on your part and on the part of the patient or the family. Such double thinking always makes the communication fragmented and not very helpful.

Where the power of reason and discussion has failed, the honest sharing of the fear of failure or the danger of no therapeutic alliance may help. No teaming equals no movement.

Paradox

The question of what happens in the use of paradox as a therapeutic technique of communication has never been clear, just like the problem of the therapeutic double message (also called "double bind") has never been clear. Part of this lack of clarity has to do with the fact that the paradox is a kind of psychological tickling or teasing and, as such, necessitates a distance from the patient. If this distance is effectively utilized, it should lead toward intimacy. If it does not lead toward intimacy, then paradox becomes a naked technique and, as such, is not useful for the patient's increasing integrity, because it does not lead to the therapist's utilizing his own integrity or his own personhood. Instead, the therapist becomes more and more a mechanic, staying at a distance merely tickling the patient as he goes by.

The successful paradox ought to be a step in the evolution toward intimacy. When the patient, having utilized the paradoxical experience for changing, wants more intimacy, it should be available. If it is not available, then the therapist may have changed the behavior but not increased the patient's integration. In essence, then, paradox opens the possibility of serving as merely a social manipulation rather than as a vehicle for genuine psychotherapy. Paradox as a naked technique is nonsymbolic, nonpersonal, and non-intimate. It leads toward more adjustment rather than more integration. Good psychotherapy should be growth-oriented; it should *not* be bettering the patient's *adaptation*, but rather increasing the patient's *power* so that he can then do what he wants with the power. All human beings organize toward health and integration, both social and interpersonal. Psychotherapy should eventuate in the same endpoint.

A Guiltless Hatred
of the Therapist

A great many of the psychological problems that are brought to the psychotherapist are centered around the problems of guilt. Many times these problems concern the difference between *real guilt* and *felt guilt*. Real guilt arises from the psychological reverberations of having behaved in a way which is unacceptable to oneself—whether it is a matter of abusing one's own child or spouse, absconding with money, having a sexual affair, or double-crossing promises or contracts that one has participated in establishing. Felt guilt, on the other hand, is a result of one's fantasy life and one's conceptual thinking rather than one's behavior. One can feel guilty about an imagined process: whether it is a child feeling guilty because father died and she is certain that it was her fault (something she said or didn't say, did or didn't do, in the previous time together); or whether it is the feeling of guilt at an anger which seems unjustified towards one's mother, father, spouse, or child. The whole process of felt guilt is one of intrapsychic war and suffering rather than the interpsychic reverberations that occur with real guilt.

The psychotherapy of either felt guilt or real guilt is frequently confused by the misguided effort to understand why it came about or how it came about. Unfortunately, this insightful discovery very frequently is of no help, or produces a kind of secondary overlay of intellectual or social imitation of recovery—pseudo recovery. I have found that *successful release of guilt may well be accomplished most effectively if the patient has an opportunity to experience a guiltless hatred of the therapist.*

I remember a particular incident in a Navy medical center when a very paranoid, psychotic sailor was brought into the staff room where five of us were having a conference. My effort to act as a consultant to his administrative physician rapidly turned into a shouting match during which I accused him of various heinous motivations, impulses, and character defects. He was prevented from physically attacking me by the sole fact that there were several officers and his attendant protecting me. The man went halfway down the stairs, turned around, came back up and stood at the door cursing me, and then went back downstairs.

It is interesting to postulate that perhaps the success and power of the "binder and grinder system of group catharsis" has to do with this evolution of guiltless hatred induced by the insulting and degrading verbalizations and the thorough defeat of anyone who tries to rebel and stand up for him/herself.

Administrative versus Symbolic Psychotherapy

All psychotherapy consists of a symbolic relationship and a real relationship. The real relationship is frequently converted into one of administrative decision-making. The patient wants to know whether she should get a divorce; the couple wants to know whether they should go on with their psychotherapy; the couple is struggling over whether you are as good a psychotherapist as their last one; or they are trying to decide whether they want to have more interviews or less.

Whenever this kind of alternation in the set develops, the therapist should also switch from being the symbolic parent—loving, demanding, probing, helping whatever way he can—to being a real person. All of a sudden he becomes the employee of the patient rather than the symbolic foster parent. All of a sudden he is dealing with his real world—that of the professional psychotherapist—and not the symbolic world of the playroom, whether it is for adults or for children.

In order to make psychotherapy successful, the administrative decisions should take precedence over all symbolic decisions. When the patient changes the focus to decision-making, she is trying to break the double bind involved in all parent-child relationships. One obvious way to respond to this shift is to offer to be fired and to make it clear to the patient that she has the right to discontinue her therapy. Another is to pull back the perspective and look at the whole situation, either with a consultant or by yourself. You may need to renegotiate a contract and to reevaluate the role with which that symbolic person whom you were five minutes ago is involved. Then you leave the decision for resolution in the hands of the patient, unless there is some serious problem that has to do with you (for example, if the patient refuses to pay the bill). Receiving payment for your professional services is an administrative decision; it should not be taken up on a symbolic level but on a real level. You need to earn your living, you have a family to support, you do not want to be their banker, and so forth.

This kind of reality testing also takes place in the playroom. The child who, after a series of play therapy interviews, says to you, "Don't you have some new toys?" or "You should see the kid next door," or "I was so busy at baseball this morning I almost forgot to come," is talking about the reality of the administrative structure. You need to answer him in this same framework: "Well, why don't we just plan on two more times, or is one more time enough?" or "I guess if you can play baseball, it's a shame for you to keep coming in here and wasting your time," or "So, if you want to quit, why don't you quit, and then if you want to tell the kid next door to come in, maybe he can get something out of coming here?"

To restate the point: The administrative decision takes precedence over the symbolic relationship while the patient is redeciding whether or not psychotherapy is valuable. On a deeper level, the patient is being offered the chance to take his life back into his own hands; to put it another way, he is being forbidden the right to leave his life in the hands of anyone else. Even if it seems that the administrative question is raised to break up the symbolic relationship, it should be accepted on that level. This is an imitation relationship; this is a pilot plant in human relationships; this is an "as if" relationship, and it should always be something that the patient can break out of. Any effort to capitalize on your symbolic role during these moments is unethical in the same sense that the mother who tries to make her child stay home from school because she is lonesome is inaugurating school phobia and taking advantage of her child by making him into her mother.

Pitfalls of Supervision

The problems of training in psychotherapy are multi-faceted. When a trainee begins the process of becoming a psychotherapist, he is informed that his *person* is the *tool* that he will use in his profession. Without then being separated from this concept, he is trained to develop the *role* of being a psychotherapist. (I call this the role of "foster parent" because it is time-limited, functionally artificial, and contains the imitation nurturant factors characteristic of mother, as well as the imitation of executive factors symbolized in father.) In the process of supervision—that is, being instructed, corrected, and directed as to how psychotherapy should be implemented—the trainee is precipitated into a transference setting. He sees the supervisor as a reincarnation of his mother, his father, and those many preliminary transference figures who populated his school system and the neighborhood community. Thus, the communication with the supervisor is overlaid with a quality of power, by virtue of which the trainee is encouraged (or at least tends) to regress to more dependent and infantile behaviors as a way of increasing the security his transference offers and currying favor with the supervisor.

Meantime, the supervisor (even a quite experienced one) is looking at a picture of himself in the past trying to gain understanding, competence, and the kind of security and power to make it possible to carry out the psychotherapy role effectively. This can involve either minor or major levels of co-transference, so that the supervisor becomes more tender, more childlike, less authoritative, less comforting, and more immersed in the co-transference process.

In addition to these intrapsychic and interpersonal complexities, the training situation is fraught with *context*. The context of training is very frequently a group phenomenon. The supervisor is behind a one-way mirror with a group of other trainees who watch the trainee on the hot seat, working with an individual patient, couple, or family. Hence the process of supervision is not only taking place, but simultaneously the metacommunication between the supervisor and the observers leaves the supervisor in the peculiar position of double thinking about the supervision, and double thinking about his explanations of the supervision and his explanations of the psychotherapy they are all watching. To add to the already considerable chaos is the effort of the observing supervisees to understand better and to evolve a better status. Thus the conversation with the supervisor becomes more complex as various supervisees ask questions, interrupt the process, and offer imitation supervision notes of their own. As the training continues, the supervisor is increasingly apt to take responsibility for making decisions which support, undercut, or dominate the ongoing process between the trainee and the patient. This means that the authenticity of any person up and down that hierarchical line is badly damaged and contaminated by the total context of the training situation.

Metaphorically speaking, in the therapy setting we have a child (whether there is an actual child, an adult individual, or couple or family) who is a real person and not a role. This real person is trying to be more of himself or herself by reliving dynamic life events that were or are painful and unresolved. Because this reliving is being done in an artificial situation with an imitation foster parent called the therapist, it is fraught with shadows and overlays of suspicion, hesitation, and sometimes even panic about the data that are emerging from the deeper levels of this intrapsychic world.

Endeavoring to cope with this artificial foster parent role is a trainee who has many of the problems of a young mother or a young father: insecurity, inexperience, self-doubt, fear of criticism, search for support and validation, and even reverberations from his personal life (concern about relationships in his real world, his anxieties about the past, and his fears for the future in that more powerful territory offstage).

On the other side of the mirror, then, is the third generation—the grandparent, if you will—who is taking the responsibility for teaching this trainee "parent" to raise "children" (the family or the patient) in the proper way. If you think about the metaphor of the child, the parent, and the grandparent, it becomes very clear that the process of supervision is not only loaded with transference factors, it is also loaded with a degrading inference that the therapist-in-training should not trust himself. Instead he should wait for detailed directives (since "mother knows best"), but *whatever* he does, he is open to correction, critique, and a confirmation of his assumption that he is a failure.

If the supervision becomes more tolerable, the role of the therapist as the parent is clarified and becomes workable; the role of the supervisor as the grandparent becomes more tolerable; and the context becomes accepting and less dangerous. Then what remains is the final challenge: How can the trainee learn to separate his *role training* from his own personhood? Central to the smooth unfolding of this project is the supervisor's awareness of his own personhood and his ability and willingness to separate the role from the fact of himself. This ability includes the very powerful capacity of the supervisor to restrain herself from amplifying the transference and producing a transference neurosis which then invades the trainee's personhood.

Partial solutions to this complex chess game include: (1) the therapist-in-training going into therapy for himself, preferably beginning with a family of origin and/or nuclear family interview so that his transference is related to someone other than a role-dominated supervisor; (2) the evolution of a peer-team relationship with one of the other supervisees so that he is not as tempted to stay in his transference neurosis after the supervision is over; and (3) the determined practice of co-therapy so that when he is in the role of being the foster parent, he at least is part of a team of parents. In the co-therapy setting, he is free to move from moment to moment in his therapeutic role, as he and his partner alternately assume the role of being the imitation foster parent. Thus the two of them form a team that has its own locus of power, security, and separateness from the supervisor. Together they are able to reassess their joint therapy experiences with each other.

Tricks of the Psychotherapy Trade

I am firmly convinced that the process of being a professional psychotherapist is like the problem of becoming a professional actor or actress. It takes training, extensive experience, and a peculiar ability to differentiate among *stage presence*, *stage process*, and *real life*. I have compiled a list of 36 "tricks" that I hope may be useful in your cultivation of your own professionalism.

1. The most prominent trick for me is the notion that play itself is a dialectic. The more you can play, the more you can be serious. The more you can transcend the set—transcend the language of complaints, the language of inferences, the language of options, or the language of irrelevancy—the more you are free to move into the *meta territory* of second-degree change. There is a long series of dialectics that is part of this process. There is a dialectic between craziness and sanity: The crazier you can be, the freer you are to be duplicitous, socially adapted, or sane. There is the same dialectic between belonging and individuating (sometimes called *empathy* and *separation*). The dialectic of belonging and individuating is a problem of great significance because the tendency is to try to find a truth: to individuate to the point of needing help, or to belong to the point of needing help. Individuating produces solitude and isolation. Belonging produces enslavement and social conformity to the point of self-destruction. The only answer is an increased tolerance for the agony and ecstasy of the dialectical change and for the impossibility of "coming to rest."

2. I am the only model I can share. Sharing information, identifying with the patient's pain by utilizing a fragment of my own pain, is one of the most repetitively valuable tricks. This process of sharing necessitates a disciplined competence in not becoming the patient, or in not playing the

game of "I know better" or "Follow me." The therapeutic intent of sharing is to make it easier for the patient and the family to experience their lives in the mirror that you hold to your life. It only takes a tiny fragment of your life for them to see the holographic whole as a proof of *your* wholeness and *their* wholeness.

3. Psychotherapy demands a cross-generational authority. The style of how this authority is expressed and how it is utilized is something each therapist should develop for him or herself, but it is certainly necessary to establish clear definitions of boundaries regarding time, space, and process. Authority becomes a more valuable trick and a more useful part of the psychotherapy trade if it is counterbalanced with a peculiar kind of one-down truthfulness. It is as though the therapist can be free to laugh at himself for using the authority to make it clear that this is a tongue-in-cheek artificial set; such a lighthearted attitude leaves the truth of their relationship as a joint project rather than as a delusional system on the part of the therapist which then is either accepted or rejected by the patient's capitulation to or rebellion from the authority.

4. The Chinese have a wonderful word called *mu* that means, in essence, to unask the question. "Back up. What you just said is not sayable, is not relevant, does not belong." English makes this concept very difficult to express. We need to pretend to stay rational, and this matter of *unasking a question* is not rational. It is a transcendence of the usual response to a question. *Mu* is an example of the above point (3). *Mu* is a way of expressing authority and, at the same time, transcending the artificiality of this therapeutic game—and the authority itself is a game.

5. The process of logic, the process of reason are both artificial. Communication involves the capacity to listen and take in what has been presented and then to respond to it as though the two I's were seeing and responding as whole people from separate places. Actually most communication is a peculiar quality of education, information exchange, or observational extras. It is probable that the only real communication that lasts is *meta communication*: that is, communication that is above the level of the usual give-and-take—whether it's talking about talking or talking out of one's fantasy rather than at the other person, or whether it is in the process of exposing oneself in a nonrational manner. This process, if it is functionally useful, produces a kind of slow burn, perhaps because it is bodily integrated or visually reinforced or physically reinforced. So the communication is double level. It may even be a direct denial of the communication, like the famous sign, "Don't Read This Sign."

6. One of the best tricks of psychotherapy is the evolution of a crisis, a kind of psychological orgasm that produces a "meta event," and then that meta event is in itself a kind of orgastic release. This release is probably most useful if it has this orgastic quality and is then left hanging in mid-air, with no effort to resolve it on the socially acceptable, duplicitous level of ordinary communication. First-degree change means increasing what is already there or decreasing what is already there, best illustrated in the traditional automobile metaphor of stepping on the gas or stepping on the brakes. Second-degree change is probably the only kind of change that is worthwhile; therapeutically, it is like shifting gears. It changes the dynamics of the whole system rather than just increasing or decreasing the power utilized.

7. Another excellent trick in doing psychotherapy is the gradual awareness and development of the capacity to produce confusion. Without confusion—your confusion and their confusion—there is no change. As long as what happened can be fitted into the patient's standard life experience, operational theory, or psychological programming of thought, nothing will be different. You will be adding to his information, you will be adding to his experience, but you will not produce a change that is second-degree and, therefore, useful therapeutically. Your own confusion is one of the parts of yourself that you can share most valuably. It really doesn't seem to make any difference what the confusion arises from. It is as though confusion by itself has the unique value of stimulating connections within the patient's thinking process and/or life experience. Then there is the hope that out of that stimulation of new connections will come an existential moment in which the past disappears, the future is unimportant, and the present becomes a fact rather than something that is being avoided in the usual manner.

8. One of the extra tricks that makes discipline more possible for the professional is the decision and the experience of writing. Writing is a method of trying to put the experience of living into a set of funny, uniquely feeble symbols in the hope that the symbolic experience itself can produce a new creative experience, with an extra value not present in the original experience being symbolized or used as a metaphor. It is best if the writing is done for yourself, because the process of writing for someone else involves a kind of double thinking that makes it into a non-experience. It is also best if this writing is irrational, if it contains your fantasies and your dreams, and if it becomes a vehicle for intrapsychic exposure.

9. The capacity of the therapist as a professional to move into the

irresponsible territory we call *play* is one of producing an unconscious-to-unconscious community with the patient. Many years ago I discovered accidentally a kind of professional pyknolepsy, a kind of sudden disappearance into sleep containing no fragment of tiredness and arising out of a need to become more profoundly invested in the interaction. As this went on over the years, it became possible for me to retrieve the dream of this moment and to learn from the experience of its timing and the patient's responsiveness.

I discovered, for example, that many times I would "click out" while patients were producing their first dreams. Gradually I decided this meant that I should not try to play with their dreams, that there was something secret and sacred about the dreams, and they belonged to the individuals. The important point was for them to hear themselves tell the dream rather than to have me try to utilize it for further understanding—which then would let them know about their unconscious but not change.

10. One of the tricks of being a professional is to be increasingly clear that you are not a peer with patients. It is not possible to do good professional therapy in a peer relationship. In the same sense the actor on the stage is never a peer with someone in the audience. That invisible separation is profoundly important and must be maintained by the actor and not by the audience—that is, by the therapist, not by the patient. The therapist must evolve and maintain the generation gap or there is no professional therapy, there is only education or adaptation training. Second-degree change may happen, of course, in any other setting, but we are talking about deliberate professional acting, not amateurish acting or game-playing. We're trying to find ways of forcing the therapeutic interaction to be useful, not waiting for it to become accidentally useful.

11. Sometimes tricks produce a strange backlash and you lose the relationship with the audience, with the foster child, by trying to be deliberate. Deliberateness means artificiality, and artificiality destroys professional acting. Pre-planning interviews, double thinking during the interview—each becomes a process of distancing yourself, and then the capacity to be a therapist is all but completely destroyed.

12. If you cannot confess your past in fragments, or if you cannot protect your future, then you should not expose your present. The *present* is the most delicate part of time, and it is usually avoided, but certainly it is acceptable or usable only if you can be clear that your past and your future are safe.

13. One who does professional therapy must be very careful about the

temptation for repetition. The compulsion for repetition, one of Freud's great discoveries, becomes a recital; the repetitive sharing of a memory is a recital, not an experience. Sharing *memories* is not a way of sharing *yourself*; it is merely a way of avoiding being who you are by talking about who you were, or when you were, or what you know.

14. A serious danger in being a professional therapist is the process of thinking abut what is happening and heading the family or the patient toward a "healthy state." It also means that you're out of yourself into your head. Therefore, you are distancing yourself from the relationship and have dropped out of the role of being the therapist. In short, the therapist needs to avoid all double thinking, and needs to avoid the application of techniques. Even things that have happened spontaneously before can become unreal when they are repeated or imitated. The problem is how to get the courage to wait for something to drop out of the therapist's creative person, to allow brainstorming rather than trying to think one's way out and thereby follow the patient's lead by becoming a peer or even a competitor. The waiting will eventually result in more freedom to free associate, to share fantasies, to move out of one's personhood rather than out of one's accumulated knowledge or rational thinking.

15. The therapist needs to establish himself as the representative of a team, a two-parent team. This may be done by such artificial means as recording the interview or having someone on the other side of the one-way window, but it probably is better when there is an actual physical presence. The patient discovers that the therapist really belongs to another world, that he has someone in whom he is more invested than this foster child called the patient, and that the therapeutic game of actor and audience is part of a real life that goes on behind the scenes of the professional interaction. This has the added advantage of forcing the patient to recognize that he also has a real life, a recognition that he may avoid with the hope that all of his life can be wrapped up in the interview—then he will not have to be responsible for those things which are so painful.

16. One of the most difficult tricks is to avoid the process of diagnosis. All efforts, all tendencies to define the other character by individual diagnosis or, if you will, system diagnosis are cop-outs. Men are not "cold," "warm," "tender." Women are not "dominating," "loving," "intelligent." These are merely adjectives that avoid the fact that an individual is a complex, impossible-to-define entity. The best description of this attitude is Gregory Bateson's statement in *Mind and Nature*, "I am a verb"—meaning, "You can't

pin me down." Whenever you start pinning somebody down, the person disappears and you're dealing with your own fantasy.

To define this more carefully, it is clear that the best diagnosis of a family scene can be gotten via the process of asking each member of the family to define relationships between others in the family, not including themselves: for example, ask father about the relationship between mother and son; ask mother about the relationship between father and son, or father and his mother. You never allow mother to talk about the relationship between herself and her son, herself and her husband, since once you start in that direction, you engage all the rationalizations and programmed concepts that belong to each of our delusional systems about ourselves.

17. While it is critical that the professional therapist develop the freedom to enjoy the foster parenthood and the psychological marriage with his partner, his teammate, he or she must also realize that this joy can only equal the fear or the pain of the empty nest: the recognition that foster parenthood is artificially inaugurated and must be artificially terminated. The fear that I have about therapy as a process is that the temptation to adopt patients because of your need to be a facilitator and their need to find a new parent produces a bilateral delusional system where the empty nest is intolerable and "motherhood" (parenthood) lasts forever.

18. Impotence is a painful discovery on the part of every parent who is engaged in an effort and/or struggle to help the child she brought into the world evolve in the fullest manner. I first thought of the impotence of the foster parent, the professional psychotherapist, as a ploy. The ploy was admitting it; the impotence was a fact. Once I realized that the impotence was for real, it became increasingly clear that the impotence is not an individual process but—like craziness, like suicide, like murder—*impotence is a two-person event*. It is part of the spirit of psychotherapy. The fact of the interaction produces impotence on the part not only of the therapist but also of the patient. The discovery of the impotence is itself a valuable one. The sharing of it then becomes a mutual recognition on the part of therapist and patient that they have this in common. It also becomes a *meta event* in the sense that they then have transcended their relationship and are jointly looking down on it. Preparing to deal with the meta event is fundamentally different from trying to become potent.

19. It seems as though the best way of teaching free association is by being creative. The capacity to share your free associations, your fantasies, your momentary breakout from the two-person event into an individual

moment of being produces a kind of freedom for the patient to disengage from his double thinking about how to satisfy you or how to further involve you in his struggle. One way of doing this is via play, and one way of playing is to engage in the kind of "muscular free association" involved in throwing a nerf ball or a nerf frisbee, or playing with a puzzle, or doing freehand drawing—some way in which you move out of the set of two people debating the horrors or the wonders of life across the table into one person experiencing more of himself, thus freeing the other to see and experience more of himself.

20. In *The Importance of Being Earnest* Oscar Wilde said, "Nothing is more real than nothing." *Silence* is its own communication. It is itself a meta event. It is an awakening, a freedom to transcend the social set, a freedom to transcend the need for progress, and arrive at a point of individuation within the freedom of the two-ness. The temptation to play social games, fill the silence, may be a serious problem for a therapist brought up in an urban culture where the demands are endless, rather than in a culture affording solitude, meditation, and the freedom to not think. I call that state in myself *vegetating*.

21. It is critical to upstage the scapegoat. Upstaging the family or establishing yourself in the foster parent role is important from the beginning. The secondary step is to upstage the scapegoat—to make sure that the frontispiece, the symptom, the façade, the persona that the family offers is accepted as a pure, artificial cover for the real pain that is underneath. Although I see no need to expose that pain, I think it is critical not to let family members go on with the delusion that the pain is the problem. Detumescing the scapegoat as a person is fairly simple; it is merely a matter of not listening to him, not listening to talk about him. That can be done by redirecting the conversation, moving from the language of pain and impotence that the family brings to the session, to the language of inference, innuendo, exploration. The therapist may even expose his fantasies, chuckling about how irrelevant they are to the family's real world. He or she thus detumesces the process of scapegoating by becoming the scapegoat and making this something that the family members have to fight, so that they destroy the therapist as the scapegoat, thus learning how to destroy their family member who has been scapegoated.

22. Learning how to carry out the act of being a professional therapist is frequently facilitated by the use of a one-way mirror. Then the person behind the one-way mirror becomes not a foster parent to the family in treatment but a third generation. It is as though the family is being foster-

parented by the therapist, who is being directed or facilitated in his effort to raise his children by a grandmother who tells him how she thinks it could be, should be, should have been, should not have been. Thus there enters a peculiar kind of cross-generational flip. It is said that grandmother and grandson get along because they have a common enemy. This takes place in the one-way mirror pattern, also. The grandparent behind the mirror identifies with the family and the therapist becomes their common enemy, so that they (the family and the "grandparent" behind the mirror) become a parental team, even though one of them has assumed superior authority even while pretending to be only a peer with the therapist.

23. Actually, the function of the supervisor might well be the function of a real grandmother to talk to the therapist about his or her life in the past, to come into the therapy room and discuss in front of the family a similar experience that the supervisor has had, with the inference that maybe the experience is relevant to what is now happening between this family and the foster parent. Such an approach necessitates a kind of humility on the part of the supervisor that makes him recognize that what was true for his generation may not be true or even relevant for the present generation. Behind this is the fact that the supervisor is massively responsible for the dignity and the uniqueness of the therapist. The therapist is an individual, not a victim. He has a life experience, and his capacity to participate is based on his life experience, not on his learning or the supervisor's life experience. This separation between the supervisor, with his conceptions, beliefs, and creative fantasies, and the therapist must be maintained by the supervisor. He then becomes a consultant.

24. The use of consultants is a critical factor in all psychotherapy. It is best to have a consultant join the second interview so that it is clear to the family that the therapist is not operating by himself. He is part of a team; he himself is open to challenge, correction, support; and the therapeutic role is endlessly variable, flexible, and available for change. In a very similar way, consultants can come in from the other side of this setting. The family can bring the grandparents, the siblings of the parents, the boyfriend or the girlfriend of the children. The oldtime fantasy of the analyst and the patient on the couch can be broken in infinite numbers of ways, and usually each of these brings new benefits rather than limitations.

25. Painful though it is, all the failures in psychotherapy are failures of the therapist. The patient never fails. The patient only loses by the therapist's failure. The therapist is in the role; he's enacting a part. To use the actor metaphor: the audience never fails. It is only the actors and the play

they are performing that fail. The audience, the *tabula rasa*, is an empty slate. The fact that there has been previous writing on the slate does not mean it is obstructed; it merely means that the therapist may fail to find a way to make an imprint.

26. In the operation of a professional therapist, there is a great deal of confusion regarding the qualities of responsibility and responsiveness. The therapist who is most responsive is the one who is most apt to be useful. On the other hand, he is responsible for the therapeutic hour and for being responsive in it. This responsibility is total. All the parameters that are present should be within the therapist's control and should be operating at his behest. In dramatic contrast to the therapist's arena of responsibility, and at the same time in direct conformity with it, the patient is responsible for his life, his decisions, his failure to make decisions, his ambivalence about deciding, and the effect of the ongoing decisions. He may or may not be responsive to the therapist or the therapy, but he is nevertheless responsible for his life.

27. Assuming that the therapist is organized and purposely structures a plan to make change come about, the response or the participation of the family can be called either *resistance* or *compliance*. Either of these is a problem and probably an error. Resistance merely means that the patient is beginning to accept more responsibility for himself, and is less and less willing to allow the therapist to be responsible. This is creative. On the other hand, the patient's compliance with or utilization of the things that the therapist is happy about may be proof that the therapist has become a victim of the patient's transference. The compliance is merely the preliminary replay of his childhood struggle with his own mother or father.

28. One of the most direct, honest, and powerful ploys of the therapist is expressed in the very simple statement, "I'm just here for the money." This notion can be expanded so that it becomes a way of transcending the set of "I'm weak, and you're wonderful." It makes the therapist more honest about the fact that he is a psychological prostitute. It can be balanced or modified by the fact, confessed or explicated by the therapist, that he is really doing this as a way of increasing the possibility of his own growth, his own change, his own increased integration, his own decreased pathology, his own efforts to make his life richer.

29. In the process of carrying out his professional role, the therapist must not become a *pseudo-therapist*; and he must *not* become role-fixated so that the role itself becomes artificial, an imitation role. That kind of fixation is very much like the actor who becomes fixed in the public eye, and

then in his own. Whether it is Bob Hope as a humorist or Marilyn Monroe as a sex object, such fixation mechanizes the process and destroys its depth, its power, and its authenticity. One of the ways of clarifying this problem is for the therapist artificially to switch roles, suddenly to ask for help from the patient with a sliver of his own pathology, seriously to share with the patient or with the family his anxiety about his own impotence, his own failure to change, his own hopes for or fears of the future.

30. One of the ways of sharing the "set of psychotherapy" is to raise the issue of the impasse: "Things are not going as fast as they should," "Maybe we're not making any progress," "I feel dissatisfied with myself," "My consultant didn't help or should be called in," or "You ought to bring in someone else to help with the system." This process of exposing an impasse triangulates the situation. All of a sudden, the two of you are working at a project which is outside of either of you, but is within the spirit, if you will, of the *set*.

31. A common source of panic in therapists is the possibility that something that happens in the interview could produce a dangerous result afterwards, or that something that happens in the room itself will be dangerous. It is clear that deliberate actions can break a pattern and make a difference. For instance, if the husband and wife get into a physical fight, the change that brings this to an end is very simple: The therapist walks out. If the therapist walks out of the hour without comment, all of a sudden the dynamics of change and the dynamics of the war are completely altered because the therapist as audience has left.

32. The fear that any professional therapist has that the patient will commit suicide, commit murder, or go crazy is profoundly significant and should never be viewed as "make-believe." However, such threats can be handled by facing the fact that any of these major events is a two-person event. Your patient will not commit suicide unless somebody in his world wants him dead. I assume that "somebody" is ordinarily a member of the family and/or the possible transference figure that the therapist represents. I do not think anybody who has gone through training and become a professional therapist would still carry this kind of pathology. So I do not expect the patient to be in danger of committing suicide while working with a therapist who cares and who is willing to expose his caring to a partner, a consultant.

33. The question of what you're working toward is probably most clearly understood if you assume that death is the only universal symptom. The one thing we have in common besides the fact of our birth is the prevailing fact of our death, so that death becomes one, if not the only,

ultimate move the therapist can make towards demanding and sharing responsiveness. This death can be in the frame of memory or anxiety about imminent death of self or some other person who symbolically represents self or, in fact, the denial of any experience with or concerns with the death of oneself or any significant other. The simple reactivation of the family's grief over a member's death quickly leads to: Who will die next? What will happen to the family then? Who thought of suicide recently? Has anyone made plans?

34. To precipitate change, it seems essential that the therapist-patient team push stress beyond the clinical tolerance of the patient. Then, the patient makes whatever moves are necessary to bring about change. But as long as the symptoms or source of stress are being relieved or modified or lessened by the efforts of the therapist, it is probable that change will not take place; the patient is enjoying the relief from stress rather than demanding more of himself. You can only run faster if you're being chased by a bull!

35. It is critical for the therapist to recognize that craziness is where life is. Life is not in social adaptation. Life is not in the therapeutic hour. Life is not in any interpersonal set. Life is in the expression of one's whole self; it is the fact of internalized individuation of personal, creative upfrontness. It is in the denial of slavery to rationality, slavery to conformity, the slavery of being culture-bound, time-bound, space-bound or anxiety-bound.

36. The last trick of the trade is the importance of disregarding *progress*. As long as the therapist is intent on making progress, he will contaminate the process of helping the patient change and instead play the game of being increasingly delusional about himself. Many parents never discover that they're not making their child progress, and that in trying to make their child progress they destroy the process of contributing to him or her making *his or her own* progress. The process of doing therapy is the ultimate effort of the professional therapist to become an actor, not just to *do* an act; to become fully invested in the role with more and more of his own creative power, his own freedom to live out the predetermined effort to be a good foster parent, not an adoptive parent or delusional change agent.

V
On Being a Therapist

Talking the Truth
in a Three-Ring Circus

I would like to see if I can be of some help in your making sure that you don't get your throat cut by your own stupidity. I think the most important aspect of becoming a therapist is that you learn how to be insulting, mean, aloof, distant, professional, and that you try hard to get over being amateur. That is a lifetime problem for all of us, including me. For 50 years I have been trying to learn how to be a professional—that is, to not be doing it for the love of it.

A person who is an amateur is a pornographer. There's a wonderful story about the U.S. senator who went to Vietnam because he heard they were having a problem with pornography. He asked this mountaineer soldier if he had any pornography and the mountaineer soldier replied, "I don't even have a pornograph."

I've been spending 50 years trying to get over being a pornographer, an amateur, someone who goes into the work for the sake of augmenting or titillating my own morbid curiosity, my own delusion of grandeur that I can cure anything that shows up in my office. I know the solution, I know the answer to everything, and I'll be glad to tell you—and if you don't make it, that's *your* problem.

I am in favor of trying to teach you how to be professional, even if I haven't been able to make it myself. One of the ways of learning to be professional is to be sure that you never buy the first presentation, and that you assume that the biggest problem of being a therapist is the politics of the group. In individual therapy you may not have to worry about politics because it is weakened and even cancelled by transference. In a family scene, you do not have a transference because all the family members are transferred to one another: he is trying to make his wife like his mother; he is trying to make believe he can be better than and different from his father; and the same thing on the wife's side. So all of the transference problems that were such a horror for poor old Freud and his friends are very different when you deal with families. You have to solve the political problem, and the first thing you need to know about the political problem is that nobody talks the truth. Nobody has any interest in saying what is really going on.

Let me tell you a crazy story. I was working at the Philadelphia Child Guidance Clinic a few years ago as "pest" after Minuchin left. I was trying to get a clinical demonstration case, and the administrator said, "Oh, we have a social worker who would like to have you see the family with schizophrenics." I said, "Fine, why don't you have her call me?" (I was in Madison, Wisconsin.) So the social worker called up and I said, "Are there other therapists involved?" and she said, "I don't know." I said, "Well, why don't you find out? I don't want to make believe I'm the first therapist." She called me back and said, "Oh, yes, I had no idea that this schizophrenic has had a therapist for years." I said, "Well, why don't you tell the therapist that you think the family ought to have family therapy, and you've asked me if I'll do it, and I had said I would be glad to but I needed to have give-and-take with the therapist to see what he wants?"

We went back and forth with about five telephone calls. It turned out this schizophrenic was in a hospital (I didn't find that out until the third telephone call) and had been there for 18 months; this was her fourth or fifth admission to the hospital; she had a therapist, she had a drug physician in the hospital, and she had her regular analyst who came to visit her every once in a while; her father had a therapist; her mother had a therapist. And the social worker didn't know about any of this! I said, "Why don't you get all these people together for the first interview and I'll be glad to go on with the family." Of course, none of them could make it because it was too expensive, they would have to take time away from their offices, they didn't want to be exposed, they didn't want to meet the other analysts of the other family members.

When I couldn't get the schizophrenic family in Philly I said, "Why don't we just have the next family that comes into the clinic, and we'll set that one up." The secretary who does all the admissions took a telephone call from a woman who had a serious problem with her three-year-old child: He wee-weed behind the TV set, and the family didn't like this. I don't know, maybe it didn't smell good, or there was a short circuit in the

TV. I asked if I could call and the secretary said, "Sure, if you want to. I was just going to make an appointment." I said, "Well, I better call first."

I called and said, "Would you please bring everybody you can find." So they all arrived: father, mother, the three-year-old, a one-year-old, a six-year-old. I endured 20 minutes of history-taking and then said, "I can't stand any more. You're going to have to go away and come back next week, and then I'll have my wife for co-therapist because your problems are too big for me to tolerate by myself, and I'm so sorry."

It turned out the one-year-old had hydrocephalus, with a swollen head, and was under the care of a neurologist. The six-year-old looked pretty good. Father had hyperventilation syndrome; that is, he would get so short of breath that he would have to stop and sit for a half-hour four times a day. In fact, he had such a severe case of this hyperventilation syndrome that for the past three years, he had gone into the hospital about once a week for serious injections, oxygen, and all such treatments.

I said, "How about your father?" and he said, "Oh, my father died." I said, "How did that happen?" and he said, "Well, he had a coronary attack and I did mouth-to-mouth resuscitation, but he died."

How to get hyperventilation syndrome in a hurry! I said, "Well, how about your mother?" and he said, "Well, my mother is all right, except she has become an alcoholic since my father died." I said, "Well, who else is alcoholic?" He said, "Well, I was an alcoholic until four years ago, but I haven't had a drop since my father died. But ever since my father died, my mother has become alcoholic."

By that time I couldn't stand any more. The next time they came back I said, "I need more people. I want both of your fathers and mothers, and any brothers and sisters," and he said, "Oh, I've got eight brothers and sisters." I said, "Wonderful, bring them all and the spouses and the babies." He said, "Well, I can't do that. I'm just on the verge of writing a letter to all of them saying I will never speak to them again." I said, "What happened?" and he said, "Well, every time mother gets drunk, she calls up all the sisters and brothers and tells them what a terrible thing the other sisters did to her. They are all beginning to blame me because I was the last one who left home, although now my older brother has come back home with his girlfriend and her two babies, and they are using up all of my mother's relief money and insurance money to support themselves, and they are stealing it from my mother."

Then it turned out that in this father's family the mother was always stealing money from the father. Every morning on the way to work, father would walk out from the house and one of the children would go with him and Daddy would say, "Now listen, you don't have to steal money from my pocket. I'll be glad to give you the money." They had never told him that his wife was doing the stealing. These children are now all grownup, married, and have children.

The problem? The baby wee-weed behind the TV set!

Muriel and I conducted 10 interviews with this family, which gradually increased in number, culminating with the arrival of the alcoholic mother who was very angry because all these children she had raised and slaved for weren't being nice to her. They had decided, the gang of them, to go to the barkeeper, whom they all knew (apparently everybody in the family had been a drunk, and the barkeeper was their best friend), and tell him that if he didn't stop selling whiskey to their mother, they would never come back to drink in his bar again. The mother broke down and cried, and Muriel cuddled her.

The final interview was an Irish fight. Having been raised up in the Adirondacks of New York state, in a kind of New England setting, it was just devastating for me to see these eight adult sisters and brothers fighting at the same time: a hundred decibels blasting in seven different directions. I just sat there with my mouth open. My mother and father had always fought in silence behind the bedroom door, I suppose, and I never heard them. But this is the politics of families, and you should assume that there is no such thing as a single-symptom family, and there is no such thing as an honest presentation. These particular people were very nice people. I was very fond of them, but the utter dishonesty of saying that the problem was with the three-year-old who wee-weed behind the TV set!

The only time you have any power is when you take the initiative of calling the family members liars about the original symptom. You start out by trying to find out some more about what is really going on. If I had accepted the original symptom of the social worker who wanted her schizophrenic patient to be in family therapy, I would have had three therapists, a hospital, and a father and mother all mad at me for trying to do something they obviously hadn't been able to do. This therapeutic project had been going on for 10 years, and the social worker naïvely assumed that she could start something cooking, as though it were the beginning. I can't tell you how many times I've had that experience!

I did a workshop in Toronto not too long ago. My demonstration family involved a stepbrother who had sexually invaded his new little stepsister. The police had arrested the stepbrother and put him in a prison.

The father and mother were in therapy, so I started with the usual problem: Who else is involved? Who saw the family first? Who knew about the symptom first? I ended up having six professional helpers who had been working with this family in various roles for the last seven years. The mother and her first husband had been going to a therapist; the father and his first wife had been going to another therapist when the new marriage took place; the new couple with their two children from each of the previous marriages were going to another therapist; and the court had appointed a social worker as the protective agent for the children who were at home once this naughty boy had invaded his little stepsister, who happened to live in the same bedroom.

I got all these mental health workers into the conference and made them tell their stories while the family members sat and listened. It was so clear that three of the six mental health workers were still competing with each other to see who was going to be the curative agent. The one woman who was representing the court was indignant about what the others were not getting from their therapists; and the one who was being the therapist to the boy in prison was indignant because they would not let this boy come out to go to interviews with the family. By the time I had gotten through all these stories, it was perfectly obvious to me that if all the mental health workers would quit, the family probably could make it. I suggested as much, and the court worker agreed. It was only four more weeks before this 17-year-old boy was to be released, and I think probably that is what happened. All of us got out of the way, and the family had a chance to live.

When somebody phones you and says, "Well, I have a problem. Could you help me?" you have to be careful because the politics may screw up everything, and what you get depends upon your courage. "I've had three previous wives, numerous past homosexual relationships and a current homosexual partner." It is amazing, all you have to do is ask! You say offhandedly, "By the way, is there any incest in the family?" and Dad says, "Well, yes, I wasn't going to mention it but . . . " It is *your* courage, and you can only be that courageous in the beginning. We are, every single one of us, supermoms, and if we didn't think we were magic supermoms, we would find another way to earn a living.

I had been doing telephone group supervision for about a year with three wonderful social workers from the country in Minnesota. I'd never seen these people—they were from the kind of rural community that has one doctor, one probation worker, a policeman, and I don't know, maybe the village postmaster. I finally went to meet them and, to my surprise, in came the three social workers, all high as kites. They had just finished three weeks of training in being auctioneers of farm machinery. They were going to do psychotherapy *one-half day a week* and sell farm machinery the rest of the week! So if, like these social workers, you can think of another job where you don't have to be super-mommy, I suggest you apply for it!

That is why I've always liked working with a co-therapist. There is a mysterious thing about co-therapy: there are two people there, just like there are two people raising a child. It is bad enough to raise a child with two people—I tell you, we tried six! It is impossible, I think, to raise a child by yourself because it automatically becomes cross-generational psychological incest. There is a mother and a child making believe that they are not only mother and child, they are also partners and peers. You know, she's a child and he's a grownup, and they go back and forth, like that famous English story about halfway up the stairs: On the stairs where I sit, there is no other stair just like it. I'm not in the nursery and I'm not in the town, and sometimes the things in my head go round and round, and I think I'm not anywhere, I'm somewhere else instead.

I think that's what happens in psychotherapy when you function all by yourself as an artificial—could I say—*prostitute.* You're faking it. It's not real love; it's an artificial, turned-on, adjudicated professional substitute for intimacy and for human relationship. You are the one who is to blame for success or failure. They have come with all they have. It may not be much, but they are coming with their whole selves. However, you are not there with your whole self. A piece of you is home with your spouse, part of you is with your own therapist, part is with your kids, part of you is at the park with your dog. There are all sorts of other places where you are, so you need to be sure that you are more paranoid than your clients. You need to be more suspicious of yourself, of them, of the possibilities of your changing a big system by your own little input. Now, some politicians think they are going to change the whole world by themselves. I hope nobody calls and asks me for help with that project. I'll just say, "I'm sorry, I'm dying."

Someone has asked me to talk more about single-parent families, since a very high proportion of women are now bringing up children alone. I am very glad to talk about that issue. I think it is tremendously sad that something like 93% of the single-parent families are headed by women. I think that's a horrible thing. I think it's horrible about men, and I'll tell you about men. I think they're utterly hopeless and will always be hopeless. They fall in love with things and never discover people until they're very old, and that's what we're stuck with. I think it's Darwinian. It is evolutionary history that the women who produced the next generation were the ones who guarded the caves and the children, and the men who produced the next generation were the ones who killed the wild animals and screwed everybody they could find. That's gone on for a hundred million generations, and we're suffering with one of the extrapolations of the same process.

When God gets tired and retires and turns over the Office to me, I'm going to arrange for the man to have the second baby. I think that would make things tremendously different. What I don't understand is why women who are functioning as single parents tend to live with just the child. Why not with another woman and her children? Why not a mother and her mother and the children? Or, what I like to guess would be great fun, why not a mother and her mother-in-law and the children? This is another generalization. For the past 20 years I have forced myself into seeing only families, and they have gradually twisted me into being a systems thinker. I take no credit for it—it was over my own dead body! But I've learned that all families are exactly the same, and that's a sad thing, but if you apply everything you know about any family to every family you see (don't expect them to agree—that's not the issue), then you're doing what I call *meta-therapy*. You're doing therapy to the family members' unconscious minds—not to their fantasies or their rationalizations or their sociopathy. You have to deal with the real family.

I think the answer to this issue is that the mother is in love with her child. I think that's why the husband leaves. The mother marries a husband thinking she can get another person who loves the way she loves, but there isn't any such thing except with another woman or a mother. What she gets is a feeble substitute and that goes sour as soon as the baby arrives, whereupon she discovers what real love is. The only unconditional positive regard in the world occurs during the first nine months after birth. Then the baby begins to play peek-a-boo, and from then on, we all get more and more sociopathic. The mother is discovering this new love, this profound biopsychosocial love with her baby, and the husband is completely outside. To compensate, maybe he falls in love with his tractor, or his Mercedes, or his psychiatric theories, or another woman. Such diversion will invariably happen unless the mother has the kind of power to hold her husband close through it all.

Let me see if I can say this more personally. I was talking on a radio program once and the interviewer asked, "How can you talk about divorce when you've been married 46 years and you've never even been divorced?" I heard myself say, "Well, I've been divorced five times but it was always from the same woman." Two days later, it got through my thick skull: after the sixth baby, I didn't get a divorce. I had felt rejected with the other five babies. When my wife turned toward the new baby, I had turned to psychiatric theories, residents, medical students, who the hell ever. But with the sixth birth, I had been around long enough—from 1937 to 1955—and I was able for the first time to stay in the intimacy, in the partnership, throughout her pregnancy and her affair with this intrauterine other.

I suppose there will come a time when men will "get it together" and discover that the kind of mother love they're looking for when they sleep with a woman isn't going to be any better with strange flesh. Gradually, if they have guts enough, if they can stick around long enough, they may get to be human beings instead of fighters and theoreticians.

I did a workshop in Minneapolis entitled "Men are Hopeless." I had 400 people: half women, half men. I spent the entire day talking about how hopeless men were, and you know what happened? Nothing. I had all sorts of applause and consternation and only one letter from one woman who mildly protested that she didn't agree. I had no letter from any man, and I had no riposte from any man in the audience during the day. You know, it was a horrible experience. I thought I was just theorizing, but it turned out I was right!

What is a Psychotherapist?

I assume that people choose their way of life, their professions, out of the quality of their psychological learning. This learning most often comes in the form of the hypnosis of the early family life, which restricts and structures one's orientation to life in the adult nuclear family, life in the family of the community, or the family of nations, or the family of friendships. As a psychiatrist I am convinced that all psychiatrists go into this field because of our preoccupation and concern with our own craziness and our hopes to get past that craziness so that we won't self-destruct. You see, craziness tends to include stupidity; in our efforts to find the infantile nurturing that craziness seeks, we invariably expose ourselves to people who are dangerously opposed to mothering in a primitive sense. In our grand stupidity, we make serious trouble for ourselves, and may even end up locked in a psychiatric hospital where the food is terrible!

The person who goes through the process of becoming a psychotherapist ordinarily does so out of two functional character evolutions. One is the effort to retaliate against what was viewed as a poor childhood with bad parenting. Then, in an effort to avoid the panic of retaliation, the person flips over into deciding to *cure* mother and father of their bad parenting qualities (or a sibling or other relative of the family). In the midst of this internally evolving fantasy program of self-hypnosis, the person becomes panicked again about the danger or the possible failure of this effort. He or she then seizes the opportunity of carrying out the same process with people who become transference objects in real life — a friend, for example, who now becomes a psychological teammate.

As this psychological process progresses, it ordinarily involves a growing preoccupation with the pathology of other people as it relates or corresponds to mother's and father's perceived pathology. The process can evolve still further into a kind of *psychological pornography*: a preoccupation with the classic kind of "dirty stories," or a treasuring and symbolic reinterpretation of real-life episodes, tragedies, failures, distortions, and so forth. These run the gamut of sexual scatological and criminal stories.

With enough opportunities or with a lucky break, the individual may move into nonprofessional psychotherapy. Here, he or she shares the parts of himself or herself that are not sociologically or psychologically tolerable in the public arena with a treasured transference object—a boyfriend, girlfriend, or support group (such as group therapy or Alcoholics Anonymous).

If all goes well, he or she may move from the experiment of nonprofessional psychotherapy into training for professional psychotherapy. This produces a peculiar, paradoxical situation in which the person is both a child and a professional foster parent—an acknowledged imitation parent. The patient is paying and is thus parent to the therapist; meanwhile, the therapist is imitating the parental role of being "in charge," being of superior status, possessing the competence and wisdom. If this therapist-to-be is fortunate, the professional psychotherapy moves him one step further and he becomes himself an amateur therapist—frequently an imitation of his own therapist, and in the process of training develops secondary transference objects (imitations of his trainer, supervisor, or a model of professionalism in his training situation).

His original move into becoming a professional therapist is usually dominated by a kind of dedicated amateurish effort to cure this introjected parent that he has been carrying in each patient he sees (or some patients he sees), and to handle his own co-transference to the patient whom he regards internally as his mother or father. This, then, makes it very difficult for him to ever terminate the therapy with this patient, because it is never quite as successful as he wants it to be. Or, if he does end therapy with this transference object that he has been trying to straighten out, he will be frightened at facing the next problem of straightening out his *real* mother and father. Better he should work at this imitation, this transference object, than be returned to that effort which he has been carrying on undercover for years without success.

In the profession of psychotherapy, this process of being a dedicated amateur becomes the basis for burnout. Burnout triggers one's technical retreat from intimacy into mechanistic manipulations, which produce counter-manipulations on the part of the patients. Furthermore, there is the tendency to become a victim of one's own delusion system. In the process of becoming a dedicated amateur to professional helpfulness, it is as though one were adopting for life any person who comes for help. Adopting people who need help is very similar in its long-term results to the process of motherhood: The therapist is so important in the beginning, and the satisfaction is so great, that he/she is tempted to assume that the infantile need of the patient will always be there, awaiting further solutions via better mothering.

The professional psychotherapist is one who recognizes his limitations and sets the situation in such a way that he can be most effective. He also separates very carefully the time, place, and method of his *being a therapist* from the fact of his *being a person* and having a life, not just a job. In fact, he moves from being a mothering person who tends to adopt everyone who is in need, to being a foster parent who recognizes the limitations of the relationship, both time-wise and by virtue of the pragmatic concerns that circumscribe foster parenthood.

Becoming a Psychological Streetwalker

In the process of becoming a professional, the therapist moves up the ladder from knowing *about* therapy to knowing *how to do* therapy (that is, the technical aspects of it); finally, if he's fortunate—or a series of patients pushes him into further integration and further professionalism—he moves into being a therapist. Being a therapist is akin to becoming a professional psychological streetwalker: a person who is openly offering to be an imitation parent, to accept the transference, to offer his imitation parenthood functions for money. The therapist is faced with still another problem at this point: how to keep from flipping back into the amateur status of doing therapy because he loves it, of doing therapy as an imitation of the problem he is still failing to solve—namely, curing his own parents.

There is one additional benefit to the professional function of therapist. This is the joint contract that both therapist and client know is artificial in the same sense that the sexual prostitute offers her body with the recognition that this imitation of love has no connection with real love. Although acknowledged, this differentiation is frequently concealed in the sexual territory, just as it is in the territory of psychological, professional contract establishment.

Intertwined with this evolving professional role set and the recognition that the therapist is an imitation or foster parent to help the patient become more and more of who he is, the therapist gets feedback that pushes his own integration, pushes his own effort to be more and more of a whole person behind his effort to be more and more of an adequate foster parent or transference object. However, the professionalism becomes further confused by the recognition that the therapist will be faced with the empty nest phenomenon. Inevitably, the patient, once he has been successfully helped to move towards adulthood, leaves home, leaves the psychological imitation of life, and moves into real life. The therapist is left with a vacuum in his imitation world. At this point he needs to go back into therapy for himself to try to clarify the separation between imitation therapist role and real-life personhood.

If the therapist has been fortunate, or determined, or had enough growth in his own years of working at this trade, he has developed a real life which transcends the role function of his professional life, so that the empty nest is recognized as painful but necessary. He tolerates the empty nest by confining his role function with all of its gains and transcending the role in his own beingness, his own personhood: in the very real loving of his real life, his real wife, his parents, his children and, hopefully, those in his friendship network. As this separation between role work and real life becomes increasingly clear, he shares more of the professional component with the patient. They are constantly aware that the specified place, time, and relationship of the therapeutic setting is not a real relationship but a *role* on the therapist's part. It does not correct the patient's relationship to his life, but it helps him get the courage within this microcasm of real life to start the struggle of straightening out his relationship to his real world.

Being Real and Losing Your Temper

The therapist is in the peculiar position of evolving a structured role, an imitation of wisdom, an imitation of being willing to fight the culture-bound rules of social interaction in a special setting with a special purpose. Given all that, he may then make his biggest contribution *by flipping out of his role and facing the fact that this was a person-to-person relationship for that moment, not just a person-to-role relationship*. I would like to offer two illustrations of this idea.

The first illustration is from a newspaper account of a policeman who discovered a man on a high bridge, ready for a jump that would mean his death. From the ground the policeman tried to talk the man down. In an effort to carry out his role of saving the man's life, the policeman began describing the suffering other people would live through—his parents, his nuclear family, his friends, and so forth. But to each of these the individual on the bridge responded with a sneer and a snort of denial. Suddenly the policeman moved out of his role, lost his temper, pulled his gun and said, "If you jump, I'll shoot you!" The shock of this statement shattered the man's rationalized decision to kill himself, and he came down off the bridge safely. This is probably the best example of a symbolic experience, or even of psychotherapy itself.

I should like to offer another example of a similar kind. Many, many years ago I worked with a 35-year-old schizophrenic who had been in and out of mental hospitals for years, had had numerous series of electroconvulsive shock treatments, and who was still very psychotic. Our relationship was structured on a once-a-week basis. Gradually, through many episodes of returning to her psychosis and many episodes of the interpersonal struggle that is psychotherapy, she became much improved. But whenever any episode of stress in her real life reappeared, she would become suicidal. After two or three years of professional relationship to me, she suddenly became very suicidal. At this point I lost my temper and told her, "If you commit suicide, I'll jump up and down on your grave and curse you!"

My words were quite shocking to her.

In subsequent years, when she had gone back into her real life, we had occasional social contacts. She explained that this had been her most powerful and therapeutic experience; it had become a kind of kernel around which she had built a capacity to tolerate the stress of her still unsatisfactory but at least valued life.

Developing Unnatural Roles

Since the therapist, like any other actor, has certain natural aptitudes, he will fashion his ordinary beginnings in psychotherapy in those roles that are natural to him. As I mentioned, the novice therapist first *learns about* psychotherapy, then *learns how to do* psychotherapy, and then, if all goes well, moves to the next step of *becoming* a psychotherapist. This means learning to adapt to various roles, depending upon the situation and the opportunities and responsibilities with which he is faced. As this process evolves, it is important to recognize that there are some roles that are not natural to a psychotherapist; there are some roles that he finds more difficult.

Usually the role of comforter, supporter, and foster mother are fairly natural and come rather easily. However, the problem of how to protect yourself from being an overprotective mother is more difficult. This is not unlike the process of raising one's own children. Comforting, feeding, and playing come rather naturally to most mothers. But as the child grows, it is increasingly difficult to learn how to utilize authority: how to make it clear that the child has rights, but that the mother also has rights; how to cultivate the child's independence and, at the same time, her own independence. Learning how to back away is frequently more difficult than learning how to join.

It would be wise for every mother to have the experience of working with children not her own before she has her own children. She thus can learn that the process of responding both to the child's needs and to her own rights, needs, and satisfactions is extremely difficult. Learning about this delicate balance with your own child is even more difficult. Usually the grandmother and the mother-in-law are not much help, and the pediatrician is not close enough or intimate enough to be a good supervisor.

In the process of psychotherapy it is possible to learn how to adapt to the different roles required by different patients and different situational stresses. The supervisor is usually considered to be a good teacher. Actually, I disagree. The usual supervisor knows what he thinks is the right way and what methods are natural to him, and tries to get the trainee to learn his special patterns and techniques. This creates a difficulty because the trainee then becomes a better and better imitator and less and less himself. Perhaps the best learning comes from doing psychotherapy with a peer, because the freedom to critique each other's work and the freedom to be creatively different in the presence of a peer is easily available. Feedback is then natural rather than artificially intellectual.

My own experience in learning how to handle my natural aggression and how to protect myself from the tendency to be overly protective and overly supportive was greatly facilitated by taking on difficult cases with a peer. Working in this kind of team relationship allows you the freedom to express your creativity, as well as your pathological impulses, with the recognition that the peer co-therapist is a protection for the patient. Thus, the therapeutic experience is a *learning by doing* rather than a learning by being taught. The panic of exposing your own pathology, your own distortions is also relieved and becomes tolerable.

When to be the Therapist

When should the therapist intervene in couples therapy or family therapy? First, if we accept Minuchin's concept that one of the things that happens when the anxiety gets too great in the dyad is that the couple triangulates a third person, then the therapy-hour fight between husband and wife or parents and children should be allowed to go its own route until some move is made to turn to the therapist. Thus the therapist can be the person who relieves the anxiety to the degree to which he thinks it is advisable, and he can also be the person who is in control of the amount of anxiety tolerated.

Secondly, the psychotherapist should be available to critique the interaction among the family members after the anxiety has settled down and the individuals have declared their separateness. He can then help them reassert their unity.

A third function of the therapist is to be the anesthetist who helps the patient (whether individual or family) tolerate the ambiguity of we-ness or separateness, or the vacillation from one to the other. The patient can then emerge as dependent child of the therapy relationship, or as stooge to the relationship, or as an individual within the relationship, or as an individual in profound and painful isolation, or as any combination of these sets.

The Parentified Patient

One solution for the inevitable ambivalence and insecurity the new parent feels as the child begins to grow and becomes more and more a separate person is to "parentify" the child. Have the child share in the decision-making; even encourage the child to take responsibility for the decisions. Experience the joy of making your child into your mother, of using your child as a security blanket. Enjoy the satisfactions, the relaxation, the freedom of not having to face the panic of being responsible for your child's growth and for the entire living process within the family.

One of the best examples of this process is a 10-year-old boy whose father was a cross-country truckdriver and only came home every week or two for a weekend. The son would say to his mother: "I'm bored, I can't think of anything to do, and I'm unhappy at being bored." The mother developed an increasing insecurity about her son's complaint. She got him ice cream. She brought him candy. She shared the TV programs that he wanted. She took him to movies. She took him out to dinner. Yet the more she tried to alleviate his boredom, the more bored he became! He had found the secret for becoming parent to his own parent, and he was wielding his power with a completely unconscious glee, with a completely unconscious sense of satisfaction. He really was bored. He really didn't get over the boredom when mother did all those things she could think of to try to make him happy. But mother became more and more insecure, more and more infantile, more and more his little girl.

A similar problem arises for inexperienced, insecure, ambivalent therapists. How do you prevent failure? How do you make the hour enjoyable? How do you make the patient feel better? How do you become more valuable to the patient who is paying you money for something you feel so insecure about? One way is to ask the patient for an answer to the issues, to ask for strokes, to ask for reassurance.

"Was that helpful? Did that make you feel better? What else can I do to make you feel better? Did I do something wrong? Are we making any progress? Should I have done this differently?"

What is the therapist's role as foster parent? How does the role evolve as an ongoing process? How do you differentiate the role of the foster parent during the first interview, after the first month, with the first change in relationship? It must be clear that the role of foster parent gives the patient lots of rights: the right to withhold, the right to secrets, the right to be angry, the right to confess, the right to complain, the right to be a brat, the right to be boring, the right to delay, the right to leave therapy, and the right to return. But the therapist as foster parent does not give the patient the right to control. To try to change the first appointment contract or the evolving contract is the patient's right, but *the capacity to control it is not acceptable*. The patient should not be the parent to the therapist. The patient should not be the therapist's security blanket. That would make the patient a parent to his own foster parent. He would become, as it were, his own grandparent.

The traditional view of *progress* is a mirage. *Process*, on the other hand, is the mandate to be all of oneself. What is the process? The process is to re-empower the patient: to give him back the power that belongs to him and that he somehow lost, frittered away, doesn't believe in or has turned his back on; to re-empower him to survive and to *live*, to be creative in spite of his pain and in spite of his impotence. The process is to help him evolve an "I position"—a personhood, a presence with form, with style, with structure, with integrity. It is the capacity to revel in *self*ness and in the freedom from the need for parenting, to revel in freedom from guilt and psychological indebtedness to the therapist.

This is the *process*, and any move away from it toward worrying or preoccupation or concern with progress is playing the game of following the mirage. *The ending is not progress; the ending is finishing the process.* The patient then will go on with the progress in his or her own time and way, and for the *self*-satisfaction.

The Therapist as Time and Place

One of the most painful experiences in being a psychotherapist is the moment of discovery that one has been displaced from being needed and relegated to the stage of being a time and a place. The importance of this time and place state is best highlighted by the fact that Carl Rogers created an entire therapeutic model around the importance of isolation in psychotherapy and the importance of the individual therapist not being triangulated. In our more modern understanding of psychotherapy it becomes clear that the therapist must be triangulated in one moment and, in the next moment, be a separate individual free of the triangulation. These two modes make possible the manipulation of the transference and the therapist's usefulness to the patient, whether individual or family.

Part of the problem with entering the therapeutic play-ring is the delusion of grandeur that is offered by the patient out of his or her need. The therapist is made into a god, taken to be omnipotent and omniscient. It is also assumed that the patient is the center of the therapist's world, just as the therapist becomes the center of the patient's world. If the therapist is seduced into this delusion of grandeur, therapy becomes useless.

The alternative decision to move in and be both useful and separate is much more precarious and difficult to maintain. One of the ways of accomplishing this is to expose the fact of the therapist's own impotence. It is really a way of learning to be more honest. If you try the impotence ploy, you may find how wonderfully it worked for Gandhi. But you must be careful not to look at the time, and you must be careful not to think, because the flash of blue light may precipitate muscular tension or diarrhea in you, the therapist. If you should get double vision, you may see yourself in reality and discover that you really are impotent. Actually, *the only person who can live the patient's life is the patient.*

When Not To Share Yourself With A Patient

In developing an existential position as a therapist, it is important to share yourself. But there are limitations, which I would like to list:

1. Do not share yourself directly with new patients when you are really not a psychotherapist but a psychiatrist or a psychologist.
2. Do not share major personal problems, only sliver problems, bits of pathology, bits of your own eccentricity, bits of your own craziness; your free associations, your fantasies, your psychosomatic symptoms (particularly the ones that happen in the middle of the interview).
3. Do not share new personal problems, since they probably have an affect load which would burden the patient, who is already struggling with his own effect.
4. Do not share parts of yourself when your need for help with them is dominant. To do so is to flip the therapy alliance so that, in essence, the patient is warned "to be good to Mama" because she's very upset.
5. When there is no other help for the therapist that is available, or when the therapist has not had therapy, the intimacy of the therapeutic relationship makes it tempting to use the patients for the therapist's growth process. However, the use of openness and requests for direct feedback should be intended to encourage the patient, not make him the therapist.
6. Do not expose your own family struggles. If the patient looks like your wife, say instead that the patient angers you because she looks like somebody who is important to you and with whom you are in conflict. It is also important that you not burden your spouse or your children with transference issues. Since they are not aware of the input, they should not have to handle the output!

Where full exposure is not appropriate, feasible, or desirable, it is possible to allude to the situation. You can say, for example:

"I'm sorry I'm not as alive this morning as I would like to be. I had to stay up all night with my sick baby."

"I'm sorry I'm not so adequate this morning. I have a hangover from a big party last night."

"I'm sorry I may seem strange to you—I'm in the midst of a personal struggle which is unrelated to us but which captures part of my interest."

"I'm sorry, you will have to give me five minutes of recovery time—I just got out of a loaded situation in the previous interview, and I haven't gotten it out of my hair yet."

Any of these indirect references gives the patient a sense that he is not fully responsible for your current existential state and allows him to recalibrate his own response to you in relation to the fact that you are not a steady-state instrument. These indirect references are similar to statements of where you are "at" or where you want to be, such as:

"I'm sorry I don't respond openly to you, but I haven't gotten to like you yet."

"You still feel like a stranger to me."

"I'm still a psychiatrist and don't feel like I'm your psychotherapist yet."

"You make me feel so much of my masculinity that it's hard for me to feel like your physician."

Sharing Your Body Experiences

Traditionally psychiatry has been concerned with the therapist's inner life on several levels. The most obvious one is his intellectual understanding of what is being experienced in the patient and what is being experienced between them. The presumption is that if the therapist can formulate in his head the dynamics that are operative, this formulation will be constructive in his planned interpretations. In later years it has become more and more acceptable for the therapist to share with the patient his free associations, his fantasies, his dream-like experiences during the interview, and to talk in considerable detail about his own personal experience of the relationship as it is unfolding in the here-and-now. With the increasing use of co-therapy and the arrival of the consultant in the therapeutic relationship, it has become more acceptable to keep a blueprint of what is operating, available on almost any level.

Unique to a very limited group of therapists, however, is the freedom to communicate with the patient by way of the therapist's body experiences. There is a surprising relevance in the therapist's gut ache, tingling in one side of his face or one side of his body, sneezing, impulse to urinate, even as with one of my colleagues, the movement of his scrotum—all are valid bits of communication usually not shared with the patient. Yet we expect the patient to move to a deeper level of his own personhood even though *we* stay on an intellectual left-brain monotone.

The process of sharing body experiences is very similar in quality to sharing the therapist's free associations and dreams during the interview, and many times results in remarkable responses from the patient. Often, the beginning of this kind of sharing on an organic body-symptom level is followed by free associations or insightful secondary movements. For example, yesterday morning a resident and I were seeing a woman who is a graduate student in physical chemistry. In the middle of the interview I began to get acid stomach. I shared this development with her and immediately recalled that part of my over-identification with her was connected to the fact that in my two years at Oak Ridge I had probably seen several hundred similar people involved in nuclear physics. Had I not consciously experienced my physical symptom, I probably would not have identified her with these other people and thus realized how quickly my transference to her had been precipitated.

If you suddenly begin to sneeze, say to the patient, "There is something about our relationship that has just made me sneeze! What do you think it is?" The patient may easily respond, "I've had a very painful butt for the last ten minutes." Now the two of you are suddenly experiencing an identification with each other which is of a profoundly personal quality.

Therapist Number N + 1

As psychotherapy becomes more and more a standard procedure and a kind of new religion, patients tend to fluctuate from church to church, from therapist to therapist. Many of our patients end up using *us* as further proof that psychotherapy won't work. Furthermore, they arrive with a set of previous experiences to support the conviction. It's a set-up.

What can you do about this when you are the *N + 1* therapist? Most of us, out of our delusion of grandeur, make believe that our techniques and our personhood will resolve the problem and the patient will be cured. To prevent the fiasco this delusion might lead to would save us much heartache and pain. One of the obvious things to do is to make sure that the first interview includes a careful survey of all previous efforts to get help, both professional and non-professional. This must include an enumeration of all previous psychotherapists, sexual affairs, psychological affairs, encounter groups, religions, and literary excursions. Such a survey gives you a sense of what you are going to face as the patient retraces the same territory and ends up in the same dead-end that made him break out of his last therapeutic effort and finally seek *your* help.

A second tactic is to be very suspicious of yourself in the beginning, before you've been deluded into guessing that you're going to be unique. One of the best ways of preventing this delusion is to have the previous therapist join you. But even this is second-best to persuading the patient to go back to his previous therapist and resolving the negative transference that made him run to you. It is that nexus of stress, anxiety, and negative transference the patient has to penetrate. Your reassurance may help him go back and do that, and you then become the previous therapist's best friend, and you are off the hook for what is most often one more fiasco.

If the patient refuses to return to the previous therapist, and you can't get the previous therapist to join you for the second interview, then try to get any one of the previous therapists to come for the second interview. Failing that, or being unwilling to do it for any number of reasons, you should bring in a consultant who becomes your *de facto* co-therapist, whether he remains or not. This consultant does not need to be a senior person. It can be a colleague or a junior person—it could almost be a non-professional person—because what is most important is that someone in the outside real world validates the fact that this is a professional effort and not one more *tête-à-tête*.

If, for whatever reasons, it is not possible to include a consultant, you can expand the group of fantasies that you have to face by having the patient bring in someone out of *his* real world. Best it should be a spouse, or mother and father, or brother and sister; but if that is not feasible, anybody in his real world would do—his girlfriend or her boyfriend, his boss, his secretary, or his latest intimate. The fact of having someone from his world or someone from your world join the session reduces the problem of what to do about "THEY." THEY are constantly contaminating all psychotherapy, and this THEY is not only a factor for the patient—it is already a powerful force for you as well. My previous therapist . . . my previous supervisor . . . my previous colleagues . . . my previous patients— all stand grouped behind my shoulder whenever I become vulnerable and personal in relating to a new patient.

The Video Machine as Co-Therapist

The video machine has many functions. I am most concerned with its function as a consultant to the family. I like to use it as consultant to myself, the therapist. It thus becomes part of that larger unit we call the therapeutic family. But I also like to use it as part of myself, the therapist, as manipulator. I use the machine to increase feedback so that I can become objective about my own subjectivity. It has long been said that one can be objective—that is, distant and cold—and I don't want any part of that. One can be *subjective*, and then one tends to be weak, distorted, and less useful. Below the level of these two, it is possible to be *objective about one's subjectivity*, and that is what the machine offers me.

One should not underestimate the machine. As a co-therapist, it helps divert you from your preoccupation with mothering the patient. It helps you dissociate. As a co-therapist, the machine can serve as a reality tester which makes it possible for you to back away and be playful rather than obsess about your internal responses or intellectual reverberations.

If providing the time and place for meta-communicating is one of the objectives of psychotherapy, then the videotape is also one way of accomplishing this. Most powerfully, the couple or family are then tempted to stop meta-communicating at home, and the constant process of disappearing into their heads is interrupted. It also makes them freer to bring their anxieties about the process back to the next interview. The office and the machine may even become the signal for a new attitude of, "Let's talk, let's back off and take a look."

One couple watched themselves on videotape just before the next interview. The husband said he was very upset and very impressed by his experience. He saw himself hide behind a tremendous wall of formality, and he noted that he hadn't looked at his wife once during the entire hour.

"I seemed artificial to myself. I got a new sense of how delusional I was about myself. As a professional I would have seemed good and competent, but as a person, I wasn't who I was in that hour at all. I wasn't letting anything come out of me. I really scared myself in the video."

The wife continued his initiative and said, "I'm anxious about us and I'm aware of my lack of feeling."

"I see that if I let the wall down," the husband responded, "I'll be taken over, and then I guess I'll be eaten up or I'll force people to take me over. My folks phoned last evening and I was that way with them. They see my formality as competence, and I hadn't known what was really there before this videotape. Now I see my role flip with my mother from mother-son to father-daughter. I have never evolved a peer relationship. I see now that my dad has done the same thing, and I'd prided myself all this time on not being like him."

Oh, the magic of pictures!

The Gift of Unconditional Positive Regard

Many years ago Carl Rogers postulated that one of the conditions necessary for successful psychotherapy was a state of unconditional positive regard. For me, unconditional positive regard only took place during the first nine months of the baby's life. I've had to reconsider that viewpoint on the basis of a unique experience with Dr. Alberto Serrano, then Director of the Child Psychiatry and Mental Health Clinic of San Antonio, Texas. I had visited Dr. Serrano many years ago on a trip back from a Mexico City convention. I had spent the day observing some of his clinical innovations in providing mental health for a large bilingual city. I had watched as the initial interview was conducted with three couples across the table from each other, with the social work therapist behind each couple. I had reveled in the excitement as couple number two and couple number three discovered things they had neglected that were similar to those told by couple number one.

Years later Dr. Serrano called to ask if I would be a speaker for his annual meeting with his community support group, many of whom were priests, nuns, and members of the mental health profession in the community. I agreed and asked, "What do you want me to talk about?" Dr. Serrano replied, "I don't care what you talk about." He had spoken in such a tone of unconditional, positive regard that I found it completely impossible to plan a topic, to plan what I wanted to say, to even decide on a brief presentation of an old theme that I had used at some other time. This block continued, not only for the several months that preceded the scheduled day, but on the journey down there, on the forenoon before the luncheon meeting, through the entire luncheon with these 70 people, through Dr. Serrano's introduction, and as I walked to the podium to begin my presentation. I had no notes, I had no theme, I had no hint of what I was going to say. In short, I was terrified. I really have no idea how I got over my stagefright, but I am aware that I gave a presentation which I thought was effective, and which was well-received by the audience and was quite acceptable to Dr. Serrano.

Only gradually did I develop the realization that Dr. Serrano's unconditional response of, "I don't care what you talk about," had been a profound, symbolic experience for me. The follow-up on this symbolic experience was a gradually evolving willingness on my part to accept what came out of me rather than trying to plan what would be useful in the interpersonal setting that I happened to be in; whether it was a psychotherapy session, in professional intercommunications with others, or in presentations to the public. It was a long time before I became aware of how profound this shift had been for me: how much Dr. Serrano had flipped me out of the world of social adaptation and cultural adaptation and into the world of creative spontaneity, of freedom to trust myself to express my living rather than manipulate my cultural adaptation for agreeable response.

It seems increasingly clear to me that one of the secrets of professional effectiveness in the field of psychotherapy is this unconditional positive regard that I so fortunately received from Dr. Serrano. I suppose this is one of the great qualities of a pastoral counselor who, in his belief that man is made in the image of God, has this unconditional positive regard "built in," even though it is many times hidden, covered with political social adaptation, and not easily apparent to those who do not have the opportunity to probe and discover its availability.

It is not easy for the psychotherapist in his professional evolution to discover that all people are identical; that just as the bodies are amazingly identical, so also the psyches are amazingly identical. Social adaptation is the result of what life has done to us. As Carl Jung so beautifully puts it, we don't live life—it lives us. We are a product of our life, not just our chronologic life, but also our intergenerational life via the influences of our parents, our extended families, our grandparents. I believe this results in the recognition that there are massive residuals of the psychological, situational, and biological experiences of the living process from birth to death.

Growing as a Therapist

Assuming that you are going through the process of *learning about* family therapy and the process of *doing* family therapy—and have even come to the point of *being* a family therapist—what comes next? With time, experience, and the use of a consultant (a peer with whom you grow), I assume that the next step is more freedom to care without the danger of becoming an adoptive parent, without the danger of being stuck in your own narrow-minded personhood. If you are always teaming with a peer, either during the second interview or during the hours when you solicit a consult because things aren't going well, you yourself expand your creative freedom and your courage to be more and more of a professional therapist. You then have more power to take the pressures of the therapy and more power to give yourself to the therapeutic act of being a good foster parent.

Another factor that is important in your growth as a professional is developing an increasing access to your free associations, to your images, to your fantasies, to your own craziness. You also need to constantly be aware that the patient is not held to any pledge of confidentiality and that everything you say or do is available for the public, the nextdoor neighbor, the newspaper reporter. You are in the public eye, and you need to protect yourself.

Still another characteristic of the growing therapist is an increasing adroitness in finding a way around those things which are important but not available for direct attack. You will have less and less delusion of grandeur and more and more awareness of the process in which you are invested, where the family are much more powerful than you yourself or even you and your co-therapy team. You will also develop a greater sense of the inferences, and have more flexible perceptions of the body, the mind, and the spirit—the *whole* that makes up personhood. You will be better able to access the multi-systems with which you are struggling; the individuals, the sub-groups, the extended family, the males, the females, the three-generation mothers, the three-generation fathers, and the many, many other kinds of triangles. Gradually, you will develop a clearer separation of your professional role from your personal life, and thereby enjoy a richer personal life. You will develop an increased security in dealing with the universals that confront you with every family: the craziness, the suicidal impulses, the fantasies of death, the fantasies of murder, of incest, of addiction in all its complexities. Finally, you will have a greater enjoyment of your role as you become more capable and less enslaved by it, and you will experience an ever-growing inner peace of your own.

Index